Life's too short
for ordinary.
That's why we've
spent 25 years
finding, visiting and
choosing brilliant
places to stay.

For people who
love special.

First edition
Copyright © 2019
Alastair Sawday Publishing Co. Ltd
Published in 2019
ISBN-13: 978-1-906136-95-6

Sawday's,
Merchants House, Wapping Road,
Bristol BS1 4RW, UK
Tel: +44 (0)117 204 7810
Email: info@sawdays.co.uk
Web: www.sawdays.co.uk

Alastair Sawday has asserted his right to be
identified as the author of this work.

Series Editor Alastair Sawday
Content Manager Carmen McCormack
Editors Nicola Crosse, Chris Elmes,
Carmen McCormack
Production coordinators Sarah Barratt,
Sarah Cottam
Writing Claire Baraowski, Sarah Barratt, Tom Bell,
Becca Bill, Jo Boissevain, Caitlin Bowring,
Nicola Crosse, Antonica Eikli, Zoe Grafton,
Carmen McCormack, Wendy Ogden, Honor Peters,
Annie Shilito
Inspections David Ashby, Mandy Barnes, Sarah
Barratt, Mike Bevens, Colin Cheyne, Sarah Cottam,
Fiona Duby, Florence Fortnam, Julie Franklin, Zoe
Grafton, Alli Liew, Carmen McCormack, Valerie
Penny, Aideen Reid, Nicky Tennent, Peter Thurlow,
Gwen Vonthron
Thanks also to others who did an inspection or two.
Designer Megan Silcocks
Marketing & PR Emily Enright, Ella Perryman
+44 (0)117 204 7801
marketing@sawdays.co.uk

We have made every effort to ensure the accuracy
of the information in this book at the time of going to
press. However, we cannot accept any responsibility
for any loss, injury or inconvenience resulting from
the use of information contained therein.

Production Pagebypage Co. Ltd
Maps Maidenhead Cartographic Services
Printing Pureprint, Uckfield
Distribution Travel Alliance, Bath
info@pelotongrey.com

LIST OF SYMBOLS

 At least one bedroom and bathroom accessible for wheelchair users. Phone for details.

 Children of all ages are welcome. Cots, highchairs etc are not necessarily available.

 Pets welcome; please let the owner know if you want to bring pets.

Cover photo, front: Artist Residence London, page 195
Cover photo, back: The Bedford (© Ben Carpenter), page 199   Photo opposite: Widbrook Grange, page 101

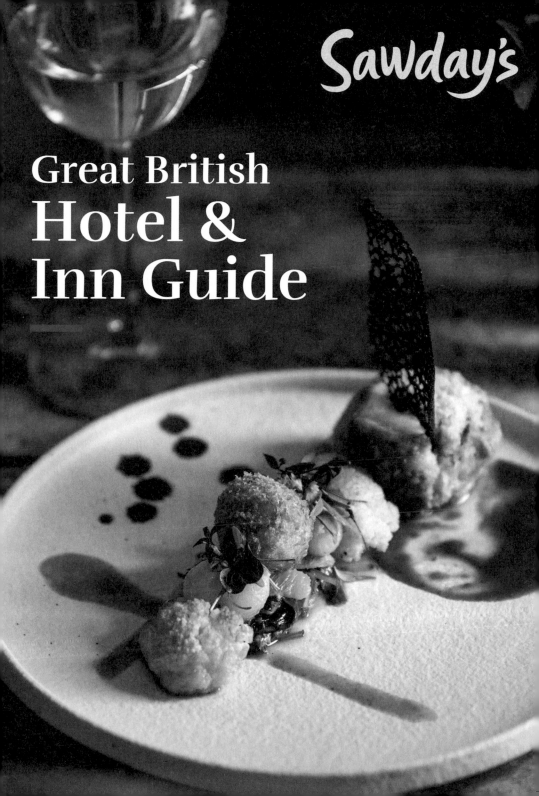

Sawday's

Great British
Hotel &
Inn Guide

Contents

SCOTLAND
p370–401

NORTH
EAST
p338–341

NORTH
WEST
p282–311

YORKSHIRE
AND
HUMBER
p314–335

EAST
MIDLANDS
p240–251

WEST
MIDLANDS
p254–278

WALES
p348–367

EAST
OF
ENGLAND
p202–236

LONDON
p190–199

SOUTH EAST
p128–187

SOUTH WEST
p28–122

CHANNEL
ISLANDS
p344–345

© Maidenhead Cartographic 2019

Ode to hotels & inns

Hotels and inns have form. They've populated novels, films, TV series and radio dramas for generations with their rich, exciting mix of romance, luxury and everything being exceedingly different to home. The tantalising bar with its rows of shining bottles, atmospheric restaurants with tempting food, kindly staff waiting to wait on you, little luxuries in your bedroom and bathroom, the joy of not needing money until you check out, ordering indulgent room service – the lovely feeling of 'real life' being suspended. These are what make staying in a hotel or inn special.

The hotels and inns in this book are the antithesis of the monolithic chains – huge investor-driven places where every square inch of space is dedicated to giving a maximum financial return. You won't find any concrete boxes and you won't find shops in the foyer trying to lure in the public – and their purses - as well as guests.

Sawday's have always championed small places. The hotels and inns we choose for our website and books are independent, often family-run places that will continue to thrive in spite of the pecking they get from the OTA vultures. We look for differences, not similarities. There are timeless old inns where mahogany panels shine with centuries of varnish, chic design hotels and second generation family-run places, where the kids have taken the reins and brought the old place kicking and screaming into the 21st century – all values intact but now Instagrammable.

We love our places for doing things on a human scale, catering for human needs and nurturing human relationships. You'll always be warmly welcomed and find people willing to go the extra mile. Our family-friendly places might have early suppers for children, highchairs, cots, special dressing gowns, safe indoor and outdoor play areas, babysitters and endless acts of kindness so parents can get a bit of a break too. Our dog-friendly places allow pets in the rooms (but not on the beds) and some provide arrival treats, dog beds, free tennis balls and the odd glass of 'pawsecco'.

Our hotels and inns are much more than rooms to sleep in. They foster a deep sense of place when you stay, with friendly staff giving you tips on their area and food nearly always sourced locally if not home grown. You might find ales from the microbrewery next door, or soaps, biscuits and even gin made by local artisans and walked round the corner to your room. Some are mini spas, where as well as being pampered by good food and general relaxation, you can bubble away in a hot tub, be pummelled by a masseuse, steam out your stress in a sauna or order a beauty treatment. At others, you can learn something new during your break, signing up for cooking classes and foraging trips, wild swimming expeditions, yoga courses or guided walks with knowledgeable locals.

Wherever you decide to stay you should be looked after by warm, affable staff. Those who know their job inside out and are contagiously enthusiastic. Not every hotel and inn will tick every box but they need to have a healthy smattering of thumbs up to make it into our collection. You'll find some earthy, straightforward inns that fit the bill for a good wholesome supper and a tumble into a comfy bed and smart hotels that are spot on for celebrating the most special of occasions.

What we can promise you is we've been to every one and, despite their differences, even because of their differences, we love them all. We know you will too.

Both images: The Masons Arms Hotel, page 246

What we look for

We look for special.
We've visited every one of them.
We've written about them honestly.

Our hotels and inns are not uniform. We look for differences not similarities, so you'll find a huge variety of places from large and swish hotels with staff on call, to tiny country inns where you'll carry your bags up ancient, uneven stairs. There are also lots of interesting places in between that defy a label. What binds them is not their outward appearance but what it feels like to be there as a guest. We look for:

Warm, affable owners and staff. Those who know their job inside out and are contagiously enthusiastic. These people have service stamped through them like a stick of rock: unobtrusive and genuine, they're often aware you need something before you realise it yourself.

Atmosphere. Good hotels and inns are ageless and classless. They encourage you to come in and join in, whether it's a buzzing city place filled with people on their laptops, a quiet, grown-up drawing room with one or two others having afternoon tea, or a boisterous family fun spot. What matters is that you feel happy when you walk in.

Character. We like our hotels and inns to be as idiosyncratic and lively as they please. Travelling is dull if you stay in places reflecting nothing more interesting than somebody else's take on the businessman's stopover. The hotels and inns we choose are shaped by the character of their owners or managers, however that manifests itself. We love surprises!

Good food. We like food that's prepared from scratch, whether it's a simple sandwich, the perfect seasonal risotto or a tasting menu for an important occasion. We like 'specials' on a blackboard, a small menu and some creativity alongside the classics. We also like to know where food, wine and beer have come from.

Generosity of spirit. Our hotels and inns are places where you can ask for things to be exactly as you want them. Need fresh milk in your room, an umbrella for your stroll through the garden, a glass of wine for watching the sunset or a feather pillow when you've been given foam? Just ask.

A sense of place. We choose places that love to celebrate their area, whether it's by offering local soaps and lotions, cheese from the artisan producer down the road, beer from a nearby microbrewery or meat and vegetables from farms and gardens just a stone's throw away. Staying at these places will teach you much about Great Britain, county by county.

Bedrooms and bathrooms better than your own. It's lovely feeling a bit cosseted when you stay in a hotel or inn, so while the style and décor will differ in each of these places, you should have: a truly comfortable sink-into bed with the crispest sheets, a warm and inviting bathroom with thick towels and plenty of stuff to slap on and smell good, something to watch or read and somewhere to sit that feels a bit special.

Both images: The Rectory Hotel, page 110

Tickton Grange, page 317

Sawday's top 6

These categories represent just some of the things we love about our hotels and inns: breathtaking views from bedroom balconies, dazzling design, food carefully sourced and cooked with flair. We've also picked our favourite places for keeping the kids entertained, travelling with your pooch or stealing away for a romantic weekend.

Every place in our collection has a warm and generous spirit so choosing just six in each category was hugely tricky, and subject to much debate. The ones we've picked stand out for the creativity and passion they show for indulging their guests, but we're confident that a visit to any hotel or inn in this book will be a memorable and enriching experience.

OUR TOP 6 FOR

Views

Our favourite places to stop and stare. Incredible views from bedrooms on the shores of lakes, terraces overlooking rambling gardens, outdoor hot tubs and restaurants by the sea.

I. PENALLY ABBEY, PEMBROKESHIRE

This beautiful country-house hotel sits high on the hill with long views over Carmarthen Bay. Outside, there's a small courtyard and five acres of lawns and woodland. Big windows in the main house flood the rooms with light, while the sunroom is a perfect spot to read the papers, dig into afternoon tea, or snooze in the sun.

PAGE 356

2. THE SCARLET, CORNWALL

The Scarlet sits above the sea with a vast wall of glass framing the view. Outside, you'll find a hot tub in the garden from which you can stargaze. Inside, there's a stylish restaurant that opens onto a decked terrace, where you eat delicious Cornish food while gazing out to sea.

PAGE 43

Another Place – The Lake, page 308

3. THE INN AT LOCH TUMMEL, PERTH & KINROSS

You weave through the forest, then arrive at this 200-year-old inn and views of fields, hills, loch and sky. Bedrooms are a treat: big, beautiful beds, chic fabrics and stunning views in almost every case. Explore the hills, whizz down mountain bike trails or head to Queen's View, one of the best lookout points in Scotland.

PAGE 384

4. ANOTHER PLACE – THE LAKE, CUMBRIA

This contemporary country house hotel sits on Ullswater in 18 beautiful acres that roll down to the lakeshore. Both hotel and water offer lots to do: paddle board on the lake, jump in for a swim or explore in a kayak. If relaxing is what you're after, there's a gorgeous terrace and a swimming pool with the most impressive views.

PAGE 308

The Scarlet, page 43

5. ALEXANDRA HOTEL & RESTAURANT, DORSET

This chic hotel has wonderful views over the Jurassic coast, all the way to Chesil Beach and on to Portland Bill. It sits high on the hill with one foot in town and the other paddling in the water. Outside, there's a sun-trapping garden where guests fall asleep in deckchairs, and a lookout tower with big sea views for a romantic dinner.

PAGE 63

6. KNOCKENDARROCH HOTEL & RESTAURANT, PERTH & KINROSS,

A grand old house with exceptional views that shoot across the valley to forested hills. Paths lead up through forest, moorland and big Highland landscapes – not a bad way to work up an appetite for some very good food. Binoculars are provided in your room so you can make the most of the stunning scenery.

PAGE 381

Penally Abbey, page 356

OUR TOP 6 FOR

Foodies

We look for places where food is sourced, cooked and served with panache. These are our top six for superb flavours and great atmosphere, whether it's a multi-course menu in a grand setting or a simple lunch in a beautiful garden.

I. THE MONTAGU ARMS, HAMPSHIRE

The Montagu Arms was originally founded in 1742, but re-modelled in 1925, giving interiors a country house feel. You'll find roaring fires, a library bar, and courtyard garden where you can eat in summer. Ambrosial food is the big draw, so expect the likes of Jerusalem artichoke salad or honey glazed duck on the menu, followed by orange soufflé and dark chocolate ice cream.

PAGE 157

2. THE DIAL HOUSE, NORFOLK

An eclectic, buzzing foodie hotel that's full of life. Inside, a blackboard announces cookery workshops and spa treatments, and a listed staircase leads to bedrooms above. Owners Hannah and Andrew were previously restaurateurs, so you won't be disappointed by their fabulous menu. Dishes are full of Norfolk-sourced produce and can be enjoyed in the elegant dining room under a large vintage chandelier.

PAGE 231

The Dial House, page 231

3. MONACHYLE MHOR, PERTH & KINROSS,

Monachyle Mhor is a unique designer hotel that started life as a B&B. Today it's one of the hippest places to stay in Scotland and still run by the same family. There's a cool little bar, a fire in the sitting room and a restaurant with impressive views. Dinners are a five-course feast with beef, lamb, pork and venison all from the farm.

PAGE 386

Abbots Oak Manor, page 240

4. THE BELL AT SKENFRITH, MONMOUTHSHIRE

This country inn sits perched on an ancient stone bridge overlooking a river snaking through the valley and glorious hills beyond. In summer, doors fly open and life spills onto a stone terrace with views of the hills, woods and the river Monnow – a fine spot for lunch in the sun. Expect Welsh rarebit, braised beef brisket and apple doughnuts with toffee sauce and mulled cider.

PAGE 348

The Dial House, page 231

5. HAMBLETON HALL HOTEL & RESTAURANT, RUTLAND

Hambleton Hall has an unbeatable position on Rutland water and a Michelin star restaurant to boot. Expect clipped lawns and gravel paths, a formal parterre garden that bursts with summer colour and a walled swimming pool. Head chef Aaron Patterson has worked with the likes of Raymond Blanc and has been crafting the elegant menu for 20 years.

PAGE 242

6. ABBOTS OAK MANOR, LEICESTERSHIRE

Sarah and Anthony brought this listed house back from the brink with style and a passion for the place. There are still elements of the old bones, but the interiors have been given a fresh new look. Dinners are a six course affair and all of the produce has been foraged and sourced locally when possible. Enjoy bell of lamb, jasmine mousse with cherry soup and lavender biscuits.

PAGE 240

The Montagu Arms, page 157

Families

These are our favourites for the combination of entertainment, comfort, generosity and creativity that elevate a place beyond family-friendly to something special where adults can enjoy themselves as much as their little ones.

1. THE ROSEVINE, CORNWALL

A superb family hotel right on the sea's edge, with backpacks and beach toys to borrow. Guests love the way children are genuinely welcome and parents are spoiled. Family apartments are brilliant, some are dog-friendly too, and there's a playroom full of DVDs, games, toys and books for rainy days. A mini football pitch is set up outside and there's a children's tea party every day.

PAGE 35

2. THE GLOBE INN AT WELLS-NEXT-THE-SEA, NORFOLK

This is a beautiful inn on a Georgian green, where you're welcomed with a relaxed and friendly vibe. The position is perfect for pottering down to the water and finding a beach for family fun. The flower-filled courtyard is great for an evening drink in summer, and the kids will love pizza made in the wood-fired oven. Rooms connect for larger families and dogs are welcome, too.

PAGE 234

Lancrigg, page 304

3. LANCRIGG, CUMBRIA

A family-friendly Lakes retreat steeped in history with acres of wild country to get lost in. A welcoming informality pervades the place, so everyone will feel completely at home, from families with young ones to lone walkers. While the kids run wild in the woodland playground, retreat to the sitting room and enjoy a drink or two as you take in the breathtaking views.

PAGE 304

4. THE FISH HOTEL, WORCESTERSHIRE

Come for Scandi chic on a smart estate with perfectly designed rooms, shepherd's huts and treehouses. It's like summer camp, for everyone – adults, children and dogs. The 400-acres of grounds have nature trails to explore from the door as well as archery and a playground. When it rains, huddle in the cosy central lodge and make use of the games room.

PAGE 257

The Fish Hotel, page 257

5. GLIFFAES HOTEL, POWYS

A beautiful old country house in 35 acres of lawns and woodland on the river Usk. There's high tea for children every night at 6:30pm, ample room to run wild in the garden and the chance to practice fishing on the lake. The Brecon Beacons are on the doorstep, so pack a picnic and head out for an adventurous day.

PAGE 349

6. AUGILL CASTLE, CUMBRIA

Augill is a one-of-a-kind castle in beautiful countryside. It's wonderfully informal and children love it. There are no uniforms, no rules, you just kick off your shoes and relax. Choose your spot in front of the fire in the hall, by a grand piano in the music room, in the honesty bar that opens onto a terrace or in the cinema in the old potting shed.

PAGE 302

The Rosevine, page 35

OUR TOP 6 FOR

Dog-friendly

Some places accept dogs, some really go the extra mile. These are our favourites for treats on arrival, dog beds in the rooms, extra sausages at breakfast and the odd glass of 'pawsecco'.

1. THE MEIKLEOUR ARMS, PERTH & KINROSS

With their own ale, over 20 malts and a bevvy of artisan gins, you'll find a toast for every occasion at this lovely country inn. The good news is, you can bring your beloved dog along with you. You'll all love walking round the estate, and spotting ospreys, otters and kingfishers down by the river. Back in the main house, interiors are pretty and the restaurant serves brilliant food.

PAGE 380

2. ROSE & CROWN, DURHAM

An idyllic country inn that dates back to 1733, set in the lovely village of Romaldkirk. Dogs are very welcome and will love trekking across the nearby fields or to the High Force waterfall. Afterwards, you'll be ready to grab a pint of local ale and retreat to the fireside. There's a peaceful sitting room for afternoon tea and a panelled restaurant for excellent food.

PAGE 338

3. WIDBROOK GRANGE, WILTSHIRE

A very loveable Georgian country house hotel in 11 acres of grounds near Bath and Bradford-on-Avon. Dogs will be in heaven here; treats and a bed wait in your room and your four-legged friend can join you in the conservatory for breakfast and afternoon tea. Expect sausages, 'pawsecco' and 'pupachinos' all round, followed by a run down the canal path.

PAGE 101

4. THE MANOR AT SWAY, HAMPSHIRE

Chic interiors, delicious food and a relaxed feel are the hallmarks of this hotel in Lymington. Inside, country house interiors have a distinctly contemporary feel; expect wooden floors, pretty wallpapers and smart sofas. Dogs are greeted with a warm smile as they join you in the bar or out on the terrace for afternoon tea. Waking up to beautiful views every morning is a real highlight.

PAGE 159

The Manor at Sway, page 159

5. LOYTON LODGE, TIVERTON

A small estate in Exmoor with open fires, pretty rooms, exceptional art and 280 beautiful acres to explore. Doggie beds, towels, bowls and treats are all provided to help your pooch settle in and they are welcome to join you in all public areas, so they won't ever need to leave your side. The food is a treat too – breakfast a feast every morning and dinner by arrangement, locally sourced and superb.

PAGE 61

6. THE GALLIVANT, SUSSEX

This cool little hotel stands across the road from Camber Sands, where five miles of pristine beach make for prime walking. Dogs are welcome in the Deck Rooms, which are decorated in relaxing coastal hues and have doors that open onto a secluded private deck. Everyone is welcome in the hotel's restaurant, so enjoy fresh seafood with your best friend by your side.

PAGE 180

The Meikleour Arms, page 380

Design

The epitome of stylishness; these places make our hearts sing the moment we walk through the door. Each one embodies a character and creativity all their own, some are bursting with colour, others are utterly chic, all are heaps of fun.

1. GILPIN HOTEL, CUMBRIA

Spa suites hang above the water on a 280-acre estate covered in ancient woodland. Cool elegance flows throughout, with Zoffany wallpapers, gilded mirrors and flowers everywhere. Bedrooms are divine: there's crisp linen, smart fabrics, smouldering fireplaces and huge bathtubs. Garden suites have hot tubs on the deck, spa suites have saunas too. Food is superb and whisked up by renowned chef, Hrishikesh Desai.

PAGE 296

2. THE BRISLEY BELL, NORFOLK

Amelia and Marcus have transformed a derelict 17th-century pub overlooking the village common into a handsome inn with two stylish dining rooms, a book-lined garden room and a cosy snug with an open fire for winter. Bedrooms are in the converted barns set around a courtyard in the garden; all have high ceilings, some have exposed brick walls, antique pieces and roll top bathtubs.

PAGE 230

Gilpin Hotel, page 296

3. ARTIST RESIDENCE BRIGHTON, BRIGHTON & HOVE

At the top of a square and looking down to the sea is this cute hotel with an arty vibe. There's something to look at in every corner; find cool art, the odd wall clad in corrugated iron and even an ornamental drainpipe. Some bedrooms have Pop Art murals, others come in Regency colours and a new batch are super-cool with roll top bathtubs in the room.

PAGE 167

4. THE TALBOT MALTON, YORKSHIRE

A 17th-century coaching inn owned by the Fitzwilliam estate. Inside, easy elegance abounds: a fire burns in the drawing room and you find fresh flowers, lovely art, the daily papers and cavernous sofas. Bedrooms are en suite with chic fabrics, warm colours and botanical prints on the walls. Several have stunning views as well.

PAGE 331

Artist Residence Brighton, page 167

5. PASCHOE HOUSE, DEVON

Guests come to this modern country house for afternoon tea, the selection of West Country gins to work through, and films to download with complimentary popcorn. Settle into chic, unstuffy rooms with views of the Devon hills, cut flowers and bathrooms with huge walk-in showers and roll top baths – pour in the Bamford bubbles and enjoy long soaks before dinner.

PAGE 56

6. THE BEDFORD, LONDON

This huge 1930s Grade II-listed building is one of London's most iconic venues. A pub, club, restaurant, music and entertainment venue, refurbished with style and flair. Spanning five floors are bars serving craft ales, artisan spirits and fine wines. Upstairs are fifteen individually designed bedrooms – roll top baths, vibrant fabrics and cool, contemporary art.

PAGE 199

The Bedford, page 199

Romance

The most romantic places have a touch
of magic that brings you closer together.
These are our grown up spaces for roaring
fires, quiet courtyards, fine dining, big baths
and funky bars.

1. MIDDLETON LODGE, YORKSHIRE

A super stylish bolthole in Yorkshire with renovated
stone barns, gorgeous rooms and delicious food.
In summer, life spills onto the courtyard for lunch
in the sun, while through the arched glass doors is
a spectacular restaurant open to the rafters.
There's a bar, treatment rooms, a two-acre kitchen
garden and bikes to borrow.

PAGE 329

2. NORTH HOUSE, ISLE OF WIGHT

An elegant townhouse with wonderful personal
service, fabulous breakfasts and cosmopolitan style.
The three listed buildings, once an 1820s theatre and
two Georgian townhouses, have been refurbished
beautifully. Bedrooms are immaculately furnished,
with well-chosen bed linen and free-standing baths.
After days out along the coast, there's nothing better
than to return to a heated pool, a well-stocked bar
and the 'Oyster Store' restaurant.

PAGE 164

The Wheatsheaf, page 120

3. THE WHEATSHEAF, GLOUCESTERSHIRE

The Wheatsheaf stands at the vanguard of a cool new movement: the village local reborn in country house style. Outside, a small courtyard garden makes the perfect spot for post-walk Pimms in summer. Inside, beautiful bedrooms come as standard and nearly all have free-standing baths. After relaxing days in the countryside, feast on local fare downstairs in the restaurant.

PAGE 120

4. CLIVEDEN HOUSE, BERKSHIRE

Cliveden is a decadent country house of epic proportions that dates from 1605. Its famous pool and beautiful new spa are at your disposal, and the old house sits in 376 acres of National Trust land. The Great Hall, a panelled masterpiece with vast portraits on the walls, is a fine spot for cocktails before dinner. Corinthian columns, muralled ceilings and exquisite food in the dining room add to the grandeur.

PAGE 148

5. ASKHAM HALL, CUMBRIA

Askham is a Grade I-listed manor house with a 12th-century Peel tower. Expect contemporary art and open fires, a beautiful drawing room and a small spa with an outdoor pool. The hall sits in 40 acres of Cumbrian countryside with paths that follow the river through glorious parkland. Romantic meals are a must; meat is reared on the estate and the produce used is all as local as possible.

PAGE 310

6. THE CARTFORD INN, LANCASHIRE

This quirky inn has a winning position overlooking the Trough of Bowland and is full of surprises. The bar, with its cool art and roaring fire, is a great place to linger over a pint of local ale, but a courtyard garden will draw you out in good weather. Bedrooms are supremely stylish: gilded sleigh beds, signature wallpapers, river views and roll top baths. The penthouse has a rooftop terrace, too.

PAGE 286

Cliveden House, page 148

North House, page 164

South West

Glazebrook House Hotel, page 50

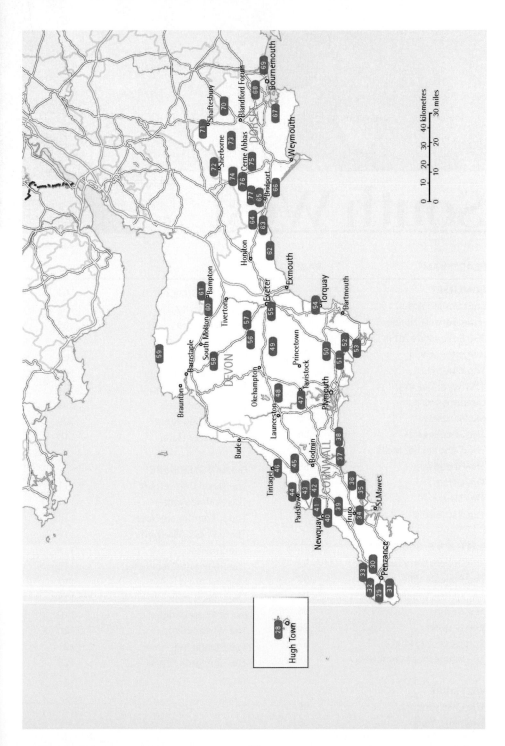

Shaftesbury 70
Blandford Forum 68 69 Bournemouth
71 67 Weymouth
DORSET
Sherborne 73
Cerne Abbas 75
72 74 76
77 65 66
64 63 Bridport
Honiton 62 Exmouth

Bampton
61
60 Tiverton
South Molton 57
58 56 55 54 Torquay
59 Barnstaple DEVON 49 Dartmouth
Braunton 48 Princetown
Okehampton 47 52
Launceston Tavistock 51 53
Bude 50
46 Bodmin 38 Plymouth
45 37
Tintagel 36
44 43 CORNWALL 35 St Mawes
Padstow 42 41 39 34 Truro
40
Newquay

33 30 Penzance
32 29 31

0   10   20   30   40 kilometres
0   10   20   30 miles

28
Hugh Town

South West

The Litton, page 89

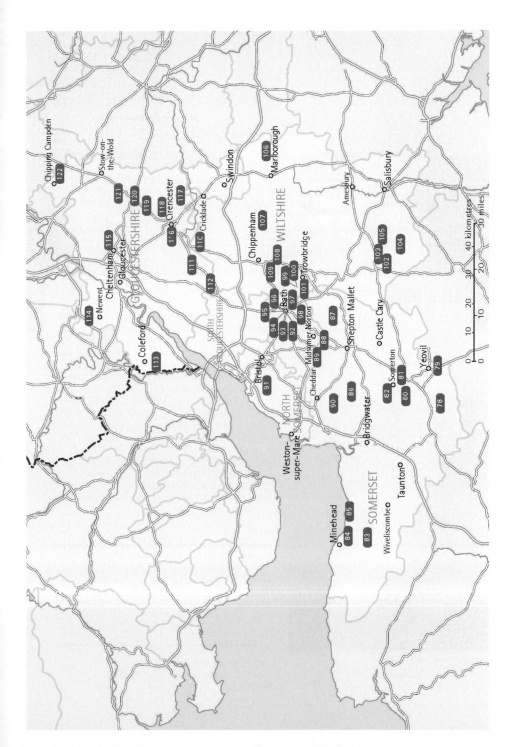

Chipping Campden

Stow-on-
the-Wold

Swindon

Marlborough

Cirencester

Amesbury

Salisbury

Cricklade

Chippenham

WILTSHIRE

Trowbridge

GLOUCESTERSHIRE

Cheltenham

Newent

Gloucester

Bath

Shepton Mallet

SOUTH
GLOUCESTERSHIRE

Coleford

Castle Cary

Bristol

Midsomer Norton

Somerton

Yeovil

NORTH
SOMERSET

Cheddar

Weston-
super-Mare

Bridgwater

SOMERSET

Taunton

Wiveliscombe

Minehead

122
121
120
119
118
117
116
115
114
113
112
111
110
109
108
107
106
105
104
103
102
101
100
99
98
97
96
95
94
93
92
91
90
89
88
87
86
85
84
83
82
81
80
79
78

40 kilometres
30 miles
30
20
20
10
10
10
0
0

Hell Bay

There are five inhabited islands here and many more that are completely empty, ranging from a jagged rock when the tide is in to beautiful sleek sand spits and your own little empire when it is out. Beach combers, adventurers, boat lovers and sea swimmers will find much to be happy about. The hotel food is stunning, most bedrooms face that sea view and the staff are the friendliest. You'll find the family's modern art collection on the walls of the sitting room, including a Barbara Hepworth. Have a drink and an amuse bouche here before heading for the sea-facing dining room – try and time supper with the sunset. Splash in the pool, wander along the lanes to discover honesty shops selling honey, homemade fudge and fresh veg, an art gallery or two, cafés and a little post office that sells everything. Boats go to other islands most days – ten minutes to Tresco for the tropical gardens, a bit further to St Mary's which is livelier. *Bags can be stored after check out until departure from Bryher.*

Rooms	25 suites for 2: £250-£640.
	Under 2s free. Singles £175-£450.
Meals	Lunch from £6.95.
	Dinner included; non-residents £45.
Closed	14 October – 16 March.

Hell Bay,
Bryher, Isles of Scilly, TR23 0PR

Tel	+44 (0)1720 422947
Email	contactus@hellbay.co.uk
Web	www.hellbay.co.uk

Chapel House

Everything here is beautiful – a stunning Georgian house; views over town that stretch out to sea; bedrooms and bathrooms to rival those in the best designer hotels. All of which would be blossom in the wind without Susan, whose instinct to go the extra mile knows no restraint – this is not just a gorgeous house, but a friendly one, too. Outside, smart red bricks give some idea of the grandeur within, but step inside and find a contemporary wonderland that took two years to refurbish. The hall is home to works from the Newlyn School of Art, the double sitting room has high ceilings, an open fire and a baby grand piano, doors lead onto a balcony and down to a courtyard garden, a peaceful retreat in summer. Bedrooms are hard to fault: white walls soak up the light; handmade beds give a fine night's sleep; super-chic wet rooms have fabulous showers. One has a wood-burner in the room, another a bath under a glass roof that slides open. There's much more: delicious kitchen suppers at weekends; cooking demonstrations with local chefs; great restaurants along the road. The magical coast awaits.

Rooms	6 doubles: £150-£300. Singles £125-£150. Dinner, B&B £90-£180 p.p. Extra bed/sofabed £20-£30 p.p.p.p.
Meals	Kitchen suppers on Friday/Saturday £22-£25; on request during the week. Sunday lunch from £14.50.
Closed	Rarely.

Tel	+44 (0)1736 362024
Email	hello@chapelhousepz.co.uk
Web	chapelhousepz.co.uk

Chapel House,
Chapel Street, Penzance, TR18 4AQ

Artist Residence Penzance

Artist Residence's Cornish offering is another cool bolthole from Justin and Charlie Salisbury. The vibe is laid-back: friendly staff stop to chat and you can turn up to dinner in your flip-flops. Choose where to eat – in the restaurant adorned with colourful pop art, in front of the wood-burner in the sitting room-bar or outside in the terrace garden. There's ping pong to play while you wait for dinner from the smokehouse. Breakfast on French toast, local eggs and homemade granola before you whisk yourself off to St Michael's Mount, glimpsed from the hotel, or the Jubilee Pool lido. There's great surfing at Sennen and paddling at Porthcurno, both ten miles, and you can catch the ferry to the Isles of Scilly direct from Penzance. *Minimum stay: 2 nights at weekends in summer. Certain bedrooms are dog-friendly.*

Rooms	14 doubles, 3 twin/doubles: £75-£180. 1 suite for 2-3: £190-£295. 1 family room for 5: £185-£225. 2 triples: £135-£180. 1 cottage for 6: £270-£385. Singles £65-£120.
Meals	Lunch & dinner, 3 courses, £20-£25.
Closed	Never.

Artist Residence Penzance,
20 Chapel Street,
Penzance, TR18 4AW

Tel	+44 (0)1736 365664
Email	penzance@artistresidence.co.uk
Web	www.artistresidence.co.uk/our-hotels/cornwall

The Old Coastguard

This seaside hotel stands by the coastal path on the way into Mousehole, one of Cornwall's nicest villages, where kids play on the harbour's sandy beach at low tide. It's a peaceful spot with a clutch of restaurants and galleries, little disturbed since the Spanish raided in 1595. Roguish brothers Edmund and Charles Inkin have form when it comes to creating small hotels of character, and this place bears all their hallmarks, being good value and casual, with relaxed staff and great food. A diverse crowd of guests – couples, families, and ladies lunching – hang out in the rustic-smart bar and dining room. Conversation may stall as you take in the outlook over hydrangeas and palms to intriguing St Clement's Isle and beyond, across the sweep of Mount's Bay to the Lizard. With Newlyn a couple of miles away, locally landed fish features at breakfast. Supper, with a modern British slant, changes with the seasons. Retreat to a lime-washed bedroom hung with Cornish art – all vary in size, character and aspect, and eight have balconies.

Rooms	8 doubles, 3 twins: £140-£225. 2 suites for 2: £245-£300. 1 family room for 4: £200-£225. Singles £110-£190. Dinner, B&B £102-£152 p.p. Extra bed £25 p.p.p.n.
Meals	Lunch from £16.50. Dinner, 3 courses, about £29. Sunday lunch from £16.
Closed	1 week in early Jan.

Tel	+44 (0)1736 731222
Email	bookings@oldcoastguardhotel.co.uk
Web	www.oldcoastguardhotel.co.uk

The Old Coastguard,
The Parade, Mousehole,
Penzance, TR19 6PR

The Gurnard's Head

This quirky inn is one of the best – the sort of place a hiker hopes to find. Outside, the wild west coast weaves up to St Ives; secret beaches appear at low tide, cliffs tumble down to the water, wild flowers streak the land pink in summer. Inside, it's earthy, warm, stylish and friendly, with rustic interiors and fires at both ends of the bar. Logs are piled high in an alcove, maps and art hang on the walls, books fill every shelf; if you pick one up and don't finish it, take it home and post it back. Comfortable, cosy bedrooms have views over the Atlantic or the moors. A short, fresh and seasonal menu that changes daily will suit walkers who need a quick fuel stop as well as serious foodies and is served in the bar, dining rooms, or in the garden on sunny days. Choose from three hand-pulled Cornish ales, a choice of good ciders and more than 20 wines by the carafe.

Rooms	3 doubles, 4 twin/doubles: £130-£195. Singles £105-£160. Dinner, B&B £92-£125 per person. Extra bed/sofabed £25 p.p.p.n.
Meals	Lunch from £12. Dinner, 3 courses from £29. Sunday lunch from £17.
Closed	Christmas.

The Gurnard's Head,
Zennor, St Ives, TR26 3DE

Tel	+44 (0)1736 796928
Email	enquiries@gurnardshead.co.uk
Web	www.gurnardshead.co.uk

Trevose Harbour House

This super-chic B&B started life in the 1850s as a fisherman's cottage. These days it's a small-scale version of a design hotel, pristine from top to toe. It's the result of an 18-month renovation and it sits in the old town, a two-minute stroll from the beach. Inside, form and function rule the roost: everything is beautiful, nothing superfluous. Interiors come in blue and white with fresh flowers, local art, beautiful ceramics, and umbrellas in case it rains.

Downstairs is open-plan – a small sitting room with an honesty bar concealed in a '50s dresser on one side, on the other a dining room where you sit at Erçol tables and tuck into an excellent breakfast under hanging lamps. Rooms have Hypnos beds, crisp linen, beautiful fabrics and impeccably upholstered armchairs. Three have sea views, all have smart TVs, coffee machines and hot-water bottles. Bathrooms are flawless: underfloor heating, walk-in showers, white robes and Neal's Yard oils, perhaps a claw-foot bath. Outside, labyrinthine lanes lead to the harbour, sandy beaches, art galleries and lots of delicious restaurants. Dreamy. *Minimum stay: 2 nights. Over 12s welcome.*

Rooms	5 doubles: £170-£290.
	1 suite for 2: £245-£290. Singles £170.
Meals	Restaurants 500m.
Closed	1 November – 12 April.

Tel	+44 (0)1736 793267	Trevose Harbour House,
Email	hi@trevosehouse.co.uk	22 The Warren, St Ives, TR26 2EA
Web	trevosehouse.co.uk	

Driftwood Hotel

A beautiful seaside boutique hotel just a mile and a half from the fishing village of Portscatho with its own beach. Gaze out to Gerrans Bay from the sheltered terrace where you eat breakfast in the sunshine. Wander the gardens, scramble down a wooded path to the beach and cove below. Hampers for beach picnics and rucksacks for walkers can be arranged; the seven-kilometre circular walk from Portscatho to Pendower Beach will take you across beach and through meadow. There's a fire to keep you cosy when it's chilly and a games room for children – special high teas too. Bedrooms vary in size and all except one have sea views, three have their own terrace. You'll eat well: Chris Eden heads up the Michelin-starred kitchen and service is on wheels. Take a digestif onto the terrace – on clear nights the sky is full of stars. *Minimum stay: 2 nights at weekends.*

Rooms	13 doubles, 1 twin: £130-£290. 1 cabin for 4: £245-£275. Dinner, B&B £125-£155 per person.
Meals	Dinner, 3 courses £55. Vegetarian tasting menu £75; 5-course tasting menu from £75; 10-course tasting menu £105.
Closed	Early Dec to early Feb.

Driftwood Hotel,
Rosevine, Portscatho, TR2 5EW

Tel	+44 (0)1872 580644
Email	info@driftwoodhotel.co.uk
Web	www.driftwoodhotel.co.uk

The Rosevine

Borrow backpacks and beach toys and stroll to the cove below, or find a spot to sit in the gardens facing the sea. This is a stylish hotel on the Roseland Peninsula where children are genuinely welcome and parents are spoiled. There's an adults-only lounge, a restaurant with tasty food, and an airy spaciousness all around. Choose between a studio or a family apartment. Studios are open-plan while apartments have separate bedrooms and bunk beds for children. Some spaces open to lovely terraces; the Slate Annexe studios are dog-friendly. Parents will appreciate the playroom with DVDs, games, toys and books, the table tennis and mini football pitch in the garden, and the children's tea party every day. Go rock pooling when the tide is out, paddle or swim when it's in and go sailing from Portscatho, a two-minute stroll away. Irresistible St Mawes is six miles away and ferries can whisk you to Falmouth for the day. *Minimum stay: 4 nights in high season.*

Rooms	8 apartments for 5 with kitchenette: £188-£390. 7 studios for 2 with kitchenette: £152-£250. Extra bed/sofabed £25 p.p.p.n.
Meals	Lunch from £8. Dinner £29-£36. Afternoon tea £4-£15.
Closed	January.

Tel	+44 (0)1872 580206
Email	info@rosevine.co.uk
Web	www.rosevine.co.uk

The Rosevine,
Rosevine, Portscatho, Truro, TR2 5EW

Trevalsa Court Hotel

Trevalsa stands at the top of a cliff with sea views stretching far and wide. In summer life spills into the garden, where you can loll about in deck chairs and fall asleep in the sun. You can nip down to a sandy beach or pick up the coastal path, which passes at the end of the garden; turn left for cliff walks or right for Mevagissey, an old fishing village of mazy lanes. Trevalsa is a treat: friendly, stylish, gently spoiling. Inside, the view is weatherproofed by an enormous mullioned window in the sitting room, a great place to watch a storm spin past. You'll find a small bar with colourful art, then a panelled dining room for tasty food, perhaps mussels steamed in Cornish cider, a bavette steak with a peppercorn sauce, treacle tart with brown bread ice cream. Bedrooms have warm colours, crisp linen, padded headboards, the odd wall of paper. Most have sea views, bigger rooms have sofas, all have excellent bathrooms, the suite has a private deck. Breakfast is served on the terrace in summer. The Lost Gardens of Heligan and St Mawes are close.

Rooms	7 doubles, 5 twin/doubles: £125-£275. 1 suite for 2: £205-£295. 2 singles: £70-£120. Dinner, B&B from £85 per person. Extra bed/sofabed £20-£60 p.p.p.n.
Meals	Dinner £31-£38.
Closed	20 November – 10 February.

Trevalsa Court Hotel,
School Hill, Mevagissey,
St Austell, PL26 6TH

Tel	+44 (0)1726 842468
Email	stay@trevalsa-hotel.co.uk
Web	www.trevalsa-hotel.co.uk

The Old Quay House Hotel

You drop down the hill, weave through mazy lanes, then pull up at this boutique hotel which started life as a seaman's mission. It's a lovely spot, the estuary lapping behind the house and a waterside terrace for dinner in summer. Inside, uncluttered bedrooms flood with light; expect good beds, goose down duvets and elegant fabrics. Most overlook the estuary, eight have balconies (some tiny), the view from the suite is hard to beat. Bathrooms are just as good: white bathrobes, free-standing baths, perhaps a walk-in shower. Downstairs, super food waits in the restaurant, so take to the terrace for a cocktail, then dig into some delicious local fare, perhaps river mussels with wild garlic and shallots, stone bass with fennel and artichoke, poached rhubarb with white chocolate mousse. Fowey is enchanting, bustles with life and fills with sailors for the August Regatta. You can take the ferry across to Bodinnick where Daphne du Maurier lived, then walk over to Lantic Bay for a picnic lunch on the beach. Breakfast on the terrace, with boats zipping past, is a treat. *Minimum stay: 2 nights at weekends in high season.*

Rooms	7 doubles, 5 twin/doubles: £145-£285. 1 suite for 2: £335. Singles from £105.
Meals	Lunch about £15, Easter-October only. Dinner £30-£37.50.
Closed	Rarely.

Tel	+44 (0)1726 833302
Email	info@theoldquayhouse.com
Web	www.theoldquayhouse.com

The Old Quay House Hotel,
28 Fore Street, Fowey, PL23 1AQ

Talland Bay Hotel

The position here is magical. First you plunge down rollercoaster lanes leaving the world behind, then you arrive at this lovely hotel and find a rather good view – a vast carpet of sea that shoots off to the horizon. Pine trees stand guard on one side, an old church crowns a hill on the other, then two acres of lawns roll down to a ha-ha before the land tumbles down to the bay. In summer, loungers and croquet hoops appear on the lawn, and you can nip down to a beach café for lunch by the water. Back at the hotel there's a conservatory brasserie, a sitting room bar and a roaring fire in the half-panelled dining room. You'll find art on the walls, polished flagstones, a terrace for afternoon tea. Follow the coastal path over the hill, then return for a good dinner, perhaps roasted scallops with caramelised orange, loin of venison with chestnut purée, lemongrass panna cotta with peach sorbet. Bedrooms have warm colours, vast beds, beautiful linen, the odd panelled wall. One has a balcony, a couple open onto terraces, all have lovely bathrooms. Gardens, beaches and the coastal path wait.

Rooms	15 twin/doubles: £160-£290. 4 suites for 2: £260-£350. 3 cottages for 2: £210-£300. Singles from £150.
Meals	Lunch from £5.50. Dinner: brasserie from £12.95; restaurant £36-£42. Sunday lunch £21.50-£25. Afternoon tea from £6.
Closed	Never.

Talland Bay Hotel,
Porthallow, Looe, PL13 2JB

Tel	+44 (0)1503 272667
Email	info@tallandbayhotel.com
Web	www.tallandbayhotel.co.uk

The Plume of Feathers

This is a popular bar-restaurant so enjoy being thrown together with diners, children, walkers and their hounds – especially in the summer. The central bar is lively with ales on tap and friendly staff zipping in and out of the kitchen. MasterChef's Nat Tallents heads up the kitchen which showcases modern dishes using local-as-can-be produce; try Cornish fish and homemade pies, lunchtime sandwiches and delicious puddings – just the sort of gastro-grub you want after a breezy walk around nearby Ladock Woods. You eat at candle-studded pine tables in front of the wood-burner or in the huge, airy conservatory. You're halfway between Newquay and Truro with wild surfing beaches to the north and gentle bucket-and-spade ones to the south plus heaps of Cornish highlights – Eden Project, Lanhydrock House and Gardens, Tehidy Woods – within a 30-minute drive. Head back for a deep sleep in boutique bedrooms dotted around the grounds in the converted barns, stables and hen houses.

Rooms	27 doubles: £90-£190.
	1 family room for 4: £130-£190.
	Dogs £15 per night.
Meals	Breakfast from £5. Lunch from £7.50.
	Dinner from £12.50.
Closed	Rarely.

Tel	+44 (0)1872 510387
Email	thelodge@hospitalitycornwall.com
Web	www.theplumemitchell.co.uk

The Plume of Feathers,
Mitchell, Newquay, TR8 5AX

Lewinnick Lodge

Oh we do love to be beside the seaside! Poised above the cliff edge to a backdrop of rustic headland (an inspiring setting for platefuls of Cornish mussels) this glass-fronted edifice overlooks the ocean; a magical setting in all weathers. Polar opposite of the 'quaint local', Lewinnick Lodge is large and luminous with a friendly modern vibe. Be wowed by a wall of glass, a sweep of oak, a sparkling bar, an open fire, efficient staff who make everyone welcome (including the dog). You can eat in or out; try feasting on light and fresh polenta-crusted squid followed by Cornish crab linguine – or tuck into a succulent steak dish, sourced from local Cornish farms. Bedrooms are light, airy and have sea views, some with a bath overlooking the ocean, all with large comfortable beds and smartly tiled bathrooms. Wander down (latest time 11.30!) to a breakfast outside on the terrace if you want: full Cornish, or Mexican-style eggs are a favourite with excellent, freshly-roasted coffee. Walk it off on the coastal path. *Minimum stay: 2 nights at weekends & in high season.*

Rooms	12 doubles, 2 twin/doubles: £120-£260. 2 suites for 2: £180-£320. 1 family room for 4: £135-£260.
Meals	Breakfast from £5. Lunch from £7.50. Dinner from £12.50. Sunday lunch £13.
Closed	Rarely.

Lewinnick Lodge,
Pentire Headland, Newquay, TR7 1QD

Tel	+44 (0)1637 878117
Email	thelodge@hospitalitycornwall.com
Web	www.lewinnicklodge.co.uk

Watergate Bay Hotel

Grab a surfboard or a kite: this hotel kits you out to ride the waves with the Extreme Academy surf school. But you can still lounge around, and if you have kids, it's a treat; young children can make friends in the popular Kids' Zone while you disappear for a massage or a swim in Swim Club. It's all about the views here, with walls of glass in The Living Space (a huge café/bar), an 25-metre infinity pool that gazes over the ocean, and a terrace strewn with loungers. This large hotel sits directly above one of the best sandy beaches in Britain – two miles long. There's a large ocean room to head home to with an open fire, a sauna and cliff-top hot tub with stunning views, and food that's fresh and delicious. Eat in the bar or Zacry's the grill, it's only 50 paces to the The Beach Hut for a burger and Jamie Oliver's Fifteen Cornwall is right next door. Coastal light floods through the windows of the sea view suites, the family suites have separate bunk rooms for children, The Village apartments have their own kitchens and open-plan lounges and many of the bedrooms are dog-friendly.

Rooms	47 twin/doubles: £190-£345. 2 suites for 2, 4 suites for 5, 18 suites for 4: £285-£450. Singles £120-£268. Dinner, B&B from £240 per night.
Meals	Lunch £10. Dinner, 2 courses, £36.50.
Closed	Never.

Tel	+44 (0)1637 860543
Email	life@watergatebay.co.uk
Web	www.watergatebay.co.uk

Watergate Bay Hotel,
On the Beach, Watergate Bay, TR8 4AA

Bedruthan Hotel & Spa

Bedruthan has the lot – stunning sea views, a couple of swimming pools, a spa with treatment rooms and restaurants galore. The sensory spa garden offers seven steps to heaven: a salt scrub; a sauna; a cold bucket shower; a dip in the hot tub; a wet scrub; a visit to the sky garden; a second bite at the hot tub. Adults get the run of the place in term time, children can come in the holidays and sign up to surf school. Qualified staff entertain younger children with fun crafty stuff or they can tire themselves out in the soft play area while their parents snooze on sunbeds by the pool. There's a wood-burner in the quiet sitting room, a cocktail bar that opens onto a terrace, then stylish bedrooms with retro colours and sparkling bathrooms. Some have separate rooms for children, others have terraces or sea views, a few overlook the car park. Younger children can have early suppers, adults return later for a slap-up meal, perhaps guinea fowl, whole lemon sole, chilled strawberry soup with prosecco sorbet. The beach is a short stroll.

Rooms	36 twin/doubles: £160-£270. 27 suites for 6: £205-£490. 32 family rooms for 4: £175-£305. 6 singles: £75-£125. Dinner, B&B from £95 per person.
Meals	Lunch from £6. Dinner £27.50-£32.50. Sunday lunch £14.50-£18.50.
Closed	2-31 January.

Bedruthan Hotel & Spa,
Mawgan Porth, Newquay, TR8 4BU

Tel	+44 (0)1637 860860
Email	stay@bedruthan.com
Web	www.bedruthan.com

The Scarlet

The Scarlet does what few others can – this may be a super-cool design hotel with one of the loveliest spas in the land, but the service here is fantastic: friendly, attentive, ready to help. As for the hotel, it sits above the sea with a vast wall of glass in reception to frame the view. Outside, you'll find a hot tub in the garden from which you can stargaze; inside, there's a stylish restaurant that opens onto a decked terrace, where you scoff delicious Cornish food while gazing out to sea. Elsewhere, an open fire in the sitting room, a pool table in the library, then a cool bar for Cornish wines and ales. Exceptional bedrooms all have sea views, then balconies or terraces, private gardens or viewing pods. Expect organic cotton, oak floors from sustainable forests, perhaps a free-standing bath or a huge walk-in shower. As for the spa, you get tented treatment rooms, chill-out pods that hang from the ceiling, and swimming pools flanked by sunbeds. Finally, the hotel is green to its core, with a biomass boiler, solar panels and state-of-the-art insulation. *Minimum stay: 2 nights at weekends.*

Rooms	21 doubles, 8 twin/doubles: £210-£405.
	8 suites for 2: £210-£460.
	Dinner, B&B £140-£280 per person.
Meals	Lunch, 3 courses, £24.95.
	Dinner, 3 courses, £45.95.
Closed	Rarely.

Tel	+44 (0)1637 861800
Email	stay@scarlethotel.co.uk
Web	www.scarlethotel.co.uk

The Scarlet,
Tredragon Road, Mawgan Porth,
Newquay, TR8 4DQ

The Seafood Restaurant

In 1975 a young chef called Rick Stein opened a restaurant in Padstow. These days he has four more as well as a deli, pâtisserie, seafood cookery schoo,l and 40 beautiful bedrooms. Despite this success, his homespun philosophy has never wavered: buy the freshest seafood from fisherman on the quay, then cook it simply and eat it with friends. The Seafood Restaurant is now a place of pilgrimage – so come to discover the Cornish coast, walk on the cliffs, paddle in the estuary, then drop into this lively restaurant for a fabulous meal, perhaps black risotto with Cornish cuttlefish, grilled Padstow lobster with fine herbs, hot chocolate fondant with toasted marshmallow ice cream. Book in for the night and a table in the restaurant is yours, though flawless bedrooms are hard to leave. They are scattered about town, some above the restaurant, others at the bistro or just around the corner at St Petroc's House. All are immaculate. Expect the best fabrics, Vi-Spring mattresses, stunning bathrooms, the odd terrace with estuary views. *Minimum stay: 2 nights at weekends.*

Rooms	32 doubles, 8 twin/doubles: £165-£315.
Meals	Lunch £38.50. Dinner £58.50.
Closed	25-26 December.

The Seafood Restaurant,
Riverside, Padstow, PL28 8BY

Tel	+44 (0)1841 532700
Email	reservations@rickstein.com
Web	www.rickstein.com/stay

St Tudy Inn

Holiday walkers and cyclists from Padstow have long loved this little pub off the beaten track, with its new slate floors and its crackling fire, Doom Bar and Tawny on tap. But it's the food that's been the biggest draw; it still is. Chef-patron Emily sailed in in 2015 with exciting plans, a friendly team and a rustic, seasonal menu. There are four cosy dining areas including the public bar and a terrace at the back, and the rooms are charming and countrified – a battered leather chair, a basket full of logs, a fine old settle. Emily heads the kitchen and creates disarmingly simple food from the best Cornish produce: lamb tagine with apricots; squash and fennel lasagne; lemon sole with new potatoes; treacle tart with clotted cream. No need to head home after you've indulged as there are now four spankingly new rooms with big comfy beds and crisply nautical colour schemes, sparkling showers and shiny Nespresso machines. Leave the little ones at home and make this your base for a grown-up getaway. *Minimum stay: 2 nights at weekends. Pets by arrangement.*

Rooms	4 doubles: £150-£225. Singles £150-£165.
Meals	Lunch & bar meals from £8.95. Dinner from £10.95.
Closed	25-26 December.

Tel	+44 (0)1208 850656
Email	sttudyinn@outlook.com
Web	www.sttudyinn.com

St Tudy Inn,
St Tudy, Bodmin, PL30 3NN

The Mill House Inn

Coast down the steep winding lane to this 1760s mill house in a woodland setting in the middle of a trio of trad Cornish villages. Trebarwith's spectacular sandy beach is a ten-minute walk away. Coastal trails lead to Tintagel, official home of the Arthurian legends, there's biking, surfing, crabbing off Port Isaac's harbour... you couldn't possibly be bored. Back at the inn, sit on squishy sofas by a wood-burning stove with a drink, fill up on some good pub grub: firecracker prawns; Cornish hake with crushed potatoes, Porthilly mussels; coconut panna cotta, torched pineapple, rum sponge to finish. Views look out over a burbling mill stream, there are great barbecues in the summer and every Thursday it's rump steak with all the trimmings for a tenner; live bands play at the weekends. Bed down in one of the simple and uncluttered bedrooms or opt for the little cottage. Four-legged friends are effusively welcomed and can join walkers on recommended stomps straight from the doorstep.

The Mill House Inn,
Trebarwith, Tintagel, PL34 0HD

Rooms	6 doubles, 1 twin/double, 1 family room for 4: £75-£130. 1 cottage for 2: £120-£160. Singles £56-£97. Dinner, B&B £60-£90 p.p. Extra bed £20 p.p.p.n.
Meals	Lunch from £7.50. Dinner from £12. Sunday lunch, 3 courses, £17.85.
Closed	Rarely.

Tel	+44 (0)1840 770200
Email	management@themillhouseinn.co.uk
Web	www.themillhouseinn.co.uk

The Horn of Plenty

The Horn of Plenty is one of those clever hotels that has survived the test of time by constantly improving itself. The latest addition is six gorgeous new rooms, four of which have terraces or balconies with 40-mile views over the Tamar Valley. Potter about outside and find six acres of gardens, then a path that leads down through bluebell woods to the river. Inside, beautiful simplicity abounds: stripped floors, gilt mirrors, fine art, fresh flowers everywhere.

Bedrooms in the main house come in country-house style, those in the garden have a more contemporary feel. All have smart colours, big comfy beds, perhaps a claw-foot bath or a ceiling open to the rafters; ten have a terrace or a balcony. Despite all this, the food remains the big draw, so come to eat well, perhaps beetroot mousse with goat's cheese parfait, grilled duck with chicory and orange, chocolate cannelloni with banana sorbet; views of the Tamar snaking through the hills are included in the price. Afternoon tea is served on the patio in summer. Tavistock, Dartmoor and the Eden Project are close.

Rooms	16 twin/doubles: £130-£275. Singles £120-£265. Dinner, B&B £107-£190 p.p. Extra bed £25 p.p.p.n.
Meals	Lunch from £21. Dinner, 3 courses, £52.50. Tasting menu £70. Afternoon tea from £9.50.
Closed	Never.

Tel	+44 (0)1822 832528
Email	enquiries@thehornofplenty.co.uk
Web	www.thehornofplenty.co.uk

The Horn of Plenty,
Gulworthy, Tavistock, PL19 8JD

Lewtrenchard Manor

A Jacobean mansion where the full aristocratic Monty is on display; *Onward Christian Soldiers* was written in the library. Although grand, with its spectacular hall, cavernous fireplace and dazzling ballroom, it's not stuffy and the Murray family run their hotel with friendly ease. Dogs are welcome here and walks shoot off in all directions. You can hire bikes nearby and explore the Camel Trail; the local Arundell Arms has fishing rights on the river Tamar and offers courses. Return for one of the hotel's relaxation therapies and an elegant afternoon tea. The silver service dinners come with vegetables from the walled garden. You can walk it off in the gardens: Gertrude Jekyll parterre, fountains, woodland and an avenue of beeches straight out of Thomas Hardy. The Dartmoor National Park can be reached on foot if you're feeling hearty. *Minimum stay: 2 nights at weekends.*

Rooms	4 doubles, 6 twin/doubles: £180-£320. 4 suites for 2: £235-£340. Singles £145-£205. Extra bed £25 p.p.p.n.
Meals	Bar meals from £5.95. Lunch from £21. Dinner, 3 courses, £49.50. Children over seven welcome in restaurant.
Closed	Never.

Lewtrenchard Manor,
Lewdown, Okehampton, EX20 4PN

Tel	+44 (0)1566 783222
Email	info@lewtrenchard.co.uk
Web	www.lewtrenchard.co.uk

Mill End

Order a hearty packed lunch the night before, and set off on the Two Moors Way. This is a walkers' hotel run by generous people in a glorious patch of Dartmoor. Tara and Nick give you cream teas, maps of walks straight from the door, high tea for children, and a boot room for your muddy things – including the dog. Outside the river Teign runs alongside the gardens (yes, you can fish; there's even an in-house fly fishing school if you want to learn) and homemade scones with clotted cream and jam are served in the sunshine. Inside are three dapper lounges where fires crackle and burn on chilly days. Order your gin and tonic, play a game of Scrabble then step into the restaurant for fresh fish, locally reared meats and gorgeous West Country cheeses. Bedrooms – some with garden views, others with French windows opening onto the lawns – are all a good size and have comfortable armchairs or sofas if you'd rather stay private. *Minimum stay: 2 nights on weekdays.*

Rooms	15 twin/doubles: £105-£200.
	6 suites for 2: £190-£260.
	Singles from £80. Extra beds from £25.
Meals	Lunch from £6. Dinner, 3 courses,
	£30-£40. Sunday lunch £22-£26.
	Afternoon tea £18.95.
Closed	Never.

Tel	+44 (0)1647 432282	Mill End,
Email	info@millendhotel.com	Chagford, Newton Abbot, TQ13 8JN
Web	www.millendhotel.com	

Glazebrook House Hotel

The front door at Glazebrook may well be a rip in the space-time continuum. Outside, English decorum reigns; inside, a wonderland for your senses waits. You don't really find a hotel, more a contemporary art installation that you get to live in for a day or two. It's a reinvention of a 19th-century collector's house and it overflows with pink flamingos, enormous chandeliers, ancient maps, a bust of the queen with a halo instead of a crown. There's a dinosaur in the library, a tasting room for whisky and wine, a red-marbled bar with sofas and armchairs, then doors onto a terrace for afternoon tea. Rooms come fully loaded: vast beds, the loveliest linen, cool design, quirky art. You get iPads, smart TVs and minibars 'on the house'. Black marble bathrooms are flawless, with walk-in showers, fluffy robes, perhaps a free-standing bath. Ambrosial food waits downstairs, maybe goat's cheese mousse, rack of lamb, hake with shellfish butter, chocolate delice with popcorn. Although the A38 passes nearby, there's only a distant hum when you're outside, so don't let that put you off visiting this exceptional hotel. Dartmoor waits.

Rooms	7 doubles, 1 twin: £199-£324. 1 single: £164-£234.
Meals	Breakfast £16.50. Lunch, 2-3 courses, £16-£20. Dinner, 3 courses, about £40; 6-course tasting menu £50; 8-course tasting menu £64.
Closed	Rarely.

Glazebrook House Hotel,
South Brent, TQ10 9JE

Tel	+44 (0)1364 73322
Email	enquiries@glazebrookhouse.com
Web	www.glazebrookhouse.com

Plantation House

This lovely small hotel delivers what so many of us want: a warm welcome, lovely food, rooms that spoil us rotten. Downstairs, a fire smoulders in the sitting-room bar; upstairs, fine Georgian windows frame views of hill and forest. Stylish bedrooms are full of comforts. They come with excellent bathrooms, lovely beds, crisp linen and warm colours. You get padded bedheads, sound systems, bowls of fruit, white robes to pad about in. Back downstairs, you'll succumb to a pre-dinner drink – in front of the fire in the bar in winter, out on the pretty terrace in summer. As for Richard's food, it bursts with flavour, so expect to eat well, perhaps Thai-style sea bass with ginger and lemongrass, local lamb with a Merlot jus, chocolate terrine with hazelnut ice cream. Soft fruits, vegetables and potatoes come from the garden in summer, as do home-laid eggs at breakfast. The river Erme passes across the road – follow it down to the sea and discover wonderful Wonwell Beach. There's lots to see around you: Dartmoor to the north, Totnes, Dartmouth, Salcombe and Slapton Sands to the south. Brilliant.

Rooms	6 doubles, 1 twin: £115-£195. 1 suite for 2: £195-£230.
Meals	Dinner, 5 courses, from £36.
Closed	Never.

Tel	+44 (0)1548 831100
Email	info@plantationhousehotel.co.uk
Web	www.plantationhousehotel.co.uk

Plantation House,
Totnes Road, Ermington,
Ivybridge, PL21 9NS

Burgh Island Hotel

When the tide is in this ocean liner of a hotel is stranded on its own island. It's romantic here and filled with history so allow yourself to be whisked back to the pre-war days of Agatha Christie and Noël Coward – both of whom were regular guests. Walk the coastline or spend idle days on the beach; there's a private cove with turquoise waters – a natural salt water swimming pool. Return to the terrace at the Palm Court Bar for afternoon tea or a cocktail with glorious sea views. You'll find a snooker room, table tennis and the library has TV. Dress up properly for three-course dinners in the Ballroom where there's usually a pianist or house band, although you can head for the Captain's Cabin or Ganges Restaurant if you prefer to be more casual. In the morning, tea or coffee is brought to your room – a nice old-fashioned touch. *Minimum stay: 2 nights at weekends.*

Rooms	10 doubles, 3 twin/doubles: £290-£510. 12 suites for 2: £420-£700. Prices include dinner.
Meals	Lunch from £16. Dinner included; non-residents £75. Afternoon tea £18.50. Sunday lunch, non-residents, £62.
Closed	2 January – 12 February.

Burgh Island Hotel,
Burgh Island, Bigbury-on-Sea,
Kingsbridge, TQ7 4BG

Tel	+44 (0)1548 810514
Email	reception@burghisland.com
Web	www.burghisland.com

The Henley Hotel

A small house above the sea with fabulous views, super bedrooms and some of the loveliest food in Devon. Despite these credentials, it's Martyn and Petra who shine most brightly, their kind, generous approach making this a memorable place to stay. Warm interiors have wooden floors, Lloyd Loom furniture, the odd potted palm, then big windows to frame the view. Below, the Avon estuary slips gracefully out to sea. At high tide surfers ride the waves, at low tide you can walk on the sands. There's a pretty garden with a path tumbling down to the beach, binoculars in each room, a wood-burner in the snug and good books everywhere. Bedrooms are a steal (one is huge). Expect warm colours, crisp linen, tongue-and-groove panelling and robes in super little bathrooms. As for Martyn's table d'hôte dinners, expect to eat very well. Fish comes daily from Kingsbridge market, you might find grilled figs with goat's cheese and Parma ham, roast monkfish with a lobster sauce, then hot chocolate soufflé with fresh raspberries. Better than the Ritz! *German spoken. Minimum stay: 2 nights at weekends.*

Rooms	2 doubles, 2 twin/doubles: £120-£137. 1 suite for 2: £150. Singles from £85. Dinner, B&B £87-£97 per person; minimum 2 nights.
Meals	Dinner £36.
Closed	November to March.

Tel	+44 (0)1548 810240	The Henley Hotel,
Email	thehenleyhotel@btconnect.com	Folly Hill, Bigbury-on-Sea,
Web	www.thehenleyhotel.co.uk	Kingsbridge, TQ7 4AR

Cary Arms & Spa

The inn is a Devon delight with interiors by way of New England: at the inn, wood-floored rooms – all but one with a private terrace or balcony – have yachting photos and breezy décor, while beach huts and suites have cantilevered sun decks. Staff go above and beyond to welcome, leaving sticks of rock on pillows and snifters of sloe gin to snaffle, delivering newspapers. Move from bedroom to spa (treatments, hydrotherapy pool, sauna and steam) to the cosy pub downstairs, all without dragging your eyes away from the sea views. You're anchored to the English Riviera, windows framing the water. Downstairs the pub serves up comforting menus – regional, ever-changing, with an emphasis on seafood and a vegan menu, too – and breakfasts of pancakes or bubble and squeak with duck eggs, plus a continental spread. Pick up the South West Coastal Path from the front door or fish with the locals from the jetty. Walk 10 minutes to Oddicombe Beach for sea kayaking, paddle boarding, snorkelling.

Rooms	7 doubles: £265-£295. 1 suite for 4, 8 suites for 2: £385-£485. 1 family room for 4: £395. Extra bed/sofabed £25 p.p.p.n.
Meals	Lunch from £7.95. Dinner £25-£35.
Closed	Never.

Cary Arms & Spa,
Beach Road, Babbacombe,
Torquay, TQ1 3LX

Tel	+44 (0)1803 327110
Email	enquiries@caryarms.co.uk
Web	www.caryarms.co.uk

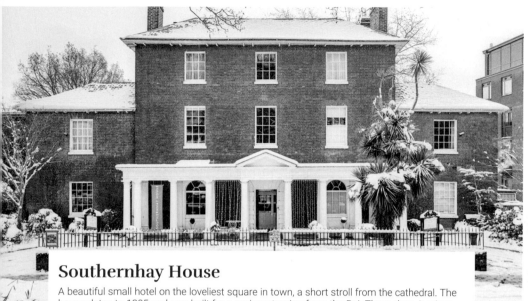

Southernhay House

A beautiful small hotel on the loveliest square in town, a short stroll from the cathedral. The house dates to 1805 and was built for a major returning from the Raj. These days, it mixes quirky design with all the comforts you'd expect of a small, city hotel. It's central, welcoming, the rooms are lovely, the dining room serves great bistro food and there's a chic bar for cocktails or a pint of local ale. Downstairs, French windows at the back of the house draw you onto a small terrace, where you can eat in good weather. Potter about and find electric blue sofas, 50s starlets framed on the wall, old style radiators and beautiful art. Stylish bedrooms wait upstairs – some are bigger, all are lovely. Expect bold colours, sumptuous fabrics, Indian art, hi-tech gadgetry. Cool bathrooms come as standard, bigger rooms have free-standing baths. Exeter has lots to offer: Roman walls, a 12th-century cathedral, the imperious Royal Albert Memorial Museum & Art Gallery. Topsham is close for river walks. *Children over 12 welcome.*

Rooms	11 doubles: £100-£288.
Meals	Breakfast, £15. Lunch from £8. Dinner, 3 courses, about £30
Closed	Never.

Tel	+44 (0)1392 435324
Email	home@southernhayhouse.com
Web	www.southernhayhouse.com

Southernhay House,
36 Southernhay East, Exeter, EX1 1NX

Paschoe House

Tabitha and team greet you warmly: afternoon tea on the house, a selection of West Country gins to work your way through and films to download with complimentary popcorn. Settle into chic, unstuffy rooms with long views of the Devon hills, flowers, chocolates and freshly baked cookies; bathrooms have cavernous walk-in showers and roll-top baths – pour in the Bamford bubbles and take a soak before dinner. The menu is seasonal, locally sourced and thoroughly modern. Dress for the space: glam and grown-up - or you can eat in the informal library, or out on the terrace with those uninterrupted countryside views. Come rain or shine there's much to do. Stroll the walled gardens and then chill with a book from the library, play tennis or garden games. Dogs are very welcome and will relish blustery walks over the Two Moors Way across Dartmoor and Exmoor. Ask about excursions: walking tours, horse riding, shooting; and there's a fixed outdoor marquee - perfect for parties and weddings. *Minimum stay: 2 nights at weekends.*

Rooms	7 doubles: £290. 1 suite for 2: £360. 1 single: £220.
Meals	Lunch £35. Dinner £60. Afternoon tea £29.50.
Closed	Monday.

Paschoe House,
Bow, Crediton, EX17 6JT

Tel	+44 (0)1363 84244
Email	stay@paschoehouse.co.uk
Web	www.paschoehouse.co.uk

The Lamb Inn

This 16th-century inn is adored by locals and visitors alike. It's a proper inn in the old tradition with gorgeous rooms and the odd touch of scruffiness to add authenticity to its earthy bones. It stands on a cobbled walkway in a village lost down tiny lanes, and those lucky enough to chance upon it leave reluctantly. Inside there are beams, but they are not sandblasted, red carpets with a little swirl, sofas in front of an open fire. Boarded menus trumpet irresistible food – carrot and orange soup, haunch of venison with a port jus, an excellent rhubarb crumble. You can eat wherever you want: in the bar, in the fancy restaurant, or out in the walled garden in good weather. There's a cobbled terrace, a skittle alley, maps for walkers and well-kept ales. Upstairs, seven rooms have a chic country style. Two have baths in the room, those in the barn have painted stone walls, the suite has a wood-burner and a private terrace. All are lovely with comfy beds, white linen, good power showers and flat-screen TVs. Kind staff chat with ease. Dartmoor waits, but you may well linger. Brilliant.

Rooms	5 doubles, 1 twin/double: £95-£140. 1 suite for 3: £145-£180. Extra bed/sofabed £22 p.p.p.n.
Meals	Lunch from £6.95. Dinner, 3 courses, £22-£35. Sunday lunch £10.95-£12.95
Closed	Rarely

Tel	+44 (0)1363 773676
Email	thelambinn@gmail.com
Web	www.lambinnsandford.co.uk

The Lamb Inn,
Sandford, EX17 4LW

Northcote Manor

A small country-house hotel built on the site of a 15th-century monastery. Those who want peace in deep country will find it here. You wind up a one-mile drive, through a wood that bursts with colour in spring, then emerge onto a lush plateau of rolling hills; the view from the croquet lawn drifts east for ten miles. As for the house, wisteria wanders along old stone walls, while the odd open fire smoulders within. There's an airy hall that doubles as the bar, a country-house drawing room that floods with light, and a sitting room where you gather for pre-dinner drinks. Super food waits in a lovely dining room, steps lead down to a pretty conservatory, doors open onto a gravelled terrace for summer breakfasts with lovely views. Bedrooms are no less appealing – more traditional in the main house, more contemporary in the garden rooms. Expect padded bedheads, mahogany dressers, flat-screen TVs, silky throws. You can walk your socks off, then come home for a good meal, perhaps Cornish crab, local lamb, strawberry soufflé with vanilla ice-cream. Exmoor and North Devon's coasts are close.

Rooms	9 twin/doubles: £170-£280. 7 suites for 2: £170-£280. Singles from £120. Extra bed £15-£25 p.p.p.n.
Meals	Light dishes from £6.50. Lunch £22.50-£25.50. Dinner, 3 courses, £45. Tasting menu £90. Sunday lunch from £28.50.
Closed	Never.

Northcote Manor,
Burrington, Umberleigh, EX37 9LZ

Tel	+44 (0)1769 560501
Email	rest@northcotemanor.co.uk
Web	www.northcotemanor.co.uk

The Old Rectory Hotel Exmoor

The road from Lynton is a great way in, through woods that cling to a hill with the sea below. As for the Old Rectory, it's a proper small hotel and a very sociable sort of place. Three acres of spectacular gardens wrap around you, and Exmoor deer drink from the pond. Inside, Huw and Sam continue to lavish love and money in all the right places. Their most recent addition is an orangery with smart sofas and warm colours, then doors onto the garden for afternoon tea in the sun. Interiors are soothing: Farrow & Ball colours, the odd stone wall, a little sitting room, fresh flowers and books everywhere. Bedrooms are just as good and heaped with treats: digital radios, flat-screen TVs, a balcony here, a leather sofa there. Spin into the restaurant for a set four-course meal: your hosts are fabulous cooks.

Rooms	3 doubles, 4 twin/doubles: £205-£245. 4 suites for 2: £260-£275. Prices include dinner.
Meals	Dinner, 4 courses, included in price; non-residents £35.
Closed	November to March

Tel	+44 (0)1598 763368
Email	info@oldrectoryhotel.co.uk
Web	www.oldrectoryhotel.co.uk

The Old Rectory Hotel Exmoor,
Martinhoe, Parracombe,
Barnstable, EX31 4QT

Ginger Peanut

Foodies will be spoilt for choice here. Award-winning chef Peter Mundy goes for taste, innovation and beauty in dishes that get rave reviews. Menus change regularly, so expect the freshest of seasonal food. The revamped pub setting has a woody, easy-going feel with the promising sparkle of well-polished glasses. It's just an after-dinner flight of stairs to sleek rooms; cleverly designed for the building's cottagey bones; each has an easy chair and Quail, the smallest, the biggest shower room. Have a lazy breakfast in bed, in the restaurant or in the café/bakery around the corner. Take a stroll around the town and church of St Michael and All Angels; there are pleasant local walks; more dramatic routes up on Exmoor (and space for clobber at the back door); ask about fishing, riding, picnic lunches – the team here are very helpful. *Minimum stay: 2 nights at weekends.*

Rooms	5 twin/doubles: £75-£135. Singles £77-£145. Dinner, B&B £80-£160 p.p.
Meals	Lunch, 2 courses, £15.50. Dinner from £13.95. Sunday lunch, 2 courses, £18.50.
Closed	Never. Restaurant closed occasionally on Mondays and Tuesdays.

Ginger Peanut,
19 Fore Street, Bampton, EX16 9ND

Tel	+44 (0)1398 332244
Email	sleep@gingerpeanut.co.uk
Web	www.gingerpeanut.co.uk

Loyton Lodge

You get the impression the tiny lanes that wrap around this small estate act as a sort of fortification, one designed to confuse invaders and protect this patch of heaven. And heaven it is – 280 acres of rolling hills and ancient woodland, with wild flowers, pristine rivers, strutting pheasants and the odd red deer commuting across the fields. It's England circa 1964 with nothing but birdsong to break the peace and glorious walks that start at the front door. As for Loyton, it's a great little base for a night or two deep in the hills. It mixes contemporary interiors with an old-school feel – roaring fires, comfy sofas, wonderful art, even a snooker room. Bedrooms have warm colours and smart fabrics, perhaps a sleigh bed or a claw-foot bath, then books and robes and crisp white linen. Breakfast is a treat – bacon and sausages from home-reared pigs, eggs from estate hens – and dinner can be arranged, perhaps local asparagus, lemon sole, walnut and fruit crumble. Take the whole house and bring the family or come for the odd night of live jazz. Exmoor waits, as do good local restaurants.

Rooms	7 doubles, 2 twin/doubles, 1 twin: £95-£130. Singles from £80. Extra beds £20; under 12s free.
Meals	Dinner, 3 courses, about £30, by arrangement.
Closed	Rarely.

Tel	+44 (0)1398 331051
Email	thelodge@loyton.com
Web	www.loyton.com

Loyton Lodge,
Morebath, Tiverton, EX16 9AS

The Mason Arms

Lose yourself in tiny lanes; follow them down to the sea. This old village pub – once a cider house - stands half a mile back from the pebble beach surrounded by lovely hills. There's a big terrace out front, a row of thatch cottages by the car park, and a restaurant and bar that feel authentic and welcoming. The beer is St Austell's, the food is great, and the spit roast gets going on Sundays. Footpaths lead in all directions: along the coast and across the hills. You can be on Beer's beach in less than an hour, or dispatching cream teas in the village. As for the rooms, there are plenty to choose from. Those above the pub are small but cosy while those in the cottages are larger. Some are quieter or quainter than others,and if you don't mind the steps, the rooms on the top level open to a terrace with gorgeous views to the sea. *Minimum stay: 2 nights at weekends in summer.*

The Mason Arms,
Branscombe, EX12 3DJ

Rooms	8 doubles, 6 twin/doubles, 6 four-posters: £80-£180. 1 family room for 4: £165-£195.
Meals	Lunch from £7.50. Bar meals from £9.95. Dinner, 3 courses, £20-£25. Sunday lunch from £9.95.
Closed	Never.

Tel	+44 (0)1297 680300
Email	masonsarms@staustellbrewery.co.uk
Web	www.masonsarms.co.uk

Alexandra Hotel & Restaurant

This chic hotel has rather good views, a clean sweep up the Jurassic coast all the way to Chesil Beach and on to Portland Bill. It sits high on the hill with one foot in town and the other paddling in the water. Directly below, the Cobb curls into the sea, the very spot where Meryl Streep withstood crashing waves in *The French Lieutenant's Woman*. Outside, there's a sun-trapping garden, where guests fall asleep in deckchairs, then a lookout tower with big sea views for a romantic dinner for two. Inside, an easy elegance flows: stripped wood floors, windows everywhere, an airy bar for pre-dinner drinks, an attractive sitting room with lots of books. There's a smart dining room that could double as a ballroom, then a conservatory brasserie that opens onto a terrace for lunch in summer. Both offer tasty, local food, perhaps Lyme Bay scallops, chicken with cavolo nero, a white chocolate mousse. Bedrooms, most with sea views, have warm colours, comfy beds, padded headboards, robes in fine bathrooms. Lyme, the beach, and the fossil-ridden coast, all wait. There's an 18th-century chapel, too.

Rooms	23 twin/doubles: £180-£390. 3 family rooms for 4: £308-£480. 1 single: £95-£130. 1 apartment for 4, 1 apartment for 6: £315-£365
Meals	Lunch from £9.90. Dinner, 3 courses, about £35. Sunday lunch from £23.
Closed	31 December – 31 January.

Tel	+44 (0)1297 442010
Email	enquiries@hotelalexandra.co.uk
Web	www.hotelalexandra.co.uk

Alexandra Hotel & Restaurant,
Pound Street, Lyme Regis, DT7 3HZ

The Anchor Inn

You're in a perfect spot here, smack-bang on the coastal path below Golden Cap and the Anchor is a thriving, lively inn that knows exactly how to make the most of its location. The big sun terrace and gardens overlook the pebbly beach; interiors evoke nautical cosiness, with open fires around which you can enjoy a pint and a crab sandwich, or a bowl of the freshest shellfish washed down with an excellent wine. There are walks from the doorstep so when you've built up an appetite the menus will tempt you with inspiring, hearty and artisanal treats that make splendid use of locally sourced produce with fish and lobsters direct from the beach. Three bedrooms with deeply comfortable king-size beds are chic – a rusty tap as a coat hook, rope buoys, trunks turned into tables – with captivating sea views; you'll think you've stepped aboard an 18th-century schooner. Bathrooms have roll-top baths, walk-in showers, the fluffiest of white towels and top-notch oils and soaps. Terrific. *Minimum stay: 2 nights.*

Rooms	3 doubles: £125-£170. Singles £125-£155.
Meals	Starters from £7. Mains from £13
Closed	Rarely.

The Anchor Inn,
Seatown, Chideock, Bridport, DT6 6JU

Tel	+44 (0)1297 489215
Email	contact@theanchorinnseatown.co.uk
Web	www.theanchorinnseatown.co.uk

The Bull Hotel

The Bull was Dorset's first boutique hotel, a cool little place with lovely staff, an informal vibe, tasty food and lots of colour. It was bought by Fullers in 2014, who immediately poured in a small fortune to make it even better. The results are dreamy: airy interiors, big art, fancy bathrooms and a chic restaurant. It remains as friendly as ever and draws a local crowd, who come for coffee and cake, a cool bar that rocks at weekends, even a masked ball on New Year's Eve; all of which makes it a lot of fun for guests passing through. Downstairs, you'll find an open fire, stripped wood floors and draft ale at the bar; in summer, life decants onto a flower-filled courtyard. Colourful bedrooms – all different – have lots of style: beautiful beds, pashmina throws, chic wallpapers, perhaps a bath at the foot of your bed. Some have sofas, family rooms have bunk beds for kids. You get digital radios and flat-screen TVs for entertainment. Don't miss the food, try pork belly croquettes followed by hake cassoulet, there are good veggie options and mezze sharing platters too. *Minimum stay: 2 nights at weekends.*

Rooms	10 doubles, 1 twin, 3 four-posters: £100-£230. 1 suite for 2: £235-£265. 3 family rooms for 4: £220-£260. 1 single: £90 £130.
Meals	Lunch, 2 courses, from £12. Dinner, 3 courses, around £35. Sunday lunch £13.50-£14.50.
Closed	Never.

Tel	+44 (0)1308 422878
Email	info@thebullhotel.co.uk
Web	www.thebullhotel.co.uk

The Bull Hotel,
34 East Street, Bridport, DT6 3LF

The Seaside Boarding House, Restaurant & Bar

You pop up the hill, come to the end of the road, then follow a track along the cliff and down to this lovely and bright small hotel. Rolling hills shoot north towards Dorchester, while the view east follows Chesil Beach, a mere 20 miles round to Portland Bill. The Boarding House's natural beauty comes courtesy of a recent facelift, proving conclusively that cosmetic surgery works. Outside, there's a dining terrace overlooking the sea, then paths that drop down to the beach. Inside, walls of glass flood big rooms with seaside light. There's a bar for cocktails and afternoon tea, a library with books and games for rainy days, then a restaurant for delicious food: perhaps cheese soufflé, whole lemon sole and chocolate and hazelnut delice. Upstairs bedrooms all have sea views and mix period furniture (some from HMS Windsor) with 21st-century design: beautiful beds, Zoffany colours, rugs on wood floors, cushioned window seats. Bathrooms have white robes and vintage tiles, then a big shower, a claw-foot bath, or both. The coastal path passes directly outside, so bring your boots. Brilliant. *Minimum stay: 2 nights at weekends.*

Rooms	9 doubles: £180-£235.
Meals	Lunch from £14. Dinner, 3 courses, about £30. Sunday lunch £25-£30. Afternoon tea from £10.
Closed	Never.

The Seaside Boarding House,
Cliff Road, Burton Bradstock, DT6 4RB

Tel	+44 (0)1308 897205
Email	info@theseasideboardinghouse.com
Web	www.theseasideboardinghouse.com

The Priory Hotel

The lawns of this 16th-century priory run down to the river Frome. Boats float past, an old church rises behind, a gorgeous garden filled with colour wraps around you. As for this lovely country house, you'll find a grand piano in the drawing room, a first-floor sitting room with garden views, then a new restaurant with walls of glass that juts into the garden giving rather good views. There's a beautiful terrace, too, where you can sit in the sun and watch the river pass. Bedrooms in the main house come in different sizes, some cosy in the eaves, others grandly adorned in reds and golds. You get Zoffany fabrics, padded window seats, bowls of fruit, the odd sofa. Eight have river views, others look onto the garden or church. Chic bathrooms – some dazzlingly contemporary – all come with white robes. Rooms in the boathouse, a 16th-century clay barn, are lavish, with oak panelling, stone walls and sublime views. Corfe Castle and Studland Bay are close. A slice of old England with delicious food to boot. *Minimum stay: 2 nights at weekends. Over 14s welcome.*

Rooms	12 twin/doubles: £220-£320.
	5 suites for 2: £350-£380.
Meals	Lunch from £14.95.
	Dinner, 3 courses, £47.50.
Closed	Never.

Tel	+44 (0)1929 551666
Email	reservations@theprioryhotel.co.uk
Web	www.theprioryhotel.co.uk

The Priory Hotel,
Church Green, Wareham, BH20 4ND

Urban Beach Hotel

A quirky little place with surfer-chic interiors, lovely staff and a happy buzz throughout. You're on a residential street 500 metres from the beach; a short stroll leads down to the promenade which you can follow into town. Back at the hotel a relaxed informality reigns. You'll find circular leather booths, driftwood lamps, a house guitar and surf boards hanging on the wall. There's a bar for cocktails, candle lanterns scattered about, a table laden with

cakes, then the daily papers and cool tunes in the air. Outside, a terrace for all seasons waits, with a roof that disappears when the sun shines and a fire pit for cooler nights. Bedrooms upstairs come in different sizes, but even the smaller rooms are lovely with warm colours, crisp linen and smart bathrooms. The beach waits at the end of the road, seven miles of sand with a surf shop on the way down. Urban Reef, Mark & Fiona's sister restaurant, has a balcony and terrace overlooking the sea, not a bad spot for dinner in summer. *Minimum stay: 2 nights at weekends; 3 nights over bank holidays.*

Rooms	9 doubles, 1 twin/double: £89-£180. 2 singles: £72.
Meals	Lunch from £6. Dinner £25-30. Sunday lunch from £14.
Closed	Never.

Urban Beach Hotel,
23 Argyll Road, Bournemouth, BH5 1EB

Tel	+44 (0)1202 301509
Email	reception@urbanbeach.co.uk
Web	www.urbanbeach.co.uk

Captain's Club Hotel and Spa

The Captain's Club stands on the banks on the Stour, where a tiny ferry potters along the river dodging swans and ducks. In summer, you decant onto its lovely terrace and watch river life float by. Inside, walls of glass weatherproof the view. The sprawling bar fills with light and comes with deep sofas, the daily papers and a grand piano. It's smart, stylish and very informal, with live music at weekends. The hotel also has its own boat, so you can take to the high seas and spin over to the Isle of Wight or Brownsea Island. Back on dry land uncluttered bedrooms have river views, low-slung beds, crisp white linen, neutral colours and excellent bathrooms. None are small, some are huge with separate sitting rooms, apartments have more than one bedroom, so perfect for families and friends. There's a spa, too, with a hydrotherapy pool, a sauna and four treatment rooms. Lovely food is on tap all day in the bar, while the mirrored restaurant ensures everyone has the view. Christchurch is a short walk upstream. Brilliant. *Minimum stay: 2 nights at weekends.*

Rooms	17 doubles: £199-£259.
	12 apartments for 6: £289-£649.
Meals	Bar meals from £6. Lunch from £15.
	Dinner £30-£35.
Closed	Never.

Tel	+44 (0)1202 475111
Email	reservations@captainsclubhotel.com
Web	www.captainsclubhotel.com

Captain's Club Hotel and Spa,
Wick Ferry, Christchurch, BH23 1HU

Castleman Hotel & Restaurant

It's a little like stepping into the pages of a Hardy novel: an untouched corner of rural Dorset; a 400-year-old bailiff's house; sheep grazing in lush fields; a rich cast of characters pottering about. The Castleman – part country house, part restaurant with rooms – is a true one-off: quirky, intimate, defiantly English (you'll think you've landed in Ambridge). It pays no heed to prevailing fashions, not least because the locals would revolt if it did. Barbara runs the place in great style. Touches of grandeur are hard to miss: a panelled hall, art from Chettle House, a magnificent Jacobean ceiling in one of the sitting rooms. Follow your nose and find a cosy bar, fresh flowers everywhere and books galore. The restaurant has garden views, though your eyes are more likely to be fixed on Barbara's delicious old-school food, perhaps potted shrimp terrine, haunch of local venison, meringues with chocolate mousse and toasted almonds. Homely bedrooms fit the bill: comfortable, delightfully priced, a couple with claw-foot baths. Magical Dorset will fill your days with splendour. Don't miss it.

Rooms	4 doubles, 1 twin/double, 1 twin, 1 four-poster, 1 family room for 4: £95-£110. Singles from £70.
Meals	Dinner, 3 courses, about £27. Sunday lunch £25.
Closed	February.

Castleman Hotel & Restaurant, Chettle, Blanford Forum, DT11 8DB

Tel	+44 (0)1258 830096
Email	enquiry@castlemanhotel.co.uk
Web	www.castlemanhotel.co.uk

The Grosvenor Arms

Shaftesbury, an ancient country seat, has seen its fair share of history. In 888 King Alfred founded an abbey here; in 1035 King Canute died within its walls. It is surrounded by flawless country, with Cranborne Chase rolling south for miles. By day you go in search of sweeping vistas, ancient woodlands, the odd prehistoric hill fort. By night you return to this cool inn to make merry. The sitting-room bar doubles as a café and acts as the hub of the inn; it's open all day and buzzes with local life, so sink into a sofa, grab the daily papers and while away the afternoon. Elsewhere, there's an airy restaurant for wood-fired pizzas and local steaks, then a conservatory that opens onto a courtyard. Bedrooms upstairs are just the ticket: none are small, some are huge, all have warm colours, big beds and sparkling bathrooms. One opens onto a balcony, one suite comes with a chaise longue, the other has a claw-foot bath in the room; all have coffee machines, flat-screen TVs and posh oils. Gold Hill, a steep cobbled street around the corner, is famous for its timeless view. *Free passes for the car park across the road.*

Rooms	6 twin/doubles: £90-£160.
	8 doubles: £95-£160.
	2 suites for 2: £140-£180.
	Dogs £10 per night.
Meals	Lunch from £5.50. Dinner, 3 courses, £20-£35. Sunday lunch from £16.
Closed	Never.

Tel	+44 (0)1747 850580
Email	info@grosvenorarms.co.uk
Web	www.grosvenorarms.co.uk

The Grosvenor Arms,
The Commons, Shaftesbury, SP7 8JA

The Eastbury Hotel

Delightful staff make you feel welcome with their smiley efficiency while local lad Matt Street, MasterChef contestant and finalist in the prestigious Roux Scholarship, heads up the kitchen. The food is great and as much thought goes into the children's menu as it does to the seven-course taster menu. You eat in the restaurant overlooking the walled garden. Elegant Sherborne is there to delve into and you can walk everywhere. The Abbey is stunning and the castle gardens (landscaped by Capability Brown) are inspiring. While away an afternoon browsing independent shops; stop in a café for tea and cake. Return to a comfortable lounge, sunny morning room with magazines and games and a library for loafing which you can also hire for special dinners. The walled garden is set in an acre of mature trees and plants, and plans are afoot for five garden rooms and a mini spa. *Minimum stay: 2 nights.*

Rooms	17 doubles: £195-£205. 4 suites for 2: £315-£350. Singles £110.
Meals	Dinner, 3 courses, £39. Three small plates £10.
Closed	Never.

The Eastbury Hotel,
Long Street, Sherborne, DT9 3BY

Tel	+44 (0)1935 813131
Email	relax@theeastburyhotel.co.uk
Web	www.theeastburyhotel.co.uk

Plumber Manor

Plumber is old school, it pays no heed to passing fashions, it just gets on with doing what it does so well – looking after guests, pouring fine libations, serving delicious food. A fine old pile of golden stone that dates to 1650, it is suitably lost in Dorset's mazy lanes and sits in a couple of acres of green and pleasant land with the river Divelish flanking one side. Outside, there's a terrace for afternoon tea with beautiful magnolias on show in summer. Inside, a pair of labradors rule the roost. There's an open fire in the sitting-room bar, fresh flowers, old clocks, a snug in cherry red. The first-floor landing has an enormous sofa, a gallery of family portraits, a grand piano for good measure. Bedrooms are split between the main house and converted barns; the latter are big and welcome dogs. Décor is dated – 1980s florals – as are bathrooms, though several now sparkle in travertine splendour. A family triumvirate oversee it all: Brian in the kitchen, Richard behind the bar, Alison everywhere. Hearty food waits, perhaps crab mousseline, rack of lamb, lemon meringue pie.

Rooms	16 twin/doubles: £160-£240. Singles from £120.
Meals	Dinner £33-£40. Sunday lunch £30.
Closed	February.

Tel	+44 (0)1258 472507
Email	book@plumbermanor.com
Web	www.plumbermanor.com

Plumber Manor,
Plumber, Sturminster Newton, DT10 2AF

The Chetnole Inn

This sweet little inn has the lot: a great position in a pretty village; lovely interiors that mix old and new; super food that draws a crowd, and three excellent, affordable bedrooms. Flagged floors, low ceilings and wood-burners keep things cosy inside, and you can eat in the dog-friendly bar or in the lively restaurant, even in the breakfast room if things get busy. The food is just what you want after a day in the hills, perhaps rabbit and pork rillettes with a pear and squash chutney, steak and ale pie with thick-cut chips, warm apple and 'Kingston black' crumble. Tea is served with homemade coconut ice, and the ales are locally sourced and constantly changing; try the Copper Hopper Gold Rush, brewed just three miles away. Spotless bedrooms upstairs fit the mood perfectly. All are big and come with comfy beds, pretty sofas, sparkling shower rooms with robes and lovely lotions. Sherborne is to the north, the coast to the south, and the Cerne Abbas giant between. Brilliant.

Rooms	2 doubles, 1 twin/double: £95. Singles £70.
Meals	Lunch & dinner £9.85-£21. Bar meals from £5. Sunday lunch from £10.50.
Closed	Rarely.

The Chetnole Inn,
Village Street, Chetnole,
Sherborne, DT9 6NU

Tel	+44 (0)1935 872337
Email	enquiries@thechetnoleinn.co.uk
Web	www.thechetnoleinn.co.uk

The New Inn Cerne Abbas

The New Inn is most certainly new; it may date to the 16th century, but recently the best part of a year has been spent refurbishing the place and now it shines. Gone are the swirly green carpets; local slate has been laid in the bar. Lots of lovely old stuff remains – timber frames, mullioned windows, the odd settle – the open-plan feel is fresh with warm colours, engineered oak floors and a smart new bar where you can order a pint of Dorset Gold or a glass of good wine. Dig into local food wherever you want, perhaps fish from Brixham, local game, sticky toffee pudding. Bedrooms – some in the main house, others in the old stables – are good value for money. You'll find Hypnos mattresses, blond wood furniture and super little bathrooms. Those in the converted stables feel more contemporary: ground-floor rooms open onto the terrace, where you eat in good weather; those above are built into the eaves. The suites come with double-ended baths in the room. Don't miss the Giant.

Rooms	7 doubles, 3 twin/doubles: £95-£140. 2 suites for 2: £160-£170. Singles £85-£160.
Meals	Lunch & dinner £5-£35.
Closed	Christmas.

Tel	+44 (0)1300 341274
Email	info@thenewinncerneabbas.co.uk
Web	www.thenewinncerneabbas.co.uk

The New Inn Cerne Abbas,
Long Street, Cerne Abbas, DT2 7JF

The Acorn Inn

Perfect Evershot and rolling countryside lie at the door of this 400-year-old gem in Thomas Hardy country. Natalie and Richard took the reins to revive its fortunes, with head chef Robert Ndungu cooking hearty food. It's very much a traditional inn; locals sup pints of Otter Ale in the long flagstoned bar and guests sample good food sourced within 25 miles. In the dining room, the atmosphere changes to rural country house with smartly laid tables, terracotta tiles, soft lighting and elegant fireplaces. Good gastropub fare is taken seriously, be it a homemade burger, or open lasagne of confit rabbit followed by twice cooked pork belly, and a warm sticky toffee pudding. Little ones have their own menu, and stacks of colouring books and crayons to keep them busy while they wait. Service is helpful and friendly. Bedrooms creak with age and style; there are antiques and fabric wall-coverings, super little bathrooms, perhaps a wonky floor or a lovely four-poster. It's worth splashing out on a larger room if you want space.

Rooms	4 doubles, 2 twin/doubles, 3 four-posters: £105-£180. 1 suite for 3: £170-£230. Singles from £89. Dinner, B&B £80-£133 p.p. Extra bed £20 p.p.p.n.
Meals	Lunch & dinner £5.25-£22.95. Bar meals from £4.95.
Closed	Rarely.

The Acorn Inn,
Evershot, Dorchester, DT2 0JW

Tel	+44 (0)1935 83228
Email	stay@acorn-inn.co.uk
Web	www.acorn-inn.co.uk

The Ollerod

Beaminster – or Emminster in Thomas Hardy's *Tess* – sits in a lush Dorset valley. From the hills above, you drop through glorious country, rolling down to this old market town, where the church tower soars towards heaven. As for this lovely hotel, it's a 13th-century priest's house and comes with original trimmings: stone flags, mullioned windows, old beams and huge inglenooks. You're looked after beautifully but it's the friendliness you'll remember – there's no pomp or ceremony, it's intimate and deeply comfortable, with something beautiful at every turn. Chris is in charge in the kitchen – he delights in local ingredients, including fish straight from the waves and cooks in a fresh, inspirational way. Bubbly Silvana is front of house and takes great care to make sure you're as happy as a sandboy. It's worth exploring the village, particularly the church and its magnificent tower with 41 'crocketted' pinnacles. You're right next door to the Beaminster Museum and when you've done with that there are five circular walks in the hills surrounding you.

Rooms	1 double, 10 twin/doubles: £99-£225.
	2 family rooms for 4: £135-£255.
Meals	Starters from £8. Mains from £17.50.
Closed	Never.

Tel	+44 (0)1308 862200
Email	reception@theollerod.co.uk
Web	www.theollerod.co.uk

The Ollerod,
3 Prout Bridge, Beaminster, DT8 3AY

Lord Poulett Arms

This 17th-century thatched inn gives you a warm welcome, rooms with views of the village and much attention to detail: bathrobes, snazzy bath stuff, fresh milk in a china jug, little bags of shortbread. Choose a table by the fireplace in the downstairs pub or in the Provençal-style courtyard and allow yourself a full Somerset breakfast – pastries, fruit compote and yoghurt; eggs with pork and marmalade sausages or scrambled eggs and smoked salmon; porridge with brown sugar and cream. The food is fresh, seasonal and local with much made, cured and smoked in-house; the atmosphere is easy going but refined, with proper silverware and linens. Walks leave from the door, to the 13th-century Grade I listed church or the famous Spreading Oak Tree, or you can drive to stately homes – Montacute House, Forde Abbey House and Gardens – in 15 minutes. The Blackdown Hills AONB and the Jurassic Coast are only half an hour's drive. Return for supper in the pub and the best night's sleep.

Rooms	4 doubles: £85-£110. 1 suite for 2: £110-£150.
Meals	Starters from £6.50. Mains from £14. Sunday lunch from £15.
Closed	Christmas.

Lord Poulett Arms,
High Street,
Hinton Saint George, TA17 8SE

Tel	+44 (0)1460 73149
Email	reservations@lordpoulettarms.com
Web	www.lordpoulettarms.com

Little Barwick House

Tim and Emma rolled west years ago and now have a legion of fans who come to feast on ambrosial food at their beautiful restaurant with rooms. Their small Georgian country house stands privately in three acres of peace. Horses graze in the paddock below, afternoon tea is served in the garden to the sound of birdsong in summer. Inside, chic interiors flood with light thanks to fine windows that run along the front. There's an open fire in the bar, eclectic reading in the sitting room, then contemporary art in the high-ceilinged dining room. Gorgeous bedrooms have a country-house feel and come with warm colours, pretty fabrics, Roberts radios, a sofa if there's room. You'll find fresh garden flowers, antique furniture, and White Company oils in compact bathrooms. Dinner is the main event, heaven in three courses. Everything is homemade and cooked by Tim and Emma, an equal partnership in the kitchen – perhaps Lyme Bay scallops, saddle of wild venison, dark chocolate tort with armagnac ice-cream. Posh wines by the glass come courtesy of clever technology. *Children over 5 welcome.*

Rooms	4 doubles, 2 twins: £100-£170. Singles £75-£140. Dinner, B&B £105-£130 per person. Extra bed £25 p.p.p.n.
Meals	Lunch, 2-3 courses, £25.95-£29.95; not Tues. Dinner, 2-3 courses, £41.95-£47.95.
Closed	Rarely.

Tel	+44 (0)1935 423902
Email	info@littlebarwick.co.uk
Web	www.littlebarwickhouse.co.uk

Little Barwick House,
Rexes Hollow Lane,
Barwick, Yeovil, BA22 9TD

The Devonshire Arms

What makes a great little inn these days? The Devonshire Arms has all the ingredients: lots of style, good prices, a community feel, some lovely rooms. It's in the right place, too, bang on the village green, with a terrace at the front, a garden at the back and a courtyard in between. Inside, is just as good. This isn't one of those places where every table is laid up for food; on the contrary, the best seats in the house are in the bar – a couple of armchairs in front of the fire. Step inside and find stylish interiors throughout. You get painted panelling in the restaurant – a sort of contemporary take on an 18th-century gentleman's club – then cool colours in the bar, where you can grab a pint of Butcombe, then spin outside to watch village life pass by. Lovely rooms have terrific prices. You'll find good beds, white linen, pretty furniture and excellent bathrooms; one has a free-standing bath. Elsewhere, red leather banquettes, fresh flowers, kind staff, the daily papers. As for the food, it's just the ticket: local partridge, fillet of bream, treacle tart with buttermilk ice cream.

Rooms	8 doubles, 1 twin/double: £95-£140. Singles from £85. Extra bed/sofabed £20 p.p.p.n.
Meals	Lunch from £5.95. Dinner, 3 courses, about £30. Sunday lunch from £12.95.
Closed	25-26 December.

The Devonshire Arms,
Long Sutton, Langport, TA10 9LP

Tel	+44 (0)1458 241271
Email	mail@thedevonshirearms.com
Web	www.thedevonshirearms.com

Kingsdon Inn

These comfy, cottagey bedrooms above a 17th-century thatched pub are accessed through an external staircase and have lovely countryside views. Adam the manager/chef and his Italian wife Cinzia live in the cottage next door and are friendly and enthusiastic. Come for the food – it attracts diners for miles – and you can eat in the garden next to masses of fragrant herbs. Food is as locally sourced as possible – sausages, eggs, homemade bread and jams for breakfast, and the pub menu is influenced by English comfort food and Italian cuisine: paella with mussel arancini, king prawn and chorizo mayo; crisp belly of cider braised pork, creamed potato, baby red chard and broccolini. It's the perfect point to break a journey between London and Cornwall, but only seven miles from Glastonbury and you're well-placed to explore the spectacular Dorset and Somerset countryside. It's also great walking and cycling country and off the beaten track so you may want to stay a few nights.

Rooms	3 doubles: £95. Singles £65.
Meals	Lunch & dinner, 2 courses, from £14. Sunday lunch, 3 courses, £17.50.
Closed	Never.

Tel	+44 (0)1935 840543	Kingsdon Inn,
Email	enquiries@kingsdoninn.co.uk	Kingsdon, Somerton, TA11 7LG
Web	www.kingsdoninn.co.uk	

The White Hart

Cool inns with lovely rooms in interesting parts of the land are a big hit with lots of us – we like the easy style, the local food, the good prices and the happy staff. The White Hart is a case in point, a beautifully refurbished inn. It sits on Somerton's ancient market square, 16th-century bricks and mortar, 21st-century lipstick and pearls. Inside, old and new mix beautifully: stone walls and parquet flooring, lovely sofas in front of the fire, funky lamps hanging above the bar. You'll find soft colours, padded window seats, country rugs, antler chandeliers. There's a cute booth in a stone turret, then lovely food waits, perhaps a chargrilled steak, Cornish crab cakes or wood-roasted pork loin. In summer, you spill onto a smart courtyard or into the garden for views of open country. Upstairs, fabulous bedrooms await. You might find timber frames, a claw-foot bath, a wall of paper or stripped boards. All have super beds, flat-screen TVs, lovely bathrooms and a nice price. Beautiful Somerset is all around, don't miss it.

Rooms	8 doubles: £85-£115.
	Dogs £10 per night.
Meals	Lunch from £6.
	Dinner, 3 courses, £25-£30.
	Sunday lunch from £15.
Closed	Never.

The White Hart,
Market Place, Somerton, TA11 7LX

Tel	+44 (0)1458 272273
Email	info@whitehartsomerton.com
Web	www.whitehartsomerton.com

The Royal Oak Inn

After a walk in Chargot Woods with the pooches, what would be nicer than to drop in at the Royal Oak? Douglas (ex Hotel du Vin) is slowly restoring this pleasing red stone pub in a deep green valley in the Exmoor Country Park. Step in to find blackened beams, ancient flags, a hotch-potch of pine tables, a rustic oak settle: this bar is the place to be, especially when the wood-burner is roaring. There's a warren of rooms, a record player at the back, vinyl to play, and Latin lessons on Thursdays (Douglas knows how to keep the locals happy). As for the food, it brings a smile to your face: mackerel quenelles with Melba toast; pheasant from the beat with allotment vegetables and crunchy roasties; apple crumble with custard, and cheeses with homemade chutney. The beer is good, the wines are global, the service is fabulous. Bedrooms ramble around the first floor (one below with its own entrance; the suite with stunning views) and have cool neutral colours, sunken spotlights, smart tartan blinds, roll top tubs, drenching showers. Breakfast, the full cooked works, is delicious. *Pets by arrangement.*

Rooms	5 doubles: £80-£100.
	1 suite for 4: £120. Singles £65.
Meals	Bar snacks available.
	Starters from £4.75. Mains from £11.
	Sunday lunch, 2-3 courses, £14-£16.
Closed	Rarely.

Tel	+44 (0)1984 641498	The Royal Oak Inn,
Email	info@theroyaloakinnluxborough.co.uk	Luxborough, Watchet, TA23 0SH
Web	www.theroyaloakinnluxborough.co.uk	

Luttrell Arms

You get a triple whammy here: spectacular Dunster Castle, its beautiful estate village and this medieval coaching inn on the high street. Inside, a recent refurbishment has brought in a warm style. You'll find a beautiful restaurant with papered walls, an attractive sitting room for afternoon tea, an open fire in the high-ceilinged bar, then a boot bar for sleeping dogs and a game of cribbage. There are a couple of terraces for lunch in the sun, sofas on a veranda that overlooks a tiny courtyard. Bedrooms are scattered about, some with village views, others overlooking the estate. Four are huge with grand four-posters, two sitting under a 500-year-old hammer beam roof. Others have period furniture, pretty wallpapers, perhaps a small private terrace; simpler rooms are smaller, but have good beds. Tasty food spans the spectrum, perhaps a posh burger in the bar to smoked haddock chowder, braised shin of beef and chocolate and raspberry tart in the restaurant. Cliff tops and wild moors wait for fabulous walking. *Minimum stay: 2 nights at weekends*

Rooms	4 doubles, 20 twin/doubles, 4 four-posters: £110-£220. Singles £90-£100.
Meals	Lunch from £4.95. Bar meals from £10.95. Dinner, 3 courses, about £30. Sunday lunch from £15.95. Afternoon tea £12.95.
Closed	Rarely.

Luttrell Arms,
36 High Street, Dunster, TA24 6SG

Tel	+44 (0)1643 821555
Email	enquiry@luttrellarms.co.uk
Web	www.luttrellarms.co.uk

Swain House

Watchet is a sleepy town on the West Somerset coast, and while its day may have passed, its medieval harbour that once made it rich inspired Coleridge to write his famous poem 'The Rime of The Ancient Mariner'. As for this stylish B&B, it makes a great little base for gentle explorations – you'll find excellent hill walking, beaches, the coastal path, even a music festival in August. Once an antiques shop, it sits on the colourful, main street with a big window looking out onto the world. Downstairs, there's a stylish dining room that doubles as a sitting room, with a sofa in front of a fire and hanging lamps at the breakfast table. Upstairs, lovely rooms wait, the sort you expect to find in a boutique inn. You get a huge noble portrait covering one wall, then pretty armchairs, smart fabrics, padded bedheads and old-style radiators. Excellent bathrooms have walk-in showers, free-standing baths, robes and REN oils – exactly what you want after a day in the hills. Pub grub waits in town, posher nosh is a little further afield. The nearby car park is nicely priced, too.

Rooms	4 doubles: £135.
	Singles from £115.
Meals	Restaurants in village.
Closed	Rarely.

Tel	+44 (0)1984 631038
Email	stay@swain-house.com
Web	www.swain-house.com

Swain House,
48 Swain Street, Watchet, TA23 0AG

The Sheppey Inn

It's a case of business in the front, party in the back: duck inside to find a cosy inn where locals clear back the tables to dance to live bands and modern art is splashed on the walls. The small snug at the front is relaxed and homely, and there's a long, light space for dining. Outside is magic: a wooden terrace lit by lanterns, the only sound the burbling river and happy hums from inside. Liz and Mark give you three upstairs bedrooms (ask for the one with the reclaimed vintage telephone doors and copper tub) or two cottages about 10 minutes across the fields. Breakfast is in the fridge for you to make yourself: croissants, cereal, fruit and more for the rooms; a full English for the cottages - generous and locally sourced (warm your crumpets on a wood-burner with a shelf). Stay for dinner and savour ales on tap, the best fish stew, or steaks with truffle sauce, chips and pickled runner beans. Dine with the locals or outside – one of the rooms has its own terrace with views of Glastonbury Tor. *Dogs are welcome in the bar, but not in the bedrooms*

Rooms	3 doubles: £100-£140. 2 self-catering cottages for 2: £130-£140.
Meals	Starters from £6.50. Mains from £13.50.
Closed	Never.

The Sheppey Inn,
Lower Godney, Wells, BA5 1RZ

Tel	+44 (0)1458 831594
Email	hi@thesheppey.co.uk
Web	www.thesheppey.co.uk

The Talbot Inn at Mells

The Talbot is an absolute stunner, one of the loveliest inns in the land. It sits in a timeless village lost in a tangle of country lanes, a 15th-century coaching inn reborn for the 21st-century. Sweep under the carriage arch and you enter a cobbled courtyard, where life gathers in good weather. There's a tithe-barn sitting room with big sofas and a Sunday cinema, then the Coach House Grill, where you eat at weekends under hanging beams. As for the main house, weave along ancient passageways and find stone walls, rugs on wood floors, crackling log fires and a low-ceilinged bar for a pint of Butcombe. The restaurant has colonised several cosy rooms and delicious food flies from the kitchen, perhaps white onion and cider soup, monkfish and mussel stew, chocolate and salted caramel sundae. Bedrooms are the best, some smaller, others huge with claw-foot baths, walk-in showers and modern four-posters. Add lovely staff to the mix and you have a slice of heaven. There's a colourful garden and great local walking, so bring your boots. The First World War poet, Siegfried Sassoon, is buried in the churchyard.

Rooms	8 doubles: £100-£160.
Meals	Lunch & dinner £5-£30.
	Sunday lunch from £15.
Closed	Rarely.

Tel	+44 (0)1373 812254
Email	info@talbotinn.com
Web	www.talbotinn.com

The Talbot Inn at Mells,
Selwood Street, Mells, Frome, BA11 3PN

The Redan Inn

The sleepy village of Chilcompton has had a culinary reawakening, thanks to the arrival of this unsuspecting roadside inn. It's had a slick new makeover from the team behind The Pump House and The Bird in Hand, and all is fresh and new: find a sturdy blue bar with chunky wooden stools; board games, vintage signs and taxidermy; long benches, fresh flowers, grey cushions. There are over 100 gins behind the bar, and a good selection of local hand-pumped

ales. Tuck into hearty fare from head chef Leon's seasonal menu – sausage rolls and ploughman's with homemade bread at lunch, slow braised brisket, caramelised onions and mash for dinner – or go all-out and choose something special from the à la carte menu: perhaps monkfish rolled in squid ink with clam velouté, fennel, and seaweed, followed by lemon meringue, tea sorbet, filo pastry. The roasts are cracking, too. Upstairs, seven stylish, spacious bedrooms gleam; all have spotless en suite bathrooms with drenching showers and Bramley smellies. Tuck into a continental breakfast before a skip around the Mendips. You're just a short drive from Bristol and Bath.

Rooms	7 doubles: £70-£130.
Meals	Bar snacks from £3. Lunch from £5. Dinner from £12.50.
Closed	Rarely.

The Redan Inn,
Fry's Well, Chilcompton, Radstock, BA3 4HA

Tel	+44 (0)1761 258560
Email	info@theredaninn.co.uk
Web	www.theredaninn.co.uk

The Litton

You're perfectly placed for Bath and Bristol here, tucked into the Mendips in a pretty village that loves its inn – and it's easy to see why. The Litton is a gem, where owner Sally and her team work hard and happily to make you feel at home. As soon as you duck inside, you're wrapped in comfort, from reindeer skins on the sofas to mulled cider warming on the bar. Tuck yourself into a corner and order a Welsh rarebit – produce is grown in the kitchen garden – or grab a

Moroccan blanket and an armful of cushions and head for the riverside terrace where there's a converted horse box bar, barbecue, fire pits and up-cycled beer barrels to perch on. The whisky bar is a temptation all of its own, as are the splendid Sunday roasts. Bedrooms, some above the bar, some in the adjoining mill, are individually and stylishly decorated. Beds are big and comfy, baths and showers sparkle. Clever cottage-style suites on the ground floor let you bring the family without feeling cramped; one is designed for the less able. It's not often an owner has thought of everything but Sally is a star, and the Litton shines out as special.

Rooms	10 doubles: £100-£180.
	2 suites for 4: £160-£320.
	Singles £100-£140.
Meals	Starters from £6. Mains from £12.
	Sunday lunch from £12.95.
Closed	Never.

Tel	+44 (0)1761 241554
Email	contact@thelitton.co.uk
Web	www.thelitton.co.uk

The Litton,
Litton, Wells, BA3 4PW

The Swan

The Swan is gorgeous, a contemporary take on a village local. It's part of a new wave of pubs that open all day and do so much more than serve a good pint. The locals love it. They come for breakfast, pop in to buy a loaf of bread, then return for afternoon tea and raid the cake stands. It's right on the bustling street, with a sprinkling of tables and chairs on the pavement in French-café style. Interiors mix old and new brilliantly. You get Farrow & Ball colours and

cool lamps hanging above the bar, then lovely old rugs on boarded floors and a wood-burner to keep things toasty. Push inland to find an airy restaurant open to the rafters that overlooks the garden. Here you dig into Tom Blake's fabulous food (he's ex-River Cottage), anything from grilled Cornish herring to a three-course feast, maybe crispy Lyme Bay cuttlefish, slow cooked Quantock venison, chocolate and salted caramel tart. Bedrooms are lovely. Two have fancy baths in the room, you get vintage French furniture, iPod docks, colourful throws and walk-in power showers. Glastonbury is close, as are the Mendips.

Rooms	5 doubles, 2 twin/doubles: £85-£135. Extra bed £20. Cots available. Dogs £10 per night.
Meals	Lunch from £5. Dinner, 3 courses, about £25. Sunday lunch from £14. Bar meals only Sun night.
Closed	Never.

The Swan,
Cheddar Road, Wedmore, BS28 4EQ

Tel	+44 (0)1934 710337
Email	info@theswanwedmore.com
Web	www.theswanwedmore.com

The Battleaxes

Originally a meeting place for workers on the Tyntesfield estate, this lovely inn now basks in a playful Victorian country-house style. Tasselled lampshades hang above the bar, the odd stately bust wears a flat cap, pot plants rise next to leather sofas. The painted bar, imaginatively stocked, features the inn's own Flatcappers Ale as well as other local brews, while The Club Room – once the village hall – is a lively dining room... though this is an informal place and you can eat wherever you want.

And eat, you will. The food is excellent, lovely pub classics that are hard to resist, perhaps local gammon, free-range eggs and hand-cut chips or shepherd's pie with a white wine gravy and pickled red cabbage. Upstairs, a clutch of beautiful bedrooms wait. All come grandly adorned: lovely big beds, fat leather armchairs, fantastic walk-in showers. You get period wallpapers and lots of colour; one has a free-standing bath and a shower for two. Pick up the papers and sink into a sofa or spin across the road and walk on the Tyntesfield estate. The coast at Clevedon is close. Brilliant.

Rooms	6 doubles: £90-£140.
Meals	Lunch & dinner from £8.95. Sunday lunch, 3 courses, £19.95.
Closed	Rarely.

Tel	+44 (0)1275 857473
Email	thebattleaxes@flatcappers.co.uk
Web	www.flatcappers.co.uk/the-battleaxes/

The Battleaxes,
Wraxall, Bristol, BS48 1LQ

The Queensberry Hotel & Olive Tree Restaurant

'No stilts, pogo sticks, space hoppers, flaming torches or whips in the bar.' Such are the rules of the house, a nod in deference to the 9th Marquis of Queensberry, whose family built this street, and who wrote the rules of boxing in 1865. As for the hotel, it occupies four gleaming Georgian townhouses on a grand old street around the corner from Royal Crescent. It's an extremely comfortable base, with an elegant sitting room, a snazzy bar, a beautiful courtyard garden and some of the best food in town. Potter about and find fresh flowers, contemporary art, the daily papers, kind staff on hand to help. Bedrooms come in different sizes, but all are full of their own delights: Vi Spring mattresses, stylish fabrics, bold colours, flat-screen TVs. Smaller rooms overlooking the garden are lovely – size doesn't matter here – though one of the suites does come with a chaise longue in its super-stylish bathroom. Chris Cleghorn's delicious food waits below, perhaps langoustine tail with cheddar gnocchi and basil or Anjou pigeon with celeriac, shallots and hazelnuts. Finish with a delicious chocolate and mandarin mousse.

Rooms	16 doubles, 10 twin/doubles: £100-£300. 3 suites for 2: £260-£460. Extra bed £25 p.p.p.n.
Meals	Bar meals from £6.95. Lunch, set menu £26-£32.50. Dinner, 3 courses, £49.50. Tasting menu, 5-7 courses, £58-£80.
Closed	Never.

The Queensberry Hotel & Olive Tree Restaurant, Russel Street, Bath, BA1 2QF

Tel	+44 (0)1225 447928
Email	reservations@thequeensberry.co.uk
Web	www.thequeensberry.co.uk

The Roseate Villa, Bath

This is a comfortable and friendly boutique-style hotel in the middle of town but hidden away on a quiet side street overlooking Henrietta Park - seven acres of green space opened to celebrate Queen Victoria's Diamond Jubilee. Stroll for five minutes to magnificent Pulteney Bridge; the station isn't much further. You can hire bikes in town, then follow a towpath along the canal out into the country. Bath will keep you busy: soak up the elegant architecture, relax at the thermae spa, eat, shop... Don't miss the Roman Baths or the Fashion Museum. Back home, there's tea and cake on arrival, buck's fizz for breakfast, even bats and balls for children who want to go to the park. Breakfast   served in an airy dining room – is excellent: smoked salmon and free-range scrambled eggs, buttermilk pancakes, the full cooked works. Bread is baked overnight by the in-house baker. Lovely staff are on hand to book restaurants, balloon flights or day trips.

Rooms	9 doubles, 11 twin/doubles: £99-£325.
	1 family room for 4: £175-£475.
	Singles from £89.
	Extra bed/sofabed £45 p.p.p.n.
Meals	Restaurant within 500m.
Closed	Never.

Tel	+44 (0)1225 466329
Email	reception.trvb@roseatehotels.com
Web	www.roseatehotels.com/
	bath/theroseatevilla/

The Roseate Villa, Bath,
Henrietta Street, Bath, BA2 6LX

No. 15 Great Pulteney

You're on the grandest street in Bath, once home to Jane Austen; the Holburne Museum of Art stands at one end, Robert Adam's famous Pulteney Bridge at the other. As for No. 15, it's a super-chic boutique hotel that doubles as a contemporary art gallery. You'll find collections of curios all over the place – art books, hand-blown lights, chandeliers by the score; there's a golden bar for drinks before dinner, a small spa with treatment rooms, a sauna and a hot tub in the original stone vaults. Bedrooms are sumptuous regardless of size, each with an original piece of art on the walls. You get Hypnos mattresses, cashmere throws, and stunning bathrooms, perhaps a copper basin, a walk-in shower or a claw-foot bath. Vast suites flood with light courtesy of high windows, while a help-yourself larder waits on the landing for popcorn, soft drinks and ice cream. Back downstairs, The Dispensary offers delicious food all day: prosecco 'on the house' at breakfast, perhaps a feisty fish pie at lunch, then chicken with lemon and thyme at dinner. There's a small garden and a car park for guests, too. Hard to beat.

Rooms	25 doubles: £140-£500. 15 suites for 2: £250-£1200.
Meals	Lunch from £6.50. Sunday brunch from £25. Dinner, 3 courses, £30-£40. Afternoon tea £28.
Closed	Never.

No. 15 Great Pulteney,
15 Great Pulteney Street, Bath, BA2 4BS

Tel	+44 (0)1225 805879
Email	enquiries@no15greatpulteney.co.uk
Web	www.no15greatpulteney.co.uk

The Griffin

What used to be a rough-and-ready ale house is now a sweet, neat city pub filled with fresh flowers and manned by young, smiley staff. The bedrooms are set above the pub and those on the top floor are the quietest, though you shouldn't hear a lot of outside noise. If you book direct you'll be offered a cooked breakfast on the house (Wednesday to Sunday) – otherwise it's a continental affair. Although Bath is brimming with good places to eat the food right here is very special, with pub classics during the week and traditional roasts on Sundays. Find piles of great books to read in both the rooms and bar area. Take a back route to Queen Square, with its boules and artisan markets. Both Bath train station and Thermae Spa are a five-minute walk and it's ten minutes (uphill) to the sweeping terrace houses of the Royal Crescent.
Pets by arrangement.

Rooms	6 doubles: £95-£145.
	2 singles: £65-£115.
Meals	Starters from £6. Mains from £15.
Closed	Rarely

Tel	+44 (0)1225 420919	The Griffin,
Email	info@thegriffinbath.co.uk	Monmouth Street, Bath, BA1 2AP
Web	www.thegriffinbath.co.uk	

Abbey Hotel

A super central hotel with views to the medieval Abbey and gentle Somerset hills. Originally three Georgian townhouses, now its rooms are bright, art-filled spaces – although not huge – best to choose one at the back if you want somewhere quieter. The feel is relaxed: chatty, professional staff look after you smoothly. Breakfast on croissants, bread from Bath's best baker, or cooked treats in the restaurant. Pierre Koffmann and Marco Pierre White are the brains behind Koffmann & Mr. White's restaurant – an English-French brasserie that's open to all. Enjoy cocktails or a G&T – the gin list is impressive – in the cool ArtBar after a full day getting acquainted with lovely Georgian architecture or walking in the surrounding Cotswolds. Bath Abbey – fan-vaulted, imposing tower, stained-glass windows – is just across the square, the Roman Baths not much further; escape the crowds and walk over Pulteney Bridge for a gentle ramble beside the river Avon. *Small doubles not dog-friendly.*

Rooms	46 doubles, 10 twin/doubles: £130-£500. 6 family rooms for 4: £200-£600.
Meals	Breakfast £10.50. Lunch from £7.50. Dinner, 3 courses, £35-£45; pre-theatre menu £21.50-£27.50; 5.30pm-7pm. Sunday lunch £24-£28.
Closed	Never.

Abbey Hotel,
North Parade, Bath, BA1 1LF

Tel	+44 (0)1225 461603
Email	reception@abbeyhotelbath.co.uk
Web	www.abbeyhotelbath.co.uk

Combe Grove Hotel

This fine old house sits above Bath in 76 acres of woodland and gardens with views that stretch for miles over unblemished country. It was recently bought by the Elmhurst Foundation and plans are afoot to expand into a centre for health and wellbeing, with retreats, talks and meditation. As for Combe Grove, it's not your average hotel, but a place to wind down; you can have a massage, swim in two pools (one in, one out), join fitness classes from yoga to spin, book a personal trainer or lounge in the sauna and steam rooms, which are shared with country club members. There's a stylish bar serving fresh juices and homemade cakes, then an outside dining terrace, where you can play boules while waiting for your dinner. Big bedrooms in the main house have padded headboards and beautiful fabrics; garden rooms – most with terraces or balconies – have cool colours and fine walk-in showers. Food is served in the muralled dining room, perhaps roasted courgettes and red quinoa, a 28-day, dry-aged ribeye, lavender meringues with Jersey cream. *Minimum stay: 2 nights at weekends in summer.*

Rooms	28 doubles, 9 twin/doubles: £100-£280. 3 suites for 2: £250-£370. Singles from £90.
Meals	Lunch from £6. Dinner, 3 courses, about £35. Afternoon tea from £15.
Closed	Never.

Tel	+44 (0)1225 834644
Email	hello@combegrove.com
Web	www.combegrove.com

Combe Grove Hotel,
Brassknocker Hill,
Monkton Combe, Bath, BA2 7HU

The Wheatsheaf Combe Hay

A hidden valley, a pretty village, a gorgeous inn, three fabulous rooms. Views from the lush terraced garden – replete with veg plot and hens – stretch across to a fine ridge of trees, the manor house and church jutting out of the woods below. In summer there are barbecues, lazy lunches, horses clopping by. This is a 15th-century farmhouse with later additions – it's all but impossible to spot the join – whose exterior comes clad in Farrow & Ball creams. Outside there

are Indian benches with seagrass cushions; inside, big sofas in front of the fire. Gastropub interiors have neutral colours to soak up the light, sandblasted beams, halogen spotlights and Lloyd Loom wicker dining chairs. Steps outside lead down to three deeply comfy bedrooms in a stone building. All come in contemporary rustic style with light wood furniture, flat-screen TVs, Egyptian cotton and deluge showers; there are bathrobes too. Climb back up for seriously good food, perhaps pork belly with quince purée, skate wing with beetroot, parmesan and capers, and Valrhona chocolate fondant. Bath is a hike across the fields.

Rooms	3 doubles: £120-£150.
Meals	Lunch & dinner £16.50-£26.
Closed	Rarely.

The Wheatsheaf Combe Hay,
Combe Hay, Bath, BA2 7EG

Tel	+44 (0)1225 833504
Email	info@wheatsheafcombehay.co.uk
Web	www.wheatsheafcombehay.com

The Castle Inn

On top of the hill that dips down to the mellow heart of Bradford-on-Avon, this renovation of a neglected Bath stone inn is the work of Flatcappers, who, in their first foray into the world of real pubs, struck gold. Enter wood-panelled dining rooms – one large, three small – in muted greys, reds and greens. Ales from local breweries – like the Kettlesmith in Bradford – dominate the bar as locals pop in for a pint and the papers, and muted jazz plays. The menu brims with British pub classics and there are specials on a board. On Sundays there's a traditional roast and children get ice creams afterwards. Above, four characterful bedrooms have views over the church and Westbury white horse, wonky door frames and period fireplaces. Breakfast can last until midday: eggs all ways, full English with braised mushrooms and sourdough toast. Fuel up before hitting Castle Combe's honeyed stone streets, or nearby Lacock Abbey.

Rooms	3 doubles: £100-£140. 1 family room for 4: £100-£140.
Meals	Lunch & dinner £7.95-£18.95.
Closed	Christmas Day & Boxing Day.

Tel	+44 (0)1275 857473
Email	thecastle@flatcappers.co.uk
Web	www.flatcappers.co.uk/the-castle-inn/

The Castle Inn,
Mount Pleasant,
Bradford-on-Avon, BA15 1SJ

Timbrell's Yard

Those lovely people at the Stay Original Company have been doing what they do so well – opening another of their small-scale pleasuredomes. Timbrell's Yard stands close to the bridge in Bradford-on-Avon with beautiful views across the river to the churchyard. Outside, a terrace at the front catches the sun, with this 18th-century listed building standing grandly behind. It's a lovely spot, good enough for Samuel Spode to paint; a copy of his work hangs in the restaurant, the real thing waits in the town's museum. Inside, you get that winning combination of stylish rooms, lovely food and well-kept ales, with cakes and coffee available all day. You'll find stripped floors, hanging lamps, exposed stone walls, then sofas in front of an open fire. Helpful staff weave about, delivering food that makes you smile, perhaps Dorset crab on toast, pork belly with sea salt crackling, vanilla panna cotta with rhubarb jelly. Bedrooms are beautiful. Fourteen have river views, two have baths in the room, mezzanine doubles have window seats where you can watch the river pass. Bathrooms are predictably divine.

Rooms	17 doubles: £85-£195. Extra beds for children £20. Dogs £10 per night.
Meals	Lunch & dinner £5-£35.
Closed	Never.

Timbrell's Yard,
49 St Margaret's Street,
Bradford-on-Avon, BA15 1DE

Tel	+44 (0)1225 869492
Email	info@timbrellsyard.com
Web	timbrellsyard.com

Widbrook Grange

Sink into the chesterfield by the fire and enjoy an outstanding G&T – with 165 craft gins on the menu and 14 tonics this is G&T Central. Not only that, the food is largely locally sourced with herbs from the garden and a sophisticated menu, and you can have your wedding party or special gathering here. We love this Georgian country-house hotel, with its rustic charm and home-from-home feel, set in the heart of Wiltshire in 11 acres of grounds at the end of a track, close to historic Bath and Bradford-on-Avon. Choose from bedrooms in the house or those in the ground-floor stables. You'll find the staff a delight and their welcome extends to families and dogs: note the dog baskets and the rabbit-rich grounds. Stroll down to the canal and walk along the tow path, or hire a narrow boat for the day. Stay put and use the gym and indoor heated pool, book a massage and treatment, have afternoon tea.

Rooms	6 doubles, 8 twin/doubles: £105-£220. 1 suite for 2: £165-£220. 4 family rooms for 3: £145-£205
Meals	Lunch from £13. Dinner, 3 courses, £35. Sunday lunch, 2 courses, £24.95. Afternoon tea from £8.95.
Closed	Never.

Tel	+44 (0)1225 864750
Email	stay@widbrookgrange.co.uk
Web	www.widbrookgrange.co.uk

Widbrook Grange,
Bradford-on-Avon, BA15 1UH

The Beckford Arms

A country-house inn on the Fonthill estate. You sweep in under the Triumphal Arch, which seems appropriate – this is one of the loveliest inns in the land. Outside, in the garden, you find hammocks in the trees and parasols on the terrace, then a church spire soaring beyond. Georgian interiors are no less lovely, a mix of original features and 21st-century style. There's a drawing room with facing sofas in front of a roaring fire; a restaurant with a wall of glass that opens onto the terrace; a bar with parquet flooring for an excellent local pint. Potter about and chance upon the odd chandelier, roaming wisteria and a rather grand mahogany table in the private dining room. Bedrooms are small but perfectly formed with prices to match: white walls, the best linen, sisal matting, good bathrooms. If you want something bigger try the pavilions on the estate; former guests include Byron and Nelson, though we doubt they had it so good. As for the food, it's lovely stuff, perhaps Brixham clam chowder, whole lemon sole, chocolate and Cointreau delice with blood orange sorbet. One of the best.

Rooms	7 doubles, 1 twin/double: £95–£120.
	2 pavilions for 2: £175–£195.
Meals	Dinner about £30.
Closed	Christmas.

The Beckford Arms,
Fonthill Gifford, Tisbury, Salisbury, SP3 6PX

Tel	+44 (0)1747 870385
Email	info@beckfordarms.com
Web	www.beckfordarms.com

The River Barn

This restaurant-with-rooms has a lovely village setting within the Fonthill Estate. The cosy beamed dining room is in the main building; bedrooms are in a rustic redbrick add-on or there's a secluded thatched barn across the road for couples. Breakfasts are so good they draw the locals most days, with much of the produce sourced fresh from the estate – smoked salmon with spinach and scrambled eggs, slow-cooked spiced chickpeas with poached eggs on sourdough, fresh fruit salad, pastries. Your room has a sofa or armchair plus good books, a hot water bottle, excellent coffee and a blanket for your dog. There are plenty of sitting areas in the wild and wonderful garden, which has an orchard, chickens and a shallow river for kids to splash in or fish for shrimps. For days out Stonehenge and Longleat are close.

Rooms	2 doubles, 1 twin: £80-£120.
	1 suite for 2: £150-£200.
Meals	Lunch £10.
	Dinner from £20; 3 courses £30.
Closed	Rarely.

Tel	+44 (0)1747 356026
Email	hello@riverbarn.co.uk
Web	www.riverbarn.co.uk

The River Barn,
Fonthill Bishop, Salisbury, SP3 5SF

The Royal Oak Inn

Philanthropic gestures don't come much better than a group of villagers financing the renovation of this once-disused pub. That's what happened to the Royal Oak, now happily restored to the heart of the community. On a quiet lane stands this whitewashed building with thatched roof and porch. Inside, neutral walls and a pastel palette are complemented by light oak furniture from a local carpenter and a cornucopia of beams. All is airy and bright with floor to ceiling windows on two walls – a great spot for breakfasts of fresh fruit, muesli, or a full English with sourdough bread from down the road. Bedrooms calm and soothe, each designed individually, with heavenly beds, Egyptian cotton linen, carefully toned fabrics and throws, and sparkling bathrooms. Open all day, this is somewhere to whittle away the hours reading the papers, playing board games, supping the regional ales, brandy and cider, and tucking into tasty food with a great provenance. Head out to walk the surrounding countryside, visit stately homes, or explore Stonehenge, Shaftesbury and Hardy's Wessex.

Rooms	4 doubles, 2 twin/doubles: £100-£150. Extra bed/sofabed £25 p.p.p.n.
Meals	Lunch from £7.95. Dinner from £13.95. Sunday lunch from £15.95.
Closed	Rarely.

The Royal Oak Inn,
Swallowcliffe, Salisbury, SP3 5PA

Tel	+44 (0)1747 870211
Email	hello@royaloakswallowcliffe.com
Web	www.royaloakswallowcliffe.com

Howard's House

This ancient village is a dream, a wormhole back in time, a fitting stage for this Grade-II listed house that dates to 1623. Outside, fine gardens sweep uphill to a ridge of old oak, where views stretch out across the valley. Inside, warm country-house interiors come with the odd beam, fine arched windows and original flagstones in the hall. You'll find smart sofas, fresh flowers and the morning papers in the cosy sitting room, where a fire crackles on colder days. In summer, doors open onto a pretty terrace, where you can breakfast in good weather. Elegant bedrooms are deeply comfortable with pretty fabrics, mullioned windows and super-comfy beds. You get bowls of fruit, a sofa if there's room, then robes in spotless bathrooms. Spin downstairs for some lovely country food, perhaps wood pigeon with garlic, lemon sole with crab bisque, passion fruit soufflé with mango sorbet; climb back up afterwards to find your bed turned down. Uplifting walks start from the front door, the renovated coach house is perfect for small parties. Salisbury, Stonehenge and the gardens at Stourhead are close.

Rooms	6 doubles, 2 twin/doubles, 1 four-poster: £150-£225. Singles £95-£120.
Meals	Lunch from £25. Dinner: seasonal menu £28-£33.50; à la carte £37-£46.50; 6-course tasting menu £80.
Closed	5 days over Christmas.

Tel	+44 (0)1722 716392
Email	enq@howardshousehotel.co.uk
Web	www.howardshousehotel.co.uk

Howard's House,
Teffont Evias, Salisbury, SP3 5RJ

The Bell at Ramsbury

Part of the Ramsbury Estate, The Bell is a classy new-wave inn and one that showcases Ramsbury Estate produce. Come for Ramsbury beers, gin and vodka, kitchen garden fruit and veg, and seasonal game. Completing this pleasing picture are nine stunning bedrooms named after game birds and fish. Cosy lodgings for fishermen, and for those exploring the glorious Marlborough Downs, they come with soothing Farrow & Ball colours, rich fabrics, down duvets, big beds, vintage books, and super bathrooms with White Company lotions and heated slate floors. Back downstairs, enjoy a pint of Gold in the smart, hop-adorned bar, or bag the sofa in the library-style lounge and entertain yourself with a copy of *The Field*. Pop into the stylish restaurant for dishes such as pan fried scallops, Kelmscott pork loin or The Bell's favourites: Ramsbury Gold battered haddock and Butts Farm rare breed steaks. As for the village, it's really pretty, and the pub, just off the main square, is 100 yards from the river bank.

Rooms	7 doubles, 2 twins: £110-£150.
Meals	Lunch £20-£25. Bar meals £7-£17. Dinner £30-£45. Sunday lunch, 2 courses, £19.50.
Closed	Rarely.

The Bell at Ramsbury,
The Square, Ramsbury,
Marlborough, SN8 2PE

Tel	+44 (0)1672 520230
Email	thebell@ramsbury.com
Web	www.thebellramsbury.com

The White Horse Inn

Whitewashed walls echo the chalk horse that gave its name to this very handsome village inn. Inside all is as neat as a new pin. Lovingly polished parquet glows beneath scrubbed wooden tables, while padded bar stools and assorted chairs – some antique and carved – are well spaced around the reclaimed oak bar, a beautiful piece of recycling. Having been a grocer's shop and a bakery during its long life the pub now focuses on what it does best: providing great food and drink to villagers and visitors. Eat by the sturdy wood-burner in the bar or in the elegant terracotta dining area with its beams and mullioned windows. Lunches are relaxed affairs of sandwiches and pub classics. Dinner lists pork and game from the pub's own farm in season – and children are well looked after. In the old stable lie eight simple but comfortable rooms, with pine furniture and pretty fabrics. Many have views to paddocks, sheep and geese, all are blissfully peaceful at night. A super pub from start to finish – very friendly, too.

Rooms	3 doubles: £85-£95.
	3 family rooms for 4: £110-£120.
	2 singles: £75-£85.
Meals	Lunch from £9.95. Bar meals from £5.95. Dinner from £11.95. Sunday lunch from £10.95.
Closed	Never.

Tel	+44 (0)1249 813118
Email	reception@ whitehorse-comptonbassett.co.uk
Web	www.whitehorse-comptonbassett.co.uk

The White Horse Inn,
Compton Bassett, Calne, SN11 8RG

Sign of the Angel

You might find the cast of *Downton Abbey* staying at this 15th-century coaching inn – and for method actors, it must be a dream. Occupying centre-stage in one the prettiest of all Cotswold villages, the Sign of the Angel is a genuine period piece: all chalky whitewash and wonky beams, artful oak furniture and flagstoned passageways. The inn was taken over by energetic young brothers Tom and Jack in 2014, and has been impeccably renovated to trumpet its age. The owners are from farming stock, and it shows in Chef Patron Jon's menu. Everything from the bread to the sorbets are locally sourced and homemade: warm mackerel rarebit, brioche and heritage tomato salad; baked tenderloin in local bacon stuffed with pear and Bath cheese; Bramley crumble with toffee apple ice cream. One word of warning for those who find stairs tricky – this place is on many levels so even to go to the gents from the bar you'll encounter steps. Bedrooms have pretty box windows, wainscotting and beams. You'll find chef's home-made cookies on your tea tray.

Rooms	5 doubles: £101-£140.
Meals	Lunch from £6. Dinner from £16. Sunday lunch, 2-3 courses, £20-£23. Cream teas from £7.50.
Closed	Never.

Sign of the Angel,
6 Church Street, Lacock, SN15 2LB

Tel	+44 (0)1249 730230
Email	info@signoftheangel.co.uk
Web	www.signoftheangel.co.uk

The Methuen Arms

The Methuen started life as a 14th-century nunnery, turned into a coaching inn in 1608, then had a Georgian facelift in the late 1700s. Now' it's a chic boutique hotel – cosy and stylish with great food and delicious Butcombe ales. It sits on the edge of the village, with an avenue of trees around the corner that lead to Corsham Court, an Elizabethan pile. As for the hotel, there's a sun-trapping courtyard where you can eat in summer, a restaurant that opens onto the garden, a locals' bar where the main currency is gossip, then a sitting-room bar where you can sink into an armchair in front of the wood-burner. It's all very pretty with an easy style that runs throughout. You'll find shuttered windows, the odd beam, the daily papers, rugs on wood floors. Gorgeous bedrooms have warm colours, padded bedheads, good art, Roberts radios. There are robes in fine bathrooms, four of which have claw-foot baths, one of which is in the bedroom. Super food waits, perhaps cream of shallot soup, venison with heritage carrots, Wiltshire honey crème caramel.

Rooms	16 doubles, 2 twin/doubles: £140-£175. 1 family room for 4: £150-£220. Singles from £90.
Meals	Lunch from £8. Dinner, 3 courses, about £35. Sunday lunch from £14.
Closed	Never.

Tel	+44 (0)1249 717060
Email	info@themethuenarms.com
Web	www.themethuenarms.com

The Methuen Arms,
2 High Street, Corsham, SN13 0HB

The Rectory Hotel

This Georgian rectory dates to 1780 and sits in two acres of English gardens, with the church tower peeping up above fine trees. From the outside, little has changed in a hundred years, but step inside and find a newly refurbished house that sparkles at every turn. There's a chic sitting with a roaring fire and beautiful art, then a restaurant that starts in a panelled dining room and flows into a conservatory, where doors open onto the garden for breakfast on the lawn in summer. Rooms above are just as good – super beds, stylish fabrics, perhaps a claw-foot bath in your room or ceilings open to the rafters. Light floods in, bigger rooms have sofas, all have contemporary elegance in spades. You get smart TVs, super-fast WiFi, then robes in magical bathrooms. Back downstairs, a chic bar opens onto the garden for Pimm's in the sun; keep going and find sunbeds circling the swimming pool. Glorious food rounds off your day, perhaps Cornish scallops, roast veal, Florentine doughnuts with Chantilly cream. Don't miss the occasional festival at their sister pub across the road.

Rooms	15 doubles: £130-£230. Child bed £25.
Meals	Lunch from £6.50. Dinner, 3 courses, about £35. Sunday lunch from £18.
Closed	Never.

The Rectory Hotel,
Crudwell, Malmesbury, SN16 9EP

Tel	+44 (0)1666 577194
Email	reception@therectoryhotel.com
Web	www.therectoryhotel.com

The Royal Oak Tetbury

Resplendent after a full refurbishment this 17th-century coaching inn is abuzz with enthusiasm. Inside, reclaimed floorboards have been artfully fitted together, a salvaged carved oak bar has its own little 'Groucho snug' at one end. Exposed stone and a real fire co-exist with a pretty Art Deco piano whose ivories are often tinkled. Cheery staff will pull you a pint of Uley or Stroud ale or perhaps an Orchard Pig cider. Treats in store on the menu from head chef Richard Simms feature pub classics with a twist: sharing or small plates, hearty salads, 'oak pots' with a veggie or meat option served with crusty bread or brown rice, and plenty of choice for vegans. Up in the roof beneath massive beams is a more formal restaurant with a spacious, calm atmosphere. Across the cobbled yard are six bedrooms – three are dog-friendly – with a restful elegance, dreamy beds and bathrooms to linger in. And if it's a special occasion then the Oak Lodge room will not fail to get things off to a very good start. Enjoy the view of the garden, glass in hand. *Minimum stay: 2 nights at weekends & in high season.*

Rooms	6 doubles: £85-£170. Extra bed/sofabed £30 p.p.p.n.
Meals	Lunch & dinner £5-£13.
Closed	Never.

Tel	+44 (0)1666 500021
Email	stay@theroyaloaktetbury.co.uk
Web	www.theroyaloaktetbury.co.uk

The Royal Oak Tetbury,
1 Cirencester Road, Tetbury, GL8 8EY

The Holford Arms

At the side of the long road that takes you into Tetbury sits this unassuming country inn with its whitewashed exterior hiding more secrets than you can shake a stick at. Owners Pete and Tor have worked a special magic here. Whether it's building more stylish 'shacks' in the big field at the back, or pressing their own apples, they have a way with food, drink and atmosphere which would be the envy of many a new pub entrepreneur. Their hands-on approach means the little inn buzzes with happy locals and nature lovers who've popped in for a pint or a Sunday roast after exploring nearby Westonbirt Arboretum. Inside, all is snug and homely. The bar winks with bottles, or try one of the local ales. Young chefs serve up tasty classics and treats; on Wednesdays you can tuck into a three-course Thai feast for a bargain price. Upstairs, six pretty bedrooms with crisp white linens and splashes of colour. Take the big twin/double under the eaves with a day bed that doubles as a window seat. Very special.

Rooms	4 doubles, 2 twin/doubles: £74-£170. Singles £74-£124. Extra bed/sofabed £30 p.p.p.n.
Meals	Starters from £5. Lunch from £10. Mains from £15.
Closed	Christmas.

The Holford Arms,
Knockdown, Tetbury, GL8 8QY

Tel	+44 (0)1454 238669
Email	info@theholfordarms.co.uk
Web	www.theholfordarms.co.uk

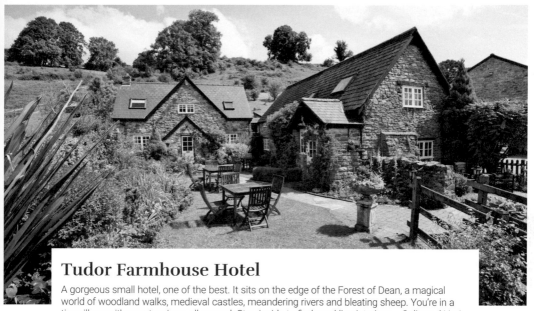

Tudor Farmhouse Hotel

A gorgeous small hotel, one of the best. It sits on the edge of the Forest of Dean, a magical world of woodland walks, medieval castles, meandering rivers and bleating sheep. You're in a tiny village with country views all around. Step inside to find sparkling interiors – Colin and Hari have spent a small fortune turning their realm into something very special. An airy elegance mixes with golden stone walls and original timber frames, the house bearing testament to its Tudor roots. Big or small, bedrooms are divine – stylishly uncluttered with smart fabrics, robes in fine bathrooms and super-comfy beds. Those in the main house have ancient beamed ceilings, those in the barns have original stone walls. The bigger rooms are faultless: the best beds, claw-foot baths, enormous showers, the lap of luxury. Lovely local food waits, cider-cured salmon, haunch of venison, rhubarb Bakewell tart; there are home-laid eggs for breakfast. You can kayak on the Wye, forage in the forest, take to cycle tracks. *Minimum stay: 2 nights at weekends. 3 dog-friendly bedrooms; only service dogs allowed in lounge, bar & dining rooms.*

Rooms	10 doubles, 3 twins, 2 four-posters: £130-£250. 5 suites for 2: £220-£250. Singles £90-£220. Extra bed/sofabed £25 p.p.p.n.
Meals	Lunch from £6.95. Dinner, 3 courses, £30-£40. Sunday lunch from £14.50.
Closed	Never.

Tel	+44 (0)1594 833046
Email	info@tudorfarmhousehotel.co.uk
Web	www.tudorfarmhousehotel.co.uk

Tudor Farmhouse Hotel,
High Street, Clearwell, GL16 8JS

Three Choirs Vineyards

England's answer to the Napa Valley. After 15 years of tilling the soil (very sandy, good drainage), Thomas's 75 acres of Gloucestershire hillside now produce 300,000 bottles a year. There are regular tastings, a shop in which to buy a bottle or two, and paths that weave through the vines – a perfect stroll after a good meal. What's more, three fabulous lodges wait down by the lake, all with decks and walls of glass. You'll find claw-foot baths and comfy beds, so camp out in grand savannah style and listen to the woodpeckers. Rooms up at the restaurant are smart and spacious with terraces that overlook the vineyard. They come with padded bedheads, walls of colour, leather armchairs, flat-screen TVs and good bathrooms. Finally, the restaurant: claret walls, lovely views, sofas in front of an open fire. Excellent food waits, perhaps twice-baked Gloucester soufflé, fillet of bream with rocket and watercress, rhubarb crème brûlée with lemon shortbread. World wines are on the list, but you'll want something from the vines that surround you; there's a microbrewery, too. Perfect. *Minimum stay: 2 nights at weekends.*

Rooms	9 doubles, 2 twins: £153-£203. Singles from £135.
Meals	Lunch from £7.50. Dinner à la carte about £35.
Closed	Christmas & New Year.

Three Choirs Vineyards,
Castle Tump, Newent, GL18 1LS

Tel	+44 (0)1531 890223
Email	info@threechoirs.com
Web	www.three-choirs-vineyards.co.uk

The Bradley

This Georgian townhouse on a leafy street is a five-minute walk from the centre of Cheltenham. Views at the back look onto the Montpellier Gardens and Cotswold Hills. Sit outside on balmy evenings on the garden terrace – it's peaceful next to the small pond. Inside all is cosy with books, boardgames, an honesty bar and a merry fire. Each bedroom has tea, coffee and homemade sloe gin. Most are large enough to have comfortable seats, and two separate suites in the garden are more modern. Breakfast is served downstairs in the dining room or the conservatory – the full works, muffins, porridge, fruit, yogurt... Cheltenham is at your feet for dinner, so stroll to smart brasserie The Ivy, French L'artisan, Thai or Indian restaurants. Beata and her small team look after you well and can help with tips about things to do. Find a fine collection of Arts & Crafts at The Wilson, discover the Montpellier Gardens or visit the Pittville Pump Room, the largest spa in town. .

Rooms	6 doubles, 2 twin/doubles: £105-£175. 2 suites: from £115. Extra bed/sofabed available. Late checkout available for an additional fee
Meals	Breakfast included.
Closed	Never.

Tel	+44 (0)1242 519077
Email	enquiries@thebradleyhotel.co.uk
Web	www.thebradleyhotel.co.uk

The Bradley,
19 Royal Parade, Cheltenham, GL50 3AY

The Fleece at Cirencester

A pretty coaching inn, The Fleece has not long been refurbished and the bar, lounge and restaurant are all scrubbed up and glowing. Open all day it has a good buzz. Drop by for coffee and egg on toast; choose a sharing platter at lunchtime with a pint of Thwaites. There are daily specials and Sunday roasts and the staff are charming, cheerful and smartly turned out. The more spacious rooms, with their beamy, up-in-the-roof feeling are the best, but all are smart with new beds and jazzy wallpapers. Face the famous market square and watch the world go by or settle more quietly into a room at the back. Set off into the Cotswolds for a hike with the dog, browse the antique shops then come back to the Fleece for the night – ask about parking before you arrive, and make sure you've booked for dinner; it can get busy.

Rooms	18 doubles, 4 twin/doubles: £85-£125. 5 suites for 2: £115-£150. 1 family room for 4: £75-£150.
Meals	Lunch from £6.95. Bar meals from £4.95. Dinner from £8.95. Sunday lunch, 2 courses, £11.95.
Closed	Rarely.

The Fleece at Cirencester,
Market Place, Cirencester, GL7 2NZ

Tel	+44 (0)1285 650231
Email	relax@thefleececirencester.co.uk
Web	www.thwaites.co.uk/hotels-and-inns/ inns/fleece-at-cirencester

Masons Arms

In a bustling Cotswolds village, the old pub owned by Arkells, the family brewery from Swindon, stands proudly by the village green. Paul Fallows first worked here aged 16; now he's head honcho and full of plans. Enter the bar, uncluttered in a stylish way, just low beams, scrubbed tables, a parquet floor, fantastic fires... the sort of place where young mums meet for coffee (beans roasted in Cirencester) and business folk for breakfast. The restaurant seats 40, with shining glasses on small square tables and good pictures on white walls. As for the food, it's simple, modern, classy: slow roast celeriac with feta and hazelnut granola; sea bream with fennel, samphire and crab salad. There are burgers too, and a dark chocolate delice, and in summer you spill onto the green. Up above: simple, comfortable bedrooms, a work in progress, great value, two for families. Paul's focus is on 'a great bed, a great shower, and excellent WiFi' – who could argue with that?

Rooms	5 doubles: £90-£100. 1 family room for 4, 1 family room for 3: £140-£150. Singles £70.
Meals	Starters from £6. Mains from £12.
Closed	Boxing Day evening & New Year's Day evening.

Tel	+44 (0)1285 850164	Masons Arms,
Email	masonsatmeysey@gmail.com	28 High Street, Meysey Hampton, GL7 5JT
Web	www.masonsarmsmeyseyhampton.com	

The Village Pub

An old favourite of locals and faithfuls from far and wide, this civilised Cotswold bolthole has been given a gentle facelift by Calcot Health & Leisure – owners of Barnsley House, the country-house hotel across the road. Expect seasonal food based on the best local produce, good-quality Hook Norton ale and decent wines. There's even a service hatch to the heated patio at the back, so you can savour the sauvignon until the sun goes down. Cotswold stone and ancient flags sing the country theme; past bar and open fires, quiet alcoves provide a snug setting that entices you to stay. If you do, tuck into crab and leek tart, rib-eye steak with béarnaise sauce, or whole plaice with crab and parsley butter; sweet tooths will love the warm ginger cake with rum and raisin ice cream. Classy, spruced-up bedrooms are equally cosy and inviting, with soothing colours, stylish fabrics, plasma screens and iPod docks. Two stunning four-poster rooms have big bathrooms with claw-foot baths, walk-in showers, posh toiletries. Roman Cirencester and gorgeous Bibury are close by.

Rooms	4 twin/doubles, 2 four-posters: £99-£174.
Meals	Appetisers from £4. Starters from £6. Mains from £13.
Closed	Rarely.

The Village Pub,
Barnsley, Cirencester, GL7 5EF

Tel	+44 (0)1285 740421
Email	info@thevillagepub.co.uk
Web	www.thevillagepub.co.uk

Inn at Fossebridge

Here, on the old Roman road (busy now with traffic), rusticity and elegance achieve the perfect balance at this gorgeous 17th-century coaching inn run with aplomb by Dee Ludlow. Stone archways divide the bar, with its flagstone floors, open fires, beamed ceilings and a hubbub at lunchtime. Throw in real ales, roast lunches and a welcome for all and you have somewhere very special. This place prides itself on serving really good pub food: prawn cocktail, fish and chips, cottage pie, good puddings. The pub garden is one of the largest and most attractive in the Cotswolds with a two-acre lake, mature trees, and barbecues in summer. Country-smart bedrooms, decorated in Georgian style, range from smallish to spacious. There's no separate sitting room but plenty of places to sit and read a paper. The two splendid holiday cottages in the grounds are perfect for big families: Stable Cottage sleeps four plus two children; Lakeside House sleeps 10. Walk from the pub up the Coln valley and revel in glorious countryside.

Rooms	8 doubles: from £110.
	1 family room for 3: from £185.
Meals	Bar meals £5.75-£9.50. Lunch & dinner £11-£21.50. Sunday lunch £14.50.
Closed	Rarely.

Tel	+44 (0)1285 720721
Email	reservations@innatfossebridge.co.uk
Web	www.innatfossebridge.co.uk

Inn at Fossebridge,
Fossebridge, Cirencester, GL54 3JS

The Wheatsheaf

The Wheatsheaf stands at the vanguard of a cool new movement: the village local reborn in country-house style. It's a winning formula with locals and travellers flocking in for a heady mix of laid-back informality and chic English style. The inn stands between pretty hills in this ancient wool village on the Fosse Way. Inside, happy young staff flit about, throwing logs on the fire, ferrying food to diners, or simply stopping for a chat. Downstairs, you find armchairs in front of smouldering fires, noble portraits on panelled walls, cool tunes playing in the background. Outside, a smart courtyard garden draws a crowd in summer, so much so it has its own bar; English ales, jugs of Pimm's and lovely wines all wait. Back inside, beautiful bedrooms come as standard, some bigger than others, all fully loaded with comfort and style. Expect period colours, Hypnos beds, Bang & Olufsen TVs, and spectacular bathrooms with beautiful baths and/or power showers. As for the food, you feast on lovely local fare, perhaps devilled kidneys, coq au vin, pear and almond tart. Don't miss it.

Rooms	14 doubles: £120-£180. Extra bed £25 child, £75 adult.
Meals	Lunch from £9. Dinner, 3 courses, about £30. Bar meals from £5.
Closed	Never.

The Wheatsheaf,
West End, Northleach,
Cheltenham, GL54 3EZ

Tel	+44 (0)1451 860244
Email	reservations@cotswoldswheatsheaf.com
Web	www.cotswoldswheatsheaf.com

The Plough Inn

Take a pint to the terrace on a summer's day and watch village life tick by. This spruced-up 17th-century inn is as inviting as can be, thanks to new owner Tom and his team. The food is locally sourced and delicious, the gins zing, and ales come straight from the cask. What's more, for the Cotswolds, the wines are very well priced. Tourists flock to Bourton on the Water with its five little bridges (two miles). The famous Daylesford Farm Shop is a 20-minute drive... pop by for an organic lunch, or a picnic for the Windrush Way. Westwards is leafy Cheltenham (15 miles), with Regency streets, a theatre, posh shops, and a racecourse in the lee of the hills. Return to sweet, cosy bedrooms upstairs. With two dog-friendly bedrooms, and dog meals on request, you're not the only one who is made welcome here.

Rooms	1 double, 2 twin/doubles: £99-£150.
Meals	Lunch from £7.50. Starters from £6.95. Mains from £13.50.
Closed	Never.

Tel	+44 (0)1451 822 602	The Plough Inn,
Email	hello@coldastonplough.com	Chapel Lane,
Web	www.coldastonplough.com	Cold Aston, GL54 3BN

The Ebrington Arms

The glorious gardens at Hidcote Manor and Kiftsgate Court are a ramble across fields from the Ebrington Arms, lovingly restored and revived by Claire and Jim. The 17th-century bar is the hub of the community and beloved by locals and tourists alike, cosy with low beams and roaring fires. Bag a seat on the settle and share organic own-brewed Yubby, Goldie or Yawnie with the regulars, or seek out the dining rooms next door. Flagstone floors, fresh flowers and a delightful mishmash of tables set the scene for some terrific pub food cooked from Soil Association certified organic ingredients. Dishes are simple yet full of flavour, so dive in to pork chop, butternut and thyme purée, cider and mustard sauce. Bedrooms (up steepish stairs) are full of charm, with chunky wooden beds, colourful throws, plump pillows, smart bathrooms and deep window seats with village or country views. Stratford-upon-Avon is close, too. A properly unpretentious inn, run by the nicest people. One of the best. *Minimum stay: 2 nights at weekends.*

Rooms	5 doubles: £130-£170.
Meals	Lunch & dinner £9-£17.50.
	Limited menu Sunday eve.
Closed	Rarely.

The Ebrington Arms,
Ebrington, Chipping Campden, GL55 6NH

Tel	+44 (0)1386 593223
Email	reservations@theebringtonarms.co.uk
Web	www.theebringtonarms.co.uk

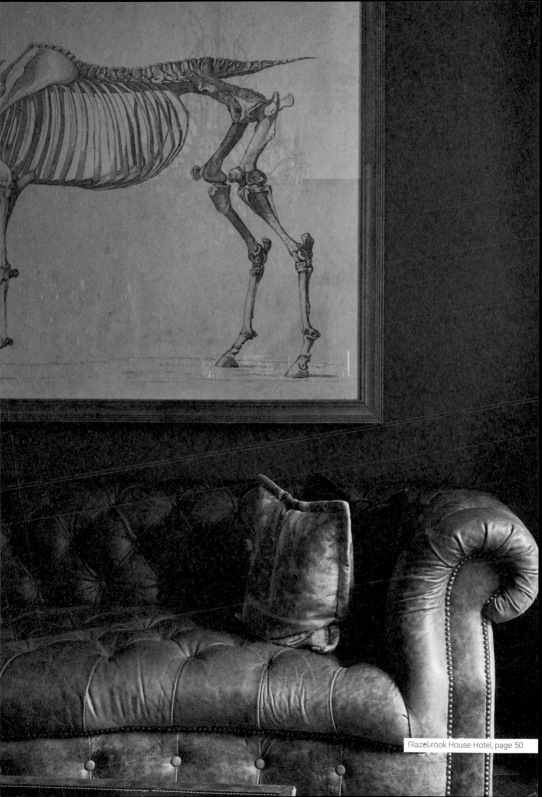

South East

The Kingham Plough, page 128

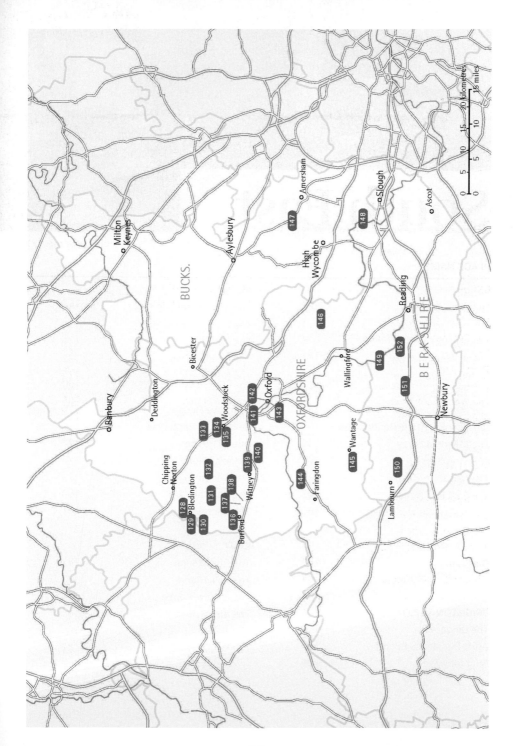

125

South East

The Milk House, page 183

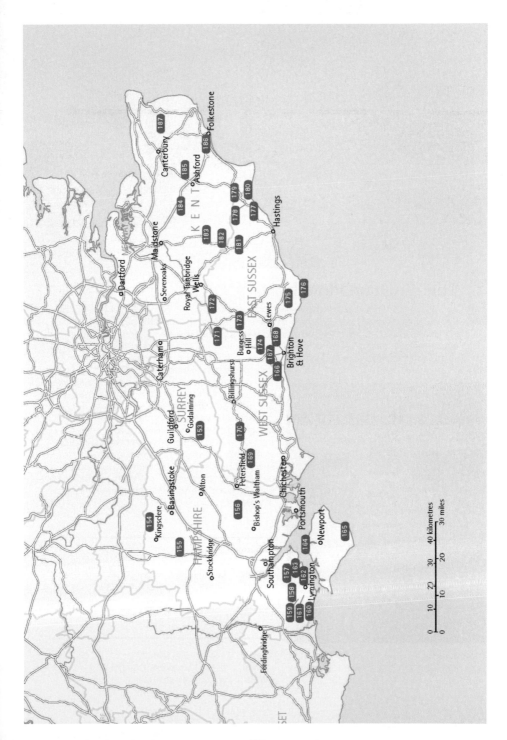

The Kingham Plough

You don't expect to find locals clamouring for a table in a country pub on a cold Tuesday in February, but different rules apply here. Provenance is king, so expect the best local ingredients cooked to perfection, delivered to you in the exquisite dining room, its ceilings open to ancient rafters. There's a terrace for summer dining, and fruit trees, herbs and lavender in the garden. Charming bedrooms have super-comfy beds, armchairs and mini bars, and sparkling bathrooms with Bramley's potions. Couples will like the privacy of the annexe rooms while families can book adjoining pairs above the pub. There are stacks of books, a games cupboard, crackling fires and plenty of nooks and crannies to hide in. Arrive by train from London to be met by a bus that delivers you to the door. The Daylesford Organic farm shop/café is close, and the village is surrounded by Cotswold countryside – perfect for a weekend of walking and exploring. *Minimum stay: 2 nights at weekends.*

Rooms	5 doubles, 1 twin: £145-£195. Singles from £110.
Meals	Lunch from £15. Bar meals from £5. Dinner, 3 courses, about £40. Sunday lunch £20.
Closed	Christmas Day.

The Kingham Plough,
The Green, Kingham, OX7 6YD

Tel	+44 (0)1608 658327
Email	book@thekinghamplough.co.uk
Web	www.thekinghamplough.co.uk

The Kings Head Inn

A beautiful English inn, a 17th-century cider house made of ancient stone that sits on the green in a Cotswold village with hens strutting their stuff and a family of ducks bathing in the pond. Inside, locals gather to chew the cud, scoff great food and wash it down with Cotswold ales. The fire burns throughout the winter, you get low ceilings, painted stone walls, the odd settle, country rugs on flagstone floors. Nicely priced bedrooms have lots of colour and style. Those in the main house have more character, those in the courtyard are bigger (and quieter). You'll find painted wood, pretty fabrics, rustic furniture, spotless bathrooms; most have great views, too. Breakfast and supper are taken in a pretty dining room (exposed stone walls, pale wood tables), while you can lunch by the fire in the bar on devilled kidneys, grilled mackerel, a plate of British cheeses. There are lovely unpompous touches like jugs of cow parsley in the loo. There's loads to do, too: antiques in Stow, golf at Burford, circular walks through gorgeous country. The front terrace teems with life in summer. *Minimum stay: 2 nights at weekends.*

Rooms	9 doubles, 3 twin/doubles: £110-£140. Singles £90-£115. Extra bed/sofabed £25 p.p.p.n.
Meals	Lunch from £7.50. Dinner, 3 courses, about £30. Sunday lunch £16.
Closed	25-27 December.

Tel	+44 (0)1608 658365
Email	info@kingsheadinn.net
Web	www.kingsheadinn.net

The Kings Head Inn,
The Green, Bledington,
Chipping Norton, OX7 6XQ

The Feathered Nest Country Inn

An appealing flagged bar steps down to a smouldering fire... contemplate the menu as you sip a fine wine. In this epicurean heaven, chef Kuba's inventiveness makes each mouthful a joy. In summer, spill into the garden where the view reaches for five miles. This 18th-century malthouse has been restored and transformed by enthusiastic owners who do nothing by halves. There are four cosy bedrooms and the sense of comfort is enveloping, the wines are wide-ranging, and the surrounding countryside is gorgeous. What's more, the kitchen churns its butter and cures its charcuterie. Burford, with its medieval three-arched bridge and wonderful church, lies five miles south; little Stow-in-the-Wold is three miles north. Visit tea shops, browse antique shops, and head for the prettiest street in the Cotswolds – or one of them: Arlington Row in Bibury.

Rooms	4 doubles: £245-£295. Dinner, B&B £185-£205 per person.
Meals	Lunch, 3 courses, £38. Dinner, 4 courses, £65; 6 courses, £95.
Closed	Monday-Wednesday.

The Feathered Nest Country Inn,
Nether Westcote,
Chipping Norton, OX7 6SD

Tel	+44 (0)1993 833030
Email	reservations@thefeatherednestinn.co.uk
Web	www.thefeatherednestinn.co.uk

The Swan

Huddled near a 13th-century church hedged by ancient limes is a mellow stone pub with an immaculate makeover. Find a peaceful alcove for a first-class negroni, or a window seat for tea. You can come by train from London, a rare treat. There are three beers on draft and many fine wines, but here at The Swan, the food is the thing. Locally sourced, it is modern British and delicious. Small plates, Sunday roasts, vegetarian: they do it all. The dining room is raftered; the courtyard can seat a hundred. Lanes, tracks and stiles start from the door; you can walk for hours. Or follow the road to Charlbury - one of the prettiest drives in the region. Honey-stone houses and wealthy wool churches abound. Then it's home, to designer wallpapers, wallowing baths, and an exciting bottle of champagne

Rooms	5 doubles, 1 twin/double: from £80. 1 family room for 4: from £130.
Meals	Starters from £5. Lunch from £8. Mains from £12.
Closed	Never.

Tel	+44 (0)1993 832332	The Swan,
Email	reservations@swanascott.com	4 Shipton Road,
Web	www.swanascott.com	Ascott-under-Wychwood, OX7 6AY

The Bull Inn

Hop on the train at Paddington for the Bull. The old pub sits on Sheep Street and ticks all the right boxes for lovers of Cotswolds' inns: great food, great service, gorgeous interiors. But it's the homely feel that pulls it into a class of its own. Warm up by log fires with a Bloody Mary (house speciality) or a pint of Fullers. The wine list is short and includes some great finds... Charlie (young, friendly, charming) recently ran a vineyard in France. Find kilim rugs on seagrass floors, white limed beams and rustic walls, a sparkling little bar with zinc tops, and wood panelling painted a Georgian slate blue. Everyone's welcome including kids and dogs, and the menu is short and delightful: baked gnocchi with mozzarella; battered whiting and chips; Pie of the Day with winter greens; chocolate sundae. The burgers (from local beef) are amazing. Upstairs are four bedrooms - with four more in the barn - modern in feel, laid-back yet luxurious: white bathrooms, wonderful wallpapers, seagrass floors, vintage chests of drawers. *Minimum stay: 2 nights at weekends.*

Rooms	8 doubles: £99-£180.
Meals	Starters from £5. Mains from £12.
Closed	Rarely.

The Bull Inn,
Sheep Street, Charlbury, OX7 3RR

Tel	+44 (0)1608 810689
Email	eat-drink-sleep@bull-inn.com
Web	www.bullinn-charlbury.com

The Killingworth Castle

The family behind The Ebrington Arms has renovated this 17th-century inn, around the corner from Blenheim Palace, to its former glory with beautifully restored bedrooms too. Wood floors sweep from side bar to main bar to dining room, burners in brick fireplaces belt out heat and the set menu is a steal. Smiling staff ferry own-brewed Yubby Bitter, Goldie and Yawnie to locals, dog walkers and drinkers; the rest are here for the food: roast venison and faggot croquette with beetroot dauphinoise, kale and juniper; blackberry and frangipane tart. And possibly the best chips in Oxfordshire! The pub won three stars from the Soil Association for its commitment to organic food but you'll also find organic wine. There's a nifty selection of malt whiskies, or try a pint of their home-brewed in the garden. Bedrooms are upstairs and down - all have original art, handmade sturdy beds and the softest linen. Muted tartan blankets keep you warm and there are organic toiletries and roll top baths.

Rooms	8 doubles: £110-£180.
Meals	Starters £6-£8. Mains £13-£21.
Closed	Rarely.

Tel	+44 (0)1993 811401	The Killingworth Castle,
Email	reservations@thekillingworthcastle.com	Glympton Road, Wootton,
Web	www.thekillingworthcastle.com	Woodstock, OX20 1EJ

The Woodstock Arms

In Woodstock – picturesque estate village to magnificent Blenheim Palace – is an old pub with a new lease of life: Johnny and Damion, seasoned operators, have turned the former boozer around. Enter a large welcoming space, be-rugged and pattern floor-tiled, with a green-painted bar and a roaring fire beneath a copper hood, sturdy tables for eating and drinking, and wing-back chairs in elegant leather. Behind the bar: real ales, cocktails, well-priced wines, and an impressive selection of soft drinks. In the dark beamed restaurant is the best of old British with a firm eye on provenance: pints of crispy whitebait from Brixham, duck salads, hearty pies (including vegetarian), crumbles and brûlées. It's a pretty stone building on Market Street, blessed with a large courtyard behind, and if you're here for the Palace and its gardens stay the night. Three bedrooms wait above, carpeted, compact, light and bright, with stylish new bathrooms. Hypnos mattresses, Roberts radios, Tassimo coffee machines, smart TVs, laptop safes... all has been properly thought through.

Rooms	3 doubles: £120-£220.
Meals	Starters from £5.50.
	Dinner from £13.50.
Closed	Rarely.

The Woodstock Arms,
6-8 Market Street,
Woodstock, Oxford, OX20 1SX

Tel	+44 (0)1993 811251
Email	info@thewoodstockarms.com
Web	www.thewoodstockarms.com

The Feathers Hotel

Woodstock is the estate village to Blenheim Palace, one of Britain's finest houses, birthplace of Winston Churchill. As for the hotel, it was once a draper's, then a butcher's, so perhaps it's no surprise it has become a stylish hotel serving excellent food. In the morning you breakfast leisurely, then stroll up to the big house and spend the day dropping your jaw before coming home for afternoon tea in the courtyard. Inside, elegant, uncluttered interiors keep things simple: beautiful art, smouldering fires, a wall or two of original panelling, flowers everywhere. Ancient windows flood rooms with light, you find colourful rugs on wooden floors, then more gin than you can shake a stick at in the sitting-room bar (over 300 different varieties). Bedrooms have a contemporary feel with smart fabrics, lovely beds, mohair throws, delicate wallpapers. Some have sofas, all have robes in fancy bathrooms. Back downstairs, delicious food waits in the restaurant, perhaps crab ravioli, loin of venison, treacle tart with blackberry sorbet. Bicester Village and Oxford are close. *Minimum stay: 2 nights at weekends in summer.*

Rooms	13 doubles, 3 twin/doubles: £99-£229. 5 suites for 2: £159-£319. Singles £99.
Meals	Lunch from £5. Sunday lunch from £14. Bar meals from £10. Dinner £37.50-£45. 5-course tasting menu £55; not Sunday eve.
Closed	Never.

Tel	+44 (0)1993 812291	The Feathers Hotel,
Email	reception@feathers.co.uk	Market Street, Woodstock, OX20 1SX
Web	www.feathers.co.uk	

The Lamb Inn

For Cotswolds, comfort and antique-lovers – a flagstoned old bar, open fires, a grown-up restaurant, bedrooms with gorgeous garden views. On Sheep Street, of course, The Lamb started life in the 15th century as a simple weaver's cottage. Now the feel is altogether more luxurious... cosy in winter, lovely in summer in the sunny, sheltered garden. After wandering down the handsome High Street with its medieval, Tudor and Georgian façades, an aperitif or a pint by the magnificent fireplace is a fine way to start the evening. You dine, in a light, elegant and slightly funky restaurant overlooking the garden, on great quality, locally sourced food like trout from Bibury, lamb from Barnsley and Wye Valley asparagus. Breakfast bacon and eggs are from a neighbouring farm. Come with your dog – there's a room with a private garden that is ideal – and delightful walking in the Windrush River Valley. *Minimum stay may apply over weekends.*

Rooms	12 doubles, 5 twin/doubles: £99-£310. Cots available free of charge.
Meals	Starters from £7. Mains from 18. Sunday lunch, 2-3 courses, £25-£29.50.
Closed	Rarely.

The Lamb Inn,
Sheep Street, Burford, OX18 4LR

Tel	+44 (0)1993 823155
Email	info@lambinn-burford.co.uk
Web	www.cotswold-inns-hotels.co.uk/ the-lamb-inn/food-drink/

The Swan

This lovely old pub sits on the river Windrush with the village cricket pitch waiting beyond. It started life as a water mill and stands on the Devonshire estate, hence the pictures of the Mitford sisters that hang on the walls. Outside, wisteria wanders across golden stone and creepers blush red in the autumn sun. Interiors hit the spot: low ceilings, open fires, beautiful windows, stone walls. Over the years thirsty feet on their way to the bar have worn grooves into ancient flagstones (including those of prime ministers and French presidents). As for the food, seasonal menus brim with local produce, offering delicious delights, perhaps game terrine with pear chutney, roast partridge with a red wine jus, rhubarb and apple crumble. Bedrooms in the old forge have 15th-century walls and 21st-century interior design; those in the cottage across the lane are yards from the river. Expect crisp linen, comfy beds, warm colours and good art. Several have claw-foot baths, one has a pink chaise longue. Burford is close. *Minimum stay: 2 nights at weekends.*

Rooms	4 doubles, 5 twin/doubles, 1 twin: £130-£160. 1 suite for 2: £210. Singles £95-£100.
Meals	Lunch from £5. Dinner, 3 courses, about £30. Sunday lunch from £16.
Closed	Christmas Day & Boxing Day.

Tel	+44 (0)1993 823339
Email	info@theswanswinbrook.co.uk
Web	www.theswanswinbrook.co.uk

The Swan,
Swinbrook, Burford, OX18 4DY

The Maytime Inn

This 17th-century coaching inn has a delightful setting in the heart of a historic Cotswold village, with the babbling Windrush river just a stone's throw away. A cool young team run this rather posh pub, headed up by Dom. Good food is sourced locally and freshly cooked in a modern British style, and drinks are taken seriously: an ever-growing choice of gins, a beer menu with craft and world beers, an excellent choice of whiskies and wines by the glass. Continental breakfast (berry compote, mini croissants and fresh smoothies) is waiting on the table in the morning; cooked breakfast includes full English, smashed avocado on toast, eggs Benedict or any way you want. Coffee is roasted locally. Walks from the door take in the peaceful countryside. It's a four-minute drive to the pretty town of Burford, which has boutiques brimming with antiques, art and gifts. Stow-on-the-Wold and Bourton-on-the Water are 20 minutes away, Oxford is 30 minutes and Cheltenham is about a 40-minute drive.

Rooms	6 doubles: £95-£150.
Meals	Starters from £6.50.
	Mains from £12.50.
Closed	Rarely.

The Maytime Inn,
Asthall, Burford, OX18 4HW

Tel	+44 (0)1993 822068
Email	info@themaytime.com
Web	www.themaytime.com

Blue Boar

Here's a pub with warmth and personality, where the main bar welcomes all-comers with signature teal blue tiles, exposed beams, comfy tweed upholstery and a sideboard full of games. Sit in the generous bay windows overlooking Witney's comings and goings, or find a corner for morning coffee or a dish from the Mediterranean-inspired menu – bruschettas, brunches, steaks, build your own pizzas or salads, plenty of gluten-free or veggie options. Behind a red velvet curtain is a more formal dining room, with vibrant pops of colour; beyond is a more rustic pizzeria with wood fired oven. The Blue Boar is now part of an award-winning group, but still retains a community pub vibe – they sponsor local events, the Witney rugby club and hold garden parties in the neatly kept courtyard garden in summer. For staying over, no two rooms are alike. Ask for a room over the lively square (triple glazing provided!) or a dog-friendly ground floor annexe room. You may find oak leaf and acorn wallpaper, smoky blues and pale yellows, quirky headboards made from old doors; all rooms have lovely Witney blanket throws.

Rooms 12 doubles, 1 twin, 1 four-poster: £95-£140. 2 family rooms for 4: £105-£140.
Meals Breakfast from £7. Lunch from £10-£12. Starters from £5. Mains from £18-£20.
Closed Rarely.

Tel +44 (0)1993 776353
Email enquiries@oakmaninns.co.uk
Web www.blueboarwitney.co.uk

Blue Boar,
28 Market Square, Witney, OX28 6BH

Artist Residence Oxford

Justin and Charlie's ability to create beautiful small hotels at the speed of light is unprecedented. Their fourth – lost in the country a few miles west of Oxford – is a reinvention of the country pub, though not as you might think. This isn't a stripped-back monument to contemporary design, rather a cool take on all things retro with quirky art and a little neon mixed in for good measure. You'll find vintage wallpapers, vivid colours, glass cabinets filled with curios, then a pink, upcycled sofa in the cocktail bar. Country rugs cover flagstone floors, a fire burns on both sides in the bar, an original pine bench comes with plumped-up cushions. You eat in the restaurant amid ferns and flock wallpaper, perhaps Dorset crab with sorrel sauce, local venison with rainbow chard, gin and tonic panna cotta; there's a pie and a pint at the bar, too, and a dining terrace that overlooks the kitchen garden. Stunning bedrooms set the standard for others to follow: fat beds, exposed timbers, robes in flawless bathrooms, old tea chests for bedside tables. We've hardly scratched the surface. Exceptional. *Minimum stay: 2 nights at weekends.*

Rooms	5 doubles, 1 twin: £140-£290. 3 suites for 2: £180-£350. Extra beds £40 p.p.p.n.; under 12s £30.
Meals	Lunch from £6.50. Dinner, 3 courses, about £40; 5-course tasting menu, £60. Sunday lunch from £15.95.
Closed	Never.

Artist Residence Oxford,
Station Road, South Leigh,
Witney, OX29 6XN

Tel	+44 (0)1993 656220
Email	oxford@artistresidence.co.uk
Web	www.artistresidence.co.uk/ our-hotels/oxford/

Old Parsonage Hotel

The Old Parsonage has been at the centre of Oxford life for over 350 years. It stands in the middle of town on land owned by University College and was once home to Oscar Wilde. It is one of the loveliest places to stay in town, its beautiful interiors touching every corner. Chief among its virtues are its shaded dining terrace, exceptional art collection, and first-floor library (curated by Philip Blackwell), which opens onto a small roof terrace. Inside, flames flicker in an ancient fireplace, newspapers wait by mullioned windows, fresh flowers scent the air. The restaurant doubles as an art gallery, its charcoal walls crammed with portraits, a theatrical setting for a good meal, perhaps Devon crab, blanquette de veau, lemon tart with crème fraîche. Bedrooms come in pale greys with the best beds, the crispest linen, pretty throws and padded headheads. Bigger rooms have sofas, some overlook the back garden, all have robes and spoiling oils and in beautiful marble bathrooms. The 'city of dreaming spires' is on your doorstep, there are bikes to borrow on which to explore. *Minimum stay: 2 nights at weekends.*

Rooms	22 doubles, 7 twins: £215-£485. 6 suites for 3: £395-£560.
Meals	Breakfast £5-£15. Lunch from £18. Dinner, 3 courses, £25-£45. Sunday lunch £25-£30. Afternoon tea £26.
Closed	Never.

Tel	+44 (0)1865 310210
Email	reservations@oldparsonage-hotel.co.uk
Web	www.oldparsonage-hotel.co.uk

Old Parsonage Hotel,
1 Banbury Road, Oxford, OX2 6NN

Turl Street Kitchen & Tower House Rooms

You land in the middle of Oxford at this quirky restaurant with rooms and find yourself surrounded by ancient colleges, with the Ashmolean Museum and the Bodleian Library both close. Interiors come in canteen style, with waitresses buzzing about, an open kitchen on display, a cool, shabby chic feel and happy chatter from people in for breakfast, lunch and dinner – this is a very popular community hub. Local food is sourced ethically and the menu changes twice a day, perhaps spiced carrot soup, steak and kidney pie, blood orange and vanilla cheesecake. There's WiFi throughout, the daily papers, a first-floor sitting room straight out of a student house. It's fun, easy going, a place for all. It's also a social enterprise, with profits going to charity, as they do 50 paces around the corner at Tower House Rooms, a terraced house with a difference: the old city wall runs through it with a 16th-century watch tower attached. Some rooms are small and share a bathroom, others are big, perhaps with a claw-foot bath. Expect good beds, smart colours, white linen, pretty throws. It's a peaceful spot, too.

Rooms	5 doubles; 3 doubles sharing 1 bathroom: £110-£170. Singles from £100. Cots for children under 5 no charge.
Meals	Lunch from £6.50. Dinner, 3 courses, £20-£25.
Closed	24 December – 2 January.

Turl Street Kitchen & Tower House Rooms,
15 Ship Street, Oxford, OX1 3DA

Tel	+44 (0)1865 246828
Email	info@towerhouseoxford.co.uk
Web	www.towerhouseoxford.co.uk

Old Bank Hotel

You're in the heart of old Oxford, with Merton College and Christ Church Meadow to the south, the Radcliffe Camera and the Bodleian Library to the north, and University College and the Botanic Gardens at Magdalen Bridge to the east. As for the Old Bank, its airy interiors are home to an exceptional collection of modern art and photography. The hub is the old tiller's hall, now a cocktail bar and brasserie, with six arched windows overlooking the high street.

Food is on tap all day long, anything from a pizza or a steak to afternoon tea, with meat from the owner's farm and fish from the Channel Islands. Bedrooms are gorgeous: beautiful beds, original art, robes in chic bathrooms. You get flat-screen TVs and good WiFi throughout. There's a peaceful library bar for residents, a decked courtyard for breakfast in summer, then the rarest commodity in Oxford, free off-street parking. The University Church of St Mary stands opposite, so climb its tower for the best views of Oxford. The Ashmolean and Pitt Rivers Museums are close. *Minimum stay: 2 nights at weekends.*

Rooms	26 doubles, 14 twin/doubles: £215-£485. 2 suites for 3: £395-£560.
Meals	Breakfast £5-£15. Lunch & dinner £5-£30. Afternoon tea from £6.95.
Closed	Never.

Tel	+44 (0)1865 799599
Email	info@oldbank-hotel.co.uk
Web	www.oldbank-hotel.co.uk

Old Bank Hotel,
92-94 High Street, Oxford, OX1 4BJ

The Lamb at Buckland

Follow the signs through picture-perfect Buckland to the 18th-century Lamb, tucked into a green corner of this historic estate village. The combined talents and enthusiasms of Shelley and chef Richard have turned this little inn into one of the best; it's an absolute gem. Step into a simple, rustic bar to find crackling logs, low beams, fat candles, old dining tables, leather wing chairs, local ales and Cotswold gin. Beyond is the more refined dining room, where modern seasonal menus champion local suppliers (Kelmscott pork, home-grown vegetables, and local game). Beautiful food flows from the kitchen: duck balls with red cabbage; roasted fillet of pork with prunes and pancetta; butternut squash and sweet potato gallette with goat's cheese and mushroom cream sauce; warm chocolate and walnut brownies. The trio of bedrooms here is delightful: crisp cotton, down duvets, colourful throws, a mix of pine and painted furniture, iPod-radios, bathrooms fresh and simple. The Thames Path, William Morris's Kelmscott Manor and Oxford are close.

Rooms	3 doubles: £80-£90.
Meals	Lunch from £9.50. Bar meals from £6. Dinner from £12.95. Sunday lunch from £12.
Closed	Rarely.

The Lamb at Buckland,
Lamb Lane, Buckland,
Faringdon, SN7 8QN

Tel	+44 (0)1367 870484
Email	thelambatbuckland@googlemail.com
Web	www.lambatbuckland.co.uk

The Greyhound Inn

This 18th-century redbrick pub is set on a quiet road in the heart of a small village close to the Uffington White Horse and is a popular draw for locals and visitors. Chef Liam Whittle produces locally-sourced menus that change with the seasons – whether you go for lamb rump with beetroot dauphinoise or twice-baked Leonard Stanley Gloucestershire cheddar soufflé, this is cooking of a high order. Two-course 'Midweek Fix' menus on Wednesdays are a steal – try confit duck leg with galette potatoes and a pickled blackberry and red wine jus followed by chocolate profiteroles. Pick up a map from the bar and explore the surrounding countryside – there are fantastic horse-riding and mountain biking routes too. Return for a pint in the back garden or inside next to the fire, and retire upstairs to bedrooms with simple country antiques. Breakfast is a treat – fresh-baked pastries, yogurt with fruit compote, Full English, eggs Benedict. *Pets by arrangement.*

Rooms	4 doubles, 2 twin/doubles: £95-£125. 1 suite for 4, 1 suite for 5: £145-£215. Singles £80-£130. Dinner, B&B £75-£100 p.p. Extra bed £20-£40 p.p.p.n.
Meals	Starters from £5.50. Lunch from £7. Dinner from £11.
Closed	Rarely.

Tel	+44 (0)1235 771969
Email	info@thegreyhoundletcombe.co.uk
Web	www.thegreyhoundletcombe.co.uk

The Greyhound Inn,
Main Street, Letcombe Regis,
Wantage, OX12 9JL

The Fat Fox Inn

A stone's throw from the big smoke yet wonderfully rural. Historic Watlington is on the edge of the Chiltern Hills, red kites wheel above beech woods and the Ridgeway runs through. The 17th-century building has been part pub, butchers, bakery and shop in its day but is now an inn to the core. The bronze buddha on the bar gazes serenely over pumps with Brakspear Bitter and Oxford Gold, the carpeted bar is cosy and simple, there's an open fire, sofas and an elegant separate dining room with oriental rugs. Consider smoked chicken and foie gras terrine, fig chutney and sourdough toast; fillet of pollock, chick pea, chorizo and sherry stew with saffron aïoli; lemon financier and thyme ice cream – just some of the delights from chef Mark Gambles and quite simply divine. Staff and owner are delightful and the whole place hums along on this team's super-friendly and engaging manner. Set well behind the bustle in several old barns are a variety of bedrooms – some with signature beds and trappings, all with antiques, beams and small neat bathrooms.

Rooms	5 doubles, 4 twins: £75-£119. Singles £65-£109. Extra bed/sofabed £20 p.p.p.n.
Meals	Lunch from £12. Bar meals from £5. Dinner from £27. Sunday lunch, 2-3 courses, £20-£25.
Closed	Never.

The Fat Fox Inn,
13 Shirburn Street,
Watlington, OX49 5BU

Tel	+44 (0)1491 613040
Email	info@thefatfoxinn.co.uk
Web	www.thefatfoxinn.co.uk

The Nags Head Inn

This was Roald Dahl's local – it features in *Fantastic Mr Fox*, half a mile out of Great Missenden. It's a beautiful old building of red brick and flint under bright red pantiles, framed by the rolling hills of the Chilterns. At the back is a vast garden with plenty of trees under which to dream and picnic tables with umbrellas. Inside, a classic refurbishment from owner Alvin Michaels of the award-winning Bricklayers Arms, with food to match: the beloved 15th-century boozer has become a great dining pub. Now low dark beams and big inglenook blend with modern oak and lemon hues, there are salt and pepper mills on shining tables and boxed shelves guarding armagnacs. The food is faultless: try pan fried wood pigeon breast with black pudding and a dry sherry jus, or slow cooked pork hock on a bed of sweet & sour cabbage. Drinks cover every aspect of the grape and globe, including London Pride, and young staff are attentive. Bedrooms above are equally good, their creams and whites complementing ancient timbers. There are ironing boards, toiletries and full-length mirrors, and the bed linen is gorgeous.

Rooms	3 doubles, 2 twins: £90-£130.
Meals	Lunch & dinner from £10.95.
	Sunday lunch, 3 courses, £23.95.
Closed	Christmas Day.

Tel	+44 (0)1494 862200	The Nags Head Inn,
Email	goodfood@nagsheadbucks.com	London Road, Little Kingshill,
Web	www.nagsheadbucks.com	Great Missenden, HP16 0DG

Cliveden House

Cliveden has no match in Britain, a country house of epic proportions that dates to 1605. It has been home to earls, dukes and one Prince of Wales, but it's best known for the Profumo affair, which almost sank a government; its famous pool and beautiful new spa are at your disposal. It sits in 376 acres of National Trust land with sublime gardens, marble fountains, sculptures by the dozen. You'll think you've arrived at Versailles and not without reason – the Astors bought Madame de Pompadour's drawing room and had it installed here! The Great Hall, a panelled masterpiece with vast portraits on its walls, is a fine spot for cocktails before dinner. Elsewhere, Corinthian columns, muralled ceilings and a dining room for ambrosial food, perhaps Orkney scallops, Anjou squab pigeon, rice pudding soufflé with Balvenie ice cream; there's a bistro in the old stables, too. Bedrooms, some in the main house, others in the wings, have huge beds, period art, white marble bathrooms. Some have hot tubs on private terraces, stately suites are vast, the riverside cottage is divine. Windsor is close.

Rooms	18 doubles, 10 twin/doubles: £445-£800. 19 suites for 2: £865-£1585. 1 cottage for 6: £2055-£2650. Extra beds £60.
Meals	Lunch from £8. Dinner, 3 courses, £55-£75; 7-course tasting menu £97.50. Sunday lunch £60. Afternoon tea £37.
Closed	Never.

Cliveden House,
Taplow, SL6 0JF

Tel	+44 (0)1628 668561
Email	reservations@clivedenhouse.co.uk
Web	www.clivedenhouse.co.uk

Miller of Mansfield

Nick Galer (ex-Fat Duck) and Mary run their inn with enthusiasm and charm. You can have breakfast in bed, bring your dog (treats on tap), arrange a cookery demo from Nick including lunch and a glass of wine or book a nine-course tasting menu. They do 'locals' dinners', wine evenings and also offer to pay £10 towards your train fare if you travel from London. Nick's style of cooking is modern British, and he's keen on spontaneity and choosing the best seasonal ingredients he can find. There are unusual gins, cocktails and an extensive wine list – each bottle comes with a story that Mary is happy to tell you. There's an informal feel throughout and you can eat where you want – cosy bar or restaurant. Most of the bedrooms are on the first floor, with two up in the eaves on the second. They all have the quirky fun touch of Mary's design, each one different, and of varying sizes. There's a small courtyard garden for having a pint in the sun.

Rooms	4 doubles: £129-£189.
	2 family rooms for 3: £199-£239.
	2 singles: £109-£149.
Meals	Lunch from £18.
	Dinner, 2 courses, from £26.
Closed	25-28 December.

Tel	+44 (0)1491 872829
Email	reservations@millerofmansfield.com
Web	www.millerofmansfield.com

Miller of Mansfield,
High Street, Goring, RG8 9AW

The Queens Arms

A wiggly country road leads to the heart of racing country – just five minutes off the M4. But you don't have to be mad about horses to be seduced by the Queens Arms. The new hands-on owners run a top team, and you feel it the moment you enter. As tasty food is ferried to groups of jolly lunchers and Barbour-wearing owners of gun dogs, the occasional champion jockey may be spotted at the bar. Families descend for roasts on Sundays; Hennessy cocktails clink with champagne glasses during Gold Cup week. The food is hearty, the portions generous and on Fridays the fish lands straight from Looe. There's beef and Guinness pie, mussels with cream and chorizo, crab gratin with parmesan, game in season, scrumptious puds. The Queens is steeped in warmth and character, with a low-beamed bar, an intimate restaurant, an awned terrace facing west, and paddocks all around. A pity not to stay the night – and dogs get their own beds. If you like character go for the rooms in the pub. Ranging from cosy to large, they have coir floors, dark woods, deep mattresses, and lovely vibrant colours on the walls.

Rooms	7 doubles, 4 twin/doubles: £110-£130. 1 family room for 3: £110-£130.
Meals	Starters from £6. Lunch from £12. Dinner from £12.
Closed	Rarely.

The Queens Arms,
East Garston, RG17 7ET

Tel	+44 (0)1488 648757
Email	info@queensarmseastgarston.co.uk
Web	www.queensarmseastgarston.co.uk

The Royal Oak

Handsome centrepiece of a handsome village, the Royal Oak is the quintessential country inn. The bar is a back-in-time proposition of original checkerboard tiles, beams, brick and panelling, four hearths ablaze, offering superb pints of Ramsbury Gold from the local Ramsbury brewery. The lobby's leather sofas and gleaming wooden floors, made homely by patterned rugs, project a smartness that carries through to the restaurant's terracotta reds and chunky beech furnishings where the likes of five-spiced duck salad with chicory, cucumber and sweet chilli and beetroot risotto, crispy sage and parmesan reflect an inventive use of local ingredients. Stay over and snuggle down in big comfy bedrooms, some classically kitted out with antiques and rich fabrics, others more contemporary. Choose between pretty views across the square or the walled garden; the quietest rooms are at the back and three are in the old staff house. A garden ringed with herbs, shrubs and trellises includes smart wicker seating and is a boon for summer. Pub quizzes and family suppers underlie links to the community.

Rooms	8 doubles, 2 twin/doubles: £95-£135.
Meals	Lunch & dinner £11-£18.
Closed	Never.

Tel	+44 (0)1635 201325
Email	info@royaloakyattendon.com
Web	www.royaloakyattendon.co.uk

The Royal Oak,
The Square, Yattendon, RG18 0UF

The Elephant at Pangbourne

In the centre of well-heeled Pangbourne, The Elephant is a stroll to chi-chi gift shops, an award-winning cheese shop – Cheese Etc – and the Thames. Amble along it; hire a boat or kayak if you fancy a splash about. This is also a handy base for the Henley Regatta. Inside, smiley staff buzz around and colonial era glamour reigns: wooden floors, club chairs to recline in, old tea chests – and quite a lot of elephants! Book in for afternoon tea or settle down for sandwiches, sharing plates or a salad in the Babar bar. The Herd Restaurant is open in the evenings – treat yourself to a steak, they are sublime. There are no fewer than 56 gins on the menu – fun to sit in the bar at a table made from an old aeroplane wing to sample a couple of them. Upstairs, grand bedrooms continue the old school sophistication. The garden annexe rooms have the best views across the gorgeous gardens to the church next door.

Rooms	20 doubles: £85-£150.
	2 singles: £65-£110.
	Extra bed/sofabed £20 p.p.p.n.
Meals	Bar meals from £6.50.
	Dinner from £11.50.
Closed	Never.

The Elephant at Pangbourne,
Church Road, Pangbourne, RG8 7AR

Tel	+44 (0)118 984 2244
Email	reception@elephanthotel.co.uk
Web	www.elephanthotel.co.uk

The Merry Harriers

Exhausted urban dwellers will unwind in this good old-fashioned pub. Remote it may be and surrounded by acres of green fields but there's lots going on. Llamas to visit, jazz in the garden, a monthly pub quiz and a lively, bustling atmosphere. Staff are friendly and chatty, head chef Sam Page turns out heart-warming pub favourite, and grows his own veg and herbs; he also does a bit of foraging – nettles, wild garlic and blackberries. They try and source everything from within 15 miles; meat from Wakelings Butchers, local ale , wine from Surrey vineyards and their own cider. Walkers rub shoulders with locals of all ages while the big fire crackles merrily and the volume increases. In summer the fun spills out onto the terrace and large rear garden – children will love tearing about and grown-ups will feel relaxed. Order a picnic and one of the llamas will carry the hamper along trails to a perfect spot along The Greensand Way. You can fall upstairs into bed too – bedrooms are not huge but are fresh and pretty, some beamed, some panelled, all with rural views. *Minimum stay: 2 nights at weekends & in high season.*

Rooms	10 doubles: £110-£160.
Meals	Starters from £6.50. Lunch from £5.95. Mains from £13.
Closed	Never.

Tel	+44 (0)1428 682883
Email	enquiries@merryharriers.com
Web	www.merryharriers.com

The Merry Harriers,
Hambleon Road, Hambledon, GU8 4DR

The Wellington Arms

Lost down a web of lanes, the 'Welly' draws foodies from miles around. Cosy, relaxed and decorated in style – old dining tables, crystal decanters, terracotta floor – the newly extended bar-dining room fills quickly, so make sure you book to sample Jason's inventive modern cooking. Boards are chalked up daily and the produce mainly home-grown or organic. Kick off with home-grown courgette flowers stuffed with ricotta, parmesan and lemon zest, follow with rack of home-reared lamb with root vegetable mash and crab apple jelly, finish with elderflower jelly, strawberry and raspberry sorbet. Migrate to the huge garden for summer meals and views of the pub's smallholding: little pigs, woolly sheep, bees and assorted hens; buy the eggs at the bar. Stay over and get cosy in any one of the four bedrooms, housed in the former wine store and pig shed. Expect exposed brick and beams, vast Benchmark beds topped with goose down duvets, fresh flowers, coffee machines, mini-fridges, and slate tiled bathrooms with underfloor heating and walk-in rain showers. Breakfast too is a treat.

Rooms	4 doubles: £125-£220.
Meals	Lunch, 2-3 courses £17.50-£20.
	Dinner £11-£21.
Closed	Rarely.

The Wellington Arms,
Baughurst Road, Baughurst, RG26 5LP

Tel	+44 (0)118 982 0110
Email	hello@thewellingtonarms.com
Web	www.thewellingtonarms.com

Watership Down Inn

A smartly-renovated 19th-century pub with seven lovely bedrooms; white linen and Watership Down lotions and potions. Breakfast is served in the main bar; locally-sourced eggs and bacon, award-winning Stornaway black pudding, Hobbs House bakery bloomer. There is an abundance of things to do and see, pop down to North Hants Bikes to rent out your own wheels, take a short stroll to the iconic Bombay Sapphire Distillery, or the multi-award winning Hardys Nursery. Head to Vale Farm Fishery for fishing in the pretty River Test, stop off at Test Valley or Drummer Golf Club for a round or head to Highclere Castle – *Downton Abbey* fans will like this one. Meals cooked by the in-house chefs are delicious and seasonal: Exmouth mussels, braised ox cheeks, celeriac mash; all paired with wine from an independent vineyard.

Rooms	6 twin/doubles: £110-£120. 1 family room for 4: £180. Singles £90. Family room for 3: £150.
Meals	Light lunch & starters from £6.50. Mains from £10.
Closed	Never.

Tel	+44 (0)1256 892254
Email	enquiries@watershipdowninn.com
Web	www.watershipdowninn.com

Watership Down Inn,
Freefolk Priors, Freefolk,
Whitchurch, RG28 7NJ

The Thomas Lord

Named after the founder of Lord's Cricket Ground, the Thomas Lord is much loved and hard to fault. Remodelling has raised the gastro credentials without losing the community vibe. Join locals (and dogs) over a trio of local Upham ales at the bar, or settle into leather armchairs around winter fires. Cricketing prints and paraphernalia decorate the walls (old bats, balls, caps, shoes) while the darkly beamed bar's weathered wooden furniture gives way to a duo of dedicated dining areas. Menus are rammed with local produce (including pickings from the pub's potager) and foodies relish it all, from the dry aged beef burgers to more sophisticated dishes such as pan fried skate wing with mussels and chilli broth. Leave room for scrumptious banana fritter with salt caramel and rum cream. Behind the pub, five double rooms in bespoke wood cabins offer comfortable and quiet beds for the night with antique touches, padded headboards, sparkling shower rooms. In summer, spill into the lovely grounds for a wander.

Rooms	5 doubles: £74-£134.
Meals	Starters from £8.50. Lunch from £13.50. Mains from £14.
Closed	Rarely.

The Thomas Lord,
West Meon, GU32 1LN

Tel	+44 (0)1730 829244
Email	info@thethomaslord.co.uk
Web	www.thethomaslord.co.uk

The Montagu Arms

Beaulieu, an ancient royal hunting ground, was gifted to Cistercian monks by King John in 1204. Their abbey took 40 years to build and you can visit its ruins in the nearby grounds of Palace House, seat of the Montagu family since 1538. As for the village, its tiny high street is a hotchpotch of 17th-century timber-framed houses that totter by the tidal estuary. The hotel dates to 1742, but was re-modelled in 1925, giving interiors an Arts & Crafts country-house feel.

You'll find roaring fires and deep sofas, then a library bar and a courtyard garden where you can eat in summer. Chic bedrooms come with period furniture, smart fabrics, fresh flowers and robes in spotless bathrooms. Downstairs, ambrosial food is the big draw, perhaps Jerusalem artichoke garden salad or honey glazed duck with Szechuan pepper, followed by orange soufflé and dark chocolate ice cream. There's a gastro pub if you want something simpler: local fish pie, ham and chips with eggs from resident hens. A kitchen garden provides much for the table, too. Beautiful walks start from the front door. *Minimum stay: 2 nights at weekends.*

Rooms	12 doubles, 1 twin, 4 four-posters: £179-£329. 7 suites for 2: £299-£399. Singles from £129.
Meals	Lunch, 3 courses, from £25. Dinner from £18. Tasting menu, 7 courses, £90. Sunday lunch from £37.
Closed	Never.

Tel	+44 (0)1590 612324
Email	reservations@montaguarmshotel.co.uk
Web	www.montaguarmshotel.co.uk

The Montagu Arms,
Palace Lane, Beaulieu,
Brockenhurst, SO42 7ZL

Daisybank Cottage Boutique B&B

This chic B&B in the New Forest mixes a warm contemporary style with some fine, old-fashioned hospitality – Ciaran and Cheryl go out of their way to make your stay special. As for their lovely Arts & Crafts house, it sits peacefully on the southern fringes of Brockenhurst with pretty gardens front and back. There's a juke box in the breakfast room, an honesty bar for pre-dinner drinks and a relaxing reading room. Spoiling bedrooms have airy colours, plantation shutters, Vi-Spring mattresses on lovely beds, then robes in stylish bathrooms. One has a claw-foot bath, another at the back opens onto the garden; keep going you'll find a shepherd's hut with its own wood-burner and a small terrace. All rooms have coffee machines, silent fridges, iPod docks and flat-screen TVs. Breakfast is a feast: local eggs, artisan jams, home-baked soda bread, bacon and sausages from a local farm. You can walk by the sea or explore the forest by foot, bike or horse. Good restaurants wait in town (a gentle ten-minute stroll), perhaps Thai, French or an excellent pizza. *Minimum stay: 2 nights at weekends. Children over 8 welcome.*

Rooms	7 doubles: £110-£155.
	1 shepherd's hut for 2: £110-£155.
	Extra bed/sofabed £35-£40 p.p.p.n.
Meals	Local restaurants within half a mile.
Closed	One week over Christmas.

Daisybank Cottage Boutique B&B,
Sway Road, Brockenhurst, SO42 7SG

Tel	+44 (0)1590 622086
Email	info@bedandbreakfast-newforest.co.uk
Web	www.bedandbreakfast-newforest.co.uk

The Manor at Sway

A big house in a small village in the middle of the New Forest – lovely gardens run down to woodland, the odd deer comes in to nibble the roses. Inside, country-house interiors have a distinctly contemporary feel – airy and nicely stylish with wood floors, pretty wallpapers and a relaxed feel. You'll find smart sofas in the sitting room, then a chic bar with a wall of glass that opens onto the terrace, perfect for afternoon tea in the sun. Bedrooms are lovely. They come in different shapes and sizes, but all have the same comforts: excellent beds, crisp linen, warm colours, sparkling bathrooms. Three are dog-friendly, those in the eaves are warmly cosy, larger rooms have armchairs, most have garden views. The big surprise is the delicious food, so work up an appetite in the forest by day, then come home for a feast, perhaps scallops with curried cauliflower, local venison in a port sauce, Bakewell tart with blackberry jam. Fabulous walking, mountain bike trails and sun loungers in the garden wait. *Minimum stay: 2 nights at weekends.*

Rooms	12 doubles, 3 twin/doubles: £90-£210.
Meals	Lunch from £6.
	Dinner, 3 courses, £30-£40.
	Sunday lunch £19.50-£24.50.
Closed	Rarely.

Tel	+44 (0)1590 682754	The Manor at Sway,
Email	info@swaymanor.com	Station Road, Sway,
Web	www.themanoratsway.com	Lymington, SO41 6BA

Chewton Glen

Chewton Glen is one of the loveliest country-house hotels in the land. It opened in 1964 with eight bedrooms, and even though it now has 70, it remains delightfully intimate. 50 years of evolution have brought a pillared swimming pool, a hydrotherapy spa, a golf course and a tennis centre. The most recent addition is The Kitchen, an informal foil to the main restaurant, where you can also come for cookery classes. As for the hotel, expect beautiful sitting rooms, roaring fires, busts and oils, a bar that opens onto a sun-trapping terrace. Bedrooms mix country-house style with contemporary flair: marble bathrooms, private balconies, designer fabrics, flawless housekeeping. You'll also find 13 treehouse suites that sit in their own valley with hot tubs on balconies and wood-burners within. Beyond, nine gardeners tend 130 acres of lawns and woodland, with a kitchen garden that serves both restaurants. The food is exceptional, perhaps twice-baked cheese soufflé, Thai lobster curry, pineapple and black pepper tarte tatin. Beach and forest wait, there's croquet on the lawn in summer. *Minimum stay: 2 nights at weekends.*

Rooms	3 doubles, 30 twin/doubles: £325-£695. 25 suites for 2: £800-£1495. 14 treehouses for 2: £850-£2850.
Meals	Breakfast £21-£26. Lunch & dinner from £10. Lunch, 3-courses, £26.50; dinner, 3 courses, £50-£70. Sunday lunch £39.50.
Closed	Never.

Chewton Glen,
Christchurch Road,
New Milton, BH25 6QS

Tel	+44 (0)1425 275341
Email	reservations@chewtonglen.com
Web	www.chewtonglen.com

The Mill at Gordleton

Another wormhole back to old England, a 400-year-old mill on Avon Water with mallards and Indian runners to watch from the terrace in summer. The house stands in three acres of gardens filled with art and beautiful things. Cosy interiors mix old and new delightfully: low ceilings, wonky walls, busts and mirrors, smouldering fires. There's a panelled bar for pre-dinner drinks, then bedrooms which are full of character. The suite above the wheelhouse has a fabulous bathroom, you'll find lots of colour, sheets and blankets, bowls of fruit. Three rooms have watery views (you can fall asleep to the sound of the river), most have fancy new bathrooms. The main suite has robes, all have White Company oils; and while a lane passes outside, you are more likely to be woken by birdsong. Downstairs, the beautifully refurbished restaurant continues to draw a happy crowd for its delicious local food, perhaps wild mushroom ravioli, Creedy Carver free-range duck, blackberry soufflé with apple crumble ice cream. The forest and coast are both on your doorstep. *Minimum stay: 2 nights at weekends April-October.*

Rooms	3 doubles, 3 twin/doubles: £150-£195.
	2 suites for 2: £150-£275.
	Singles from £115.
Meals	Lunch from £6.95. Dinner £22.50-£27.50;
	à la carte about £40.
	Sunday lunch from £21.50.
Closed	Christmas Day.

Tel	+44 (0)1590 682219
Email	info@themillatgordleton.co.uk
Web	www.themillatgordleton.co.uk

The Mill at Gordleton,
Silver Street, Sway,
Lymington, SO41 6DJ

The East End Arms

A good little local hidden down New Forest lanes, winningly unpretentious and owned by John Illsley of Dire Straits. Walkers, wax jackets and locals congregate in the small, rustic Foresters Bar with its chatty community vibe, and walls lined with the famous. The carpeted-cosy dining room, all cottagey furniture and roaring log fire, cocks a snook at gastropub remodelling, but the menus change twice daily – a rare treat – and make the best of seasonal produce. Try saddle of venison, whole baked seabass or locally caught Lymington crab. A paved terrace invites al fresco drinking, while bedrooms on the back add va-va-voom. Fresh, clean-lined and cosy, in fashionably neutral tones that bring the forest indoors, they sport roman blinds and Mulberry fabrics. Stylish bathrooms and paintings by John himself add warmth and class; fine breakfasts are the cherry on the cake. A great little find for anyone who loves the New Forest – neither new nor a forest, but fine open heathland nonetheless and excellent hiking terrain.

Rooms	5 twin/doubles: £110-£130. Singles £100-£110. Extra bed/sofabed available £20 p.p.p.n.
Meals	Lunch from £8.50. Dinner from £12.95; not Sunday eves.
Closed	Rarely.

The East End Arms,
Lymington Road, East End,
Lymington, SO41 5SY

Tel	+44 (0)1590 626223
Email	managereastendarms@yahoo.co.uk
Web	www.eastendarms.co.uk

The Master Builder's House Hotel

The position here is hard to beat: lawns run down to the river, yacht flags flutter in the breeze, ancient woodland runs along the water, soundproofing this beautiful landscape. As for the house, it dates to 1729 and was home to the shipwrights who built Nelson's fleet; several ships built here saw action at Trafalgar. These days peace reigns. A chic sitting room opens onto a smart garden, where gravel paths weave past colourful beds to tables for lunch in the sun. There's a lovely old bar and an airy restaurant – both have terraces that drink in the view, and both serve locally sourced seasonal food, perhaps a pizza or posh fish and chips in the bar; or rack of lamb with heritage carrots and black garlic compote in the restaurant. Bedrooms in the main house have big views, Indian furniture, then colour and character in spades. Those in the annexe, recently refurbished (a few await their turn), come in crisp blues and whites, with a wall of wood, Bose sound systems and excellent walk-in showers. As for the New Forest, walk, cycle or kayak though it. A great forest base.

Rooms	17 doubles, 9 twin/doubles: £95-£320. 2 cottages for 4: £500-£1400. .
Meals	Lunch from £5.50. Dinner: in bar from £13.50; in restaurant, 3 courses, £30-£35. Sunday lunch £24.95-£29.50
Closed	Never.

Tel	+44 (0)1590 616253
Email	enquiries@themasterbuilders.co.uk
Web	www.themasterbuilders.co.uk

The Master Builder's House Hotel,
Bucklers Hard, Beaulieu, SO42 7XB

North House

Here's an Isle of Wight hotel beautifully remodelled in chic cosmopolitan style, while keeping lovely old fireplaces and other period features intact. Three listed buildings – an 1820s built theatre and two Georgian townhouses – are combined with an impressive frontage on a quiet road. A couple of minutes away downhill is Cowes High Street, with shops, restaurants and a hubbub of boatie endeavours, at its most lively during race weeks. Bedrooms come in three sizes, all immaculately furnished with well-chosen bed linens and metro-tiled bathrooms; from some you can watch the water traffic passing on the Solent. Larger rooms have free-standing baths, perfect after blowy coastal walks or days out at island attractions. There's no hotel parking, but staff are happy to advise. Downstairs, there are stylish spaces to relax – the traditional library is perfect for reading or catching up with some work, the bar and restaurant are also open to the public. Outside, take a dip in the small heated pool all year round, with deckchairs and a neat suntrap terrace for summer.

Rooms	14 twin/doubles: £145-£245.
Meals	Dinner, 3 courses, £20-£45.
	Pubs/restaurants 2-minute walk.
Closed	Never.

North House,
Sun Hill, Cowes, PO31 7HY

Tel	+44 (0)1983 209453
Email	reservations@northhousecowes.co.uk
Web	www.northhousecowes.co.uk

Hillside

Is it an art gallery, a smallholding or a cool hotel? Whatever it is, Hillside is a great little place to wash up for a couple of nights. It stands at the foot of forested hills with views over Ventnor and out to sea. Outside, five acres of lawn, field and woodland are home to Hebridean sheep, free-range chickens, red squirrels and white doves; there are beehives, too, and a stunning kitchen garden that provides much for the table. Inside, you find a wonderland in white. There's a cute bar with a wood-burner, a sitting room with Danish leather sofas, an airy restaurant for the freshest food, then a conservatory that opens onto a terrace for afternoon tea in the sun. Inside, 286 pieces of art hang on the walls, but it's the food that counts most; the hotel has its own fishing boat and rears cattle in nearby fields. And it's delicious stuff, as fresh as can be, perhaps Ventnor Bay scallops with chorizo and Hillside honey, local rack of lamb with a red wine jus and garden greens, pear tarte tatin with edible wild flowers. Uncluttered bedrooms are a treat, those at the front have the view. *Minimum stay: 2 nights at weekends.*

Rooms	6 doubles, 2 twin/doubles, 1 twin: £156-£206. 3 singles: £78-£143. 2 apartments for 4: £206-£292. Dinner, B&B from £108 per person.
Meals	Lunch, 2 courses, £20. Dinner £24-£28.
Closed	Never.

Tel	+44 (0)1983 852271
Email	mail@hillsideventnor.co.uk
Web	www.hillsideventnor.co.uk

Hillside,
151 Mitchell Avenue,
Ventnor, PO38 1DR

The Ginger Pig

Everyone loves this pub minutes from the beach. The décor is fresh, contemporary and open-plan and the food is consistently brilliant. Whether it's poached skate wing terrine, a chargrilled rib-eye with hand-cut chips, or a blackboard special (slow-braised lamb with spiced cabbage and garlic mash perhaps) this is a serious destination for those who love British food. The friendly team has created a balanced mix of drinking bar frequented by locals and dining area decked with modern art. It's all down to experienced restaurateur Ben McKeller who's created the first in the funky, family-friendly Gingerman group. Upstairs: two floors of elegant new bedrooms with state-of-the-art bathrooms. Ginger cocktails await, as do super-comfy beds and posh coffee machines. The paved, sheltered garden is a little oasis. Breakfast can be taken in the pub's dining room and includes treats such as roast tomato rarebit and ham hock hash topped by a fried egg. Wander down to the seafront for a dose of ozone, or pop to Brighton for the buzz. *Minimum stay: 2 nights at weekends. Nearest car park on Princes Crescent, Hove, BN3 4GS.*

Rooms	8 doubles: £100-£150.
Meals	Breakfast from £6. Starters from £4. Lunch from £12. Dinner, 3 courses, from £25. Sunday lunch £15.50.
Closed	Never.

The Ginger Pig,
3 Hove Street, Brighton, BN3 2TR

Tel	+44 (0)1273 736123
Email	rooms@gingermangroup.com
Web	thegingerpigpub.com

Artist Residence Brighton

At the top of a square, looking down to the sea, a cute hotel with an arty vibe. You're bang in the middle of Brighton with all the stuff you'd want on your doorstep: galleries, bars, the Pier and the Royal Pavilion. As for the hotel, good food, great staff, relaxed informality and a playful style are the hallmarks here. You get stripped boards, exposed brick walls and an old garage door that slides back to reveal the Set Restaurant with an open kitchen. It's one of the best places to eat in Brighton with seasonal, modern British food as well as a 10-course tasting menu on the Chef's Table. You'll find cool art, the odd wall clad in corrugated iron, even an ornamental drainpipe! Bedrooms come in different styles. Some have Pop Art murals, others come in Regency colours, a new batch are super-cool with baths in the room. Most have small, stylish shower rooms, one has a decked terrace. There's the quirky cocktail bar, overlooking the West Pier, a ping pong table that doubles as a boardroom, then lunch in the restaurant with views through big windows down to the sea. *Minimum stay: 2 nights at weekends.*

Rooms	17 doubles, 5 twins: £95-£250. 1 suite for 6: £280-£380. 1 quadruple: £145-£190. Singles £95-£165.
Meals	Breakfast £2.50-£8. Lunch from £7. Dinner, 4 courses, about £30. Restaurants within 500m.
Closed	Never.

Tel	+44 (0)1273 324302
Email	brighton@artistresidence.co.uk
Web	www.artistresidence.co.uk/ our-hotels/brighton/

Artist Residence Brighton,
34 Regency Square, Brighton, BN1 2FJ

Brightonwave

A small, friendly, boutique B&B hotel in the epicentre of trendy Brighton. The beach and the pier are a two-minute walk, the bars and restaurants of St James Street are around the corner. An open-plan sitting room/dining room comes in cool colours with big suede sofas, fairy lights in the fireplace and ever-changing art on the walls. Bedrooms at the front are big and fancy, with deluge showers in sandstone bathrooms. Those at the back may be smaller, but so is their price and they come with spotless compact showers; if you're out more than in, why worry? All rooms have fat duvets, white linen, flat-screen TVs and DVD players; the lower-ground king-size has its own whirlpool bath and garden. Richard and Simon are easy-going and happy for guests to chill drinks in the kitchen (there are corkscrews in all the rooms). Breakfast, served late at weekends, includes pancakes, the full English or sautéed tarragon mushrooms on toast. Good food waits on your doorstep: Riddle and Finns, The Salt Rooms, an Italian restaurant up the road. Fabulous Brighton waits. *Over 14s welcome.*

Rooms	3 doubles, 4 twin/doubles, 1 four-poster: £90-£190. Singles £75-£80.
Meals	Restaurants nearby.
Closed	1 week over Christmas & 2 weeks in January.

Brightonwave,
10 Madeira Place, Brighton, BN2 1TN

Tel	+44 (0)1273 676794
Email	info@brightonwave.co.uk
Web	www.brightonwave.co.uk

Park House, Hotel & Spa

This splendid country-house hotel sits in 10 acres of English gardens with quilted fields circling the grounds and the South Downs Way passing within a mile. Potter about outside and find a croquet lawn, grass tennis courts and a six-hole golf course that slips into the country. Shrubberies burst with colour, there's a terrace for afternoon tea, wellies wait at the door for country walks. You can snooze on sunbeds while listening to birdsong by the outdoor pool, or nip in to the indoor pool and spa which has treatment rooms, saunas, steam rooms and a gym. The hotel is just as good, its country-house interiors filled with colour and style. The relaxed bar overlooks the garden, there's a sitting room with the daily papers and a conservatory that opens onto a terrace for scrumptious breakfasts. Smart rooms have heavenly beds, chic bathrooms, big country views, perhaps a terrace. Delicious food is the final delight, perhaps crab and ginger risotto, duck with honey-glazed parsnips, mint chocolate soufflé with passion fruit sorbet. Exceptional. *Minimum stay: 2 nights at weekends.*

Rooms	6 doubles, 10 twin/doubles: £135-£370. 4 family rooms for 4: £240-£370. 1 cottage for 4: £250-£385.
Meals	Lunch from £25. Dinner from £45. Afternoon tea £25.
Closed	24-26 December.

Tel	+44 (0)1730 819020
Email	reservations@parkhousehotel.com
Web	www.parkhousehotel.com

Park House, Hotel & Spa,
Bepton, Midhurst, GU29 0JB

The Horse Guards Inn

After a visit to Petworth House, head to the sleepy village of Tillington and this pub on the park's western edge. The lovely All Hallows church with its unusual spire is opposite and views sweep towards the South Downs from the leafy garden; a sunny spot for lunch or an evening gin and tonic. Inside there's a series of rambling rooms furnished with quirky pieces, fresh flowers, wonky beams and old pine tables in front of log fires. Sam and Misha love this pub: they've created a real community feel and their passion is reflected in their championing of local producers and imaginative menus, including veg from their patch and good stuff foraged from the local hedgerows. Bread is baked daily and they sell eggs from their own chickens – the closest shop is in nearby Petworth (a mile's walk along the park). Each of the three bedrooms is characterful with a sleek bathroom. Two are upstairs in the pub, one is in an adjacent 'one-up, one-down' cottage. Wake to a breakfast feast.

Rooms	2 twin/doubles: £85-£140. 1 double: £105-£140.
Meals	Starters from £6. Mains from £15.50.
Closed	Christmas.

The Horse Guards Inn,
Tillington, Petworth, GU28 9AF

Tel	+44 (0)1798 342332
Email	info@thehorseguardsinn.co.uk
Web	www.thehorseguardsinn.co.uk

The Cat

Owner Andrew swapped grand Gravetye Manor for the buzzy, pubby atmosphere of The Cat in 2009; he hasn't looked back. The 16th-century building, a fine medieval hall house with a Victorian extension, has been comfortably modernised without losing its character. Inside are beamed ceilings and panelling, planked floors, splendid inglenooks, and an airy room that leads to a garden at the back, furnished with teak and posh parasols. Harvey's Ale and some top-notch pub food, passionately put together from fresh local ingredients by chef Alex Jacquemin, attract a solid, old-fashioned crowd: retired locals, foodies and walkers. Tuck into rare roast beef and horseradish sandwiches, Rye Bay sea bass with brown shrimp and caper butter, South Downs lamb chops with dauphinoise (and leave room for treacle tart!). The setting is idyllic, in a pretty village opposite a 12th-century church – best viewed from two of four bright and comfortable bedrooms. Crisp linen on big beds, rich fabrics, fawn carpets, fresh bathrooms and antique touches illustrate the style. A special retreat in a charming village backwater.

Rooms	4 doubles: £130-£165. Singles £95-£110.
Meals	Lunch & dinner from £12. Bar meals from £6. Sunday lunch, 3 courses, £26.
Closed	Rarely.

Tel	+44 (0)1342 810369
Email	thecatinn@googlemail.com
Web	www.catinn.co.uk

The Cat,
Queen's Square, West Hoathly,
East Grinstead, RH19 4PP

The Dorset Arms

Set back from the road, the striking façade of the Dorset Arms oozes history and charm. Inside: thick beams, wall studs, an ancient Sussex oak floor, and an enormous log fire in the bar. An ale house since 1735, its fortunes have been revived by the current Lord De La Warr, with Lady De La Warr lending her astute eye for detail to the rooms. Locals love the candles on old tables, colourful cushions on benches, and family paintings and photos. Ale from local Larkins, Tonbridge and Black Cat micro-breweries and a changing menu from the Buckhurst Estate. Try pan-seared scallops with smoked bacon, peas and saffron cream sauce, then venison steak with stilton mash, and vanilla panna cotta to finish. Or go for the locally famous Buckhurst Park sausages, made to the Lord's own recipe reminiscent of his childhood. Six lovely bedrooms are housed in the attractive red brick cottage detached from the pub; beautifully comfy beds with upholstered headboards, spotless bathrooms, and a shared sitting room on the ground floor. Marvellous.

Rooms	6 doubles, 1 twin: £85-£130. 1 family room for 4: £130-£180.
Meals	Starters from £5. Mains from £11.
Closed	Rarely.

The Dorset Arms,
Buckhurst Park, Withyham, TN7 4BD

Tel	+44 (0)1892 770278
Email	enquiries@dorset-arms.co.uk
Web	www.dorset-arms.co.uk

The Griffin Inn

The Griffin is English to its core, a posh inn with a streak of scruffiness, a community local that draws a devoted crowd. They come for the lively bar, the attractive restaurant and the club room for racing on Saturdays. In summer, life spills onto a smart terrace for local food cooked in a wood-fired oven. There's a bar in the garden, weekend barbecues, deckchairs scattered across the lawns for ten-mile views over Pooh Bear's Ashdown forest to Sheffield Park. Quirky bedrooms are nicely-priced. Some have wonky floors, others a four-poster, you'll find timber frames, lovely old furniture, then robes and free-standing baths; those in the coach house are quieter. Seasonal menus offer tasty rustic food, perhaps rabbit gnocchi, local pheasant, dark chocolate tort with honey ice cream; excellent wines help you wash it all down. The pub has three cricket teams that travel the world in pursuit of glory – you may find them in the bar on a summer evening after a hot day in the field. *Minimum stay: 2 nights bank holiday weekends.*

Rooms	6 doubles, 7 four-posters: £85-£150. Singles £70-£80 (Sun-Thur).
Meals	Bar meals from £6.50. Dinner, 3 courses, £30-£40.
Closed	Christmas Day.

Tel	+44 (0)1825 722890
Email	info@thegriffininn.co.uk
Web	www.thegriffininn.co.uk

The Griffin Inn,
Fletching, Uckfield, TN22 3SS

The Bull

This 16th-century inn on the South Downs has won awards and with good reason – a cracking bar, beautiful bedrooms, tasty local food and an excellent array of ales and craft beers. Step inside where all is freshly and carefully made-over with extra space to dine among the many happy locals who gather for a pint of Bedlam, the pub's own brew. From the spanking new kitchen: menus using meat from Sussex farms, game from local estates, fish from short-range boats – try hay-smoked venison haunch with chervil root, chanterelles and kale, followed by rhubarb and citrus cheesecake with brown butter and Muscat. After dark, the big garden glows with light, fire pits are lit and blankets offered. Upstairs are stylish bedrooms with bags of character. Expect chic fabrics, old-style radiators and comfy beds. Bigger rooms have sofas, all have flat-screen TVs, rain showers in sparkling bathrooms, and freshly-baked cookies. Bring walking boots and mountain bikes, and scale the Ditchling Beacon for big views. Brighton and Gatwick are close. Don't miss Sunday lunch. *Minimum stay: 2 nights at weekends.*

Rooms	4 doubles, 2 twin/doubles; 2 rooms can interconnect to form a family suite: £115-£195.
Meals	Lunch & dinner from £13. Dinner, 3 courses, £25-£35. Sunday lunch from £15.
Closed	Never.

The Bull,
2 High Street, Ditchling, BN6 8TA

Tel	+44 (0)1273 843147
Email	info@thebullditchling.com
Web	www.thebullditchling.com

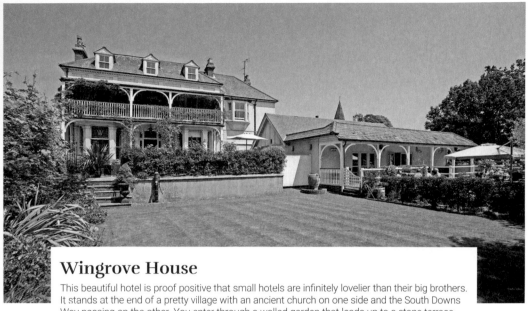

Wingrove House

This beautiful hotel is proof positive that small hotels are infinitely lovelier than their big brothers. It stands at the end of a pretty village with an ancient church on one side and the South Downs Way passing on the other. You enter through a walled garden that leads up to a stone terrace, where wisteria hangs from the balcony and bamboo sways in the breeze, a lovely spot to linger in good weather. In winter you retreat to the sitting room, where wood floors, an open fire and painted panelling give a warm contemporary feel.

Super bedrooms have cool colours, smart fabrics and robes in excellent bathrooms. Two open onto the veranda, the biggest at the back overlooks the churchyard, some have double-ended baths, others vast walk-in showers. The restaurant, recently refurbished, has a chic rustic feel. An open fire keeps things cosy on colder nights, a wall of glass opens onto a dining terrace in summer. Delicious food waits, perhaps locally smoked salmon, slow-braised venison, sticky toffee pudding with salted caramel ice cream. Walks start from the front door: Cuckmere Haven and Beachy Head wait.

Rooms	16 doubles: £100-£195.
	1 cottage for 5: £750-£1200 per week.
Meals	Light meals from £6.50.
	Dinner from £16; Mon-Sat.
	Sunday lunch from £16.
Closed	Never.

Tel	+44 (0)1323 870276
Email	info@wingrovehousealfriston.com
Web	www.wingrovehousealfriston.com

Wingrove House,
High Street, Alfriston,
Polegate, BN26 5TD

Belle Tout Lighthouse

A fine old lighthouse atop a white cliff with stunning views in every direction. To your left, Beachy Head, to your right, Birling Gap – it's a magical position with the South Downs rolling down into the English Channel. As for the lighthouse, it dates to 1832. It was once moved 57 feet back to stop it crumbling into the sea and it featured prominently in the BBC's production of *The Life and Loves of a She-Devil*. It re-opened in 2010 after a splendid renovation as a lovely

little B&B hotel. Bedrooms are rather wonderful: not huge, but all have windows that bring the outside in. You get white walls to soak up the light, fantastic views of rolling hills, pretty fabrics, lovely linen, the odd exposed brick wall; shower rooms are small but sweet, one room has a bath. Ian's legendary breakfasts are served on high with views of sea and cliff. There's a wood-burner in the sitting room, where guests gather each night before climbing up to explore the lantern. Good food waits in the village: a lovely pub and an excellent Thai restaurant. Magnificent walking waits. *Minimum stay: 2 nights. Over 15s welcome.*

Rooms	6 doubles: £160-£240.
	Singles £108-£204.
Meals	Pub/restaurant within 1 mile.
Closed	Christmas & New Year.

Belle Tout Lighthouse,
Beachy Head Road, Beachy Head,
Eastbourne, BN20 0AE

Tel	+44 (0)1323 423185
Email	info@belletout.co.uk
Web	www.belletout.co.uk

Strand House

As you follow the Royal Military Canal down to miles of sandy beach, bear in mind that 600 years ago, you'd have been swimming in the sea. This is reclaimed land and Strand House, built in 1425, originally stood on Winchelsea Harbour. Outside, you find wandering wisteria, colourful flowerbeds and a woodland walk that leads up to the village. Inside, medieval interiors have low ceilings, timber frames and mind-your-head beams. There are sofas galore, a wood-burner in the sitting room, an honesty bar from which to help yourself. It's a home-spun affair: Hugh cooks breakfast, Mary looks after guests in style. Quirky bedrooms sweep you back in time. One has an ancient four-poster, some have wonky floors, three open onto a terrace, all have good beds and robes for tiny shower rooms. The suite, with its balcony and views across fields, is a treat. The house, once a work house, was painted by Turner and Millais. Local restaurants wait: Webbe's at the Fish Café, The Kings Head in Rye, the Curlew in Bodiam. Dogs are very welcome. *Minimum stay: 2 nights at weekends & in high season.*

Rooms	5 doubles, 1 twin/double; 1 double with separate bath: £80-£150. 1 suite for 4: £180. 5 triples: £80-£150. Singles from £60. Extra beds £25 p.p. Dogs £7.50.
Meals	Dinner for groups by arrangements; minimum 8 people.
Closed	Rarely.

Tel	+44 (0)1797 226276
Email	info@thestrandhouse.co.uk
Web	www.thestrandhouse.co.uk

Strand House,
Tanyards Lane,
Winchelsea, Rye, TN36 4JT

Jeake's House

Rye is gorgeous, one of those lovely English towns that's been around for centuries, but has never lost its looks. The same is true of Jeake's House, which sits in the old town on a pretty cobbled street away from the crowds. In its 300-year history it's been a wool store, a school and the home of American poet Conrad Potter Aiken. Inside, style abounds. The galleried dining room – once an old Baptist chapel – is now painted deep red and full of busts, books, clocks and mirrors, a fine setting for your bacon and eggs. There's a raffish bar, where a fire burns in winter, then a pretty sitting room with a Broadwood square piano. Potter about and find timber frames, ancient beams and some strikingly furnished bedrooms; several have four-posters, one has a telly concealed in the wood-burner, all are deeply comfortable and excellent value for money. As for Rye, art galleries, antiques shops, old churches and river walks wait; don't miss the Summer Exhibition in early September. All this would be blossom in the wind without Jenny, whose natural joie de vivre makes this a very special place. *Children over 8 welcome.*

Rooms	7 twin/doubles; 1 double with separate bath: £99-£130. 3 four-poster suites for 2: £135-£155.
Meals	Restaurants within walking distance.
Closed	Never.

Jeake's House,
Mermaid Street, Rye, TN31 7ET

Tel	+44 (0)1797 222828
Email	stay@jeakeshouse.com
Web	www.jeakeshouse.com

The George in Rye

Rye is beautiful, old England trapped in aspic. It was a Cinque Port, Henry James lived here and the oldest church clock in England chimes at the top of the hill. The George stands on its cobbled High Street right in the thick of things. Built in 1575 from reclaimed ships' timbers, its exposed beams and panelled walls remain on display. Inside, old and new mix beautifully – expect Jane Austen in the 21st century. There's a roaring fire in the bar, screen prints of the Beatles on the walls in reception, a sun-trapping courtyard for lunch in summer. Beautiful bedrooms come in all shapes and sizes (a couple are small), but chic fabrics, Frette linen and Vi-Spring mattresses are standard, as are good books, fine bathrooms, white robes and cashmere covers on hot water bottles. Some are huge with zinc baths in the room, one has a round bed. You eat in the George Grill, an open kitchen on display, perhaps Provençal fish soup, grilled rib-eye with hand-cut chips, gooseberry soufflé with bay leaf ice cream. Walk it off by following the river down to the sea.

Rooms	8 doubles, 21 twin/doubles: £135-£195. 5 suites for 2: £295-£325. Singles from £95.
Meals	Lunch from £6. Dinner, 3 courses, £30-£40. Afternoon tea £12.50.
Closed	Never.

Tel	+44 (0)1797 222114
Email	stay@thegeorgeinrye.com
Web	www.thegeorgeinrye.com

The George in Rye,
98 High Street, Rye, TN31 7JT

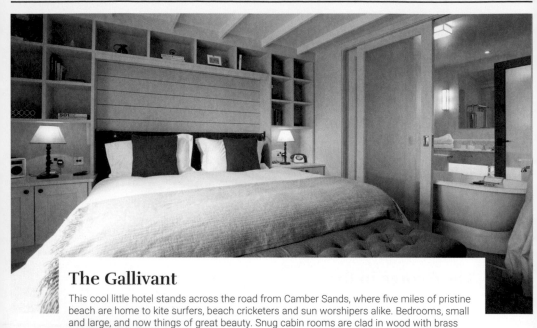

The Gallivant

This cool little hotel stands across the road from Camber Sands, where five miles of pristine beach are home to kite surfers, beach cricketers and sun worshipers alike. Bedrooms, small and large, and now things of great beauty. Snug cabin rooms are clad in wood with brass lamps hanging from the ceiling; baby Hamptons have daybeds and marble bathrooms; deck rooms at the back come in cool whites with doors onto private terraces. Then come the garden rooms – heaven for hedonists – with double-ended baths in the room (and doors that slide for privacy), then small decks in the garden, where you'll also find a massage hut and deckchairs in summer. All have great storage, flawless bathrooms and crisp linen for Hypnos beds. As for the food, most is sourced within 10 miles and you eat in an airy restaurant that opens onto a terrace in summer, perhaps cod with lime and cucumber, salt marsh lamb with root veg, chocolate torte with Frangelico jelly. There's tea and cake 'on the house' every afternoon, too. *Minimum stay: 2 nights at weekends.*

Rooms	20 doubles: £135-£245. Singles £85-£240.
Meals	Lunch from £16. Dinner, 3 courses, from £35.
Closed	Rarely.

The Gallivant,
New Lydd Road, Camber, Rye, TN31 7RB

Tel	+44 (0)1797 225057
Email	enquiries@thegallivant.co.uk
Web	www.thegallivant.co.uk

The George Inn

This handsome old inn in pretty Robertsbridge has a warm welcome for all. The bare-boarded, earthy-hued bar/dining area is the perfect setting for richly textured fabrics, wool and leather chairs and sofas, painted tables and beautiful period pieces. Family portraits gaze serenely down as you enjoy a pint of Rother Valley Level Best and get cosy by the brick inglenook – famously favoured by Hilaire Belloc. If you're peckish, look to the chalkboards for the day's local and seasonal dishes: locally landed lemon sole, Rye Bay scallops, slow-roasted pork belly with Bramley apple spiced compote, chargrilled lamb rump with minted rösti. Or opt for a chargrilled rib eye steak, cut to size and order. Leave room for lovely puddings, especially the chocolatey ones. Upstairs, money has been lavished on four gorgeous luxury-steeped rooms with superb Hypnos beds, signature wallpapers, rich fabrics, antique furniture and beautiful en suite shower rooms. Perfect for visiting nearby Battle, Bodiam Castle, Pashley Manor Gardens and more besides.

Rooms	4 twin/doubles: £95-£150. Singles £89 £140. Extra bed/sofabed £35-£45 p.p.p.n.
Meals	Lunch from £5. Bar meals from £9.75. Dinner from £10. Sunday roast £10.75. Not Sun eve.
Closed	Rarely.

Tel	+44 (0)1580 880315
Email	info@thegeorgerobertsbridge.co.uk
Web	www.thegeorgerobertsbridge.co.uk

The George Inn,
High Street, Robertsbridge,
Battle, TN32 5AW

The Queen's Inn

Sharon and Sally-Anne took on the run-down Queen's Inn in 2014 having run a successful catering company for many years. This rambling old village inn was the perfect venue to showcase Sally-Anne's cooking. Revived with panache, the wisteria-festooned Georgian façade hides a cosy, beamed 16th-century interior: a bar with wooden floor and huge fireplace, and upstairs, wonky corridors leading to quirky, hugely individual rooms. Expect a retro feel throughout with chunky dial phones, old-style radios, painted furniture and jazzy fabrics and lamps, plus goose down duvets, coffee and homemade brownies. Bathrooms are smart; room five boasts a free-standing tub in the room. Downstairs, rustic and modern combine in the dining room, with its ancient plank floor, brick fireplace and contemporary print wallpaper. In the bar, relax with a pint of Hophead or tuck into Moroccan spiced rack of lamb, sea bass with samphire, crab and chive sauce, Park Farm sausages and mash, baked vanilla cheesecake. National Trust treasures and Pashley Manor Gardens are close.

Rooms	5 doubles: £95-£180.
	1 family room for 4: £135. Singles £85.
Meals	Starters from £5. Mains from £12.50
Closed	Never.

The Queen's Inn,
Rye Road, Hawkhurst, TN18 4EY

Tel	+44 (0)1580 754233
Email	info@queensinn.co.uk
Web	www.thequeensinnhawkhurst.co.uk

The Milk House

The gardens at Sissinghurst Castle were designed by Vita Sackville-West and are of the loveliest in the land; if you stay at this charming village pub, you can stroll over after breakfast, through apple orchards and bluebell woods. As for the Milk House, it's a great base from which to explore – stylish, welcoming, nicely priced. In summer, you decant onto a big terrace with an outside bar and a wood-fired pizza oven, not a bad spot for a crispy margherita and a glass of Pimm's. There's a duck pond, a lawned garden, views over open country, even a four-day festival in August (local bands, theatre, face painting, lots of food). Interiors have an easy style: woven willow lampshades, a sofa in front of the fire, a timber-framed dining room for fabulous food – mostly sourced within 20 miles – perhaps twice-baked Stilton soufflé, grilled mackerel with roasted fennel, After Eight crème brûlée with brandy butter brioche. And the Sunday lunch is fabulous. Beautiful bedrooms are crisply uncluttered. Expect chic fabrics, super beds, excellent bathrooms, a sofa if there's room.

Rooms	3 doubles, 1 twin: £120-£150. Extra bed/sofabed £10 p.p.p.n.
Meals	Lunch from £6. Dinner, 3 courses, about £30. Sunday lunch from £15.
Closed	Rarely.

Tel	+44 (0)1580 720200	The Milk House,
Email	fresh@themilkhouse.co.uk	The Street, Sissinghurst,
Web	www.themilkhouse.co.uk	Cranbrook, TN17 2JG

The Barrow House

You get a little time travel at the Barrow House: a 14th-century inn, 17th-century timber frames, 21st-century comfort and design. It's a great little place – friendly and stylish with super food and all sorts of libations waiting at the bar. It sits in a pretty village surrounded by open country with Leeds Castle up the road. Known as the George for centuries, it changed its name in deference to the Bronze Age barrow that rises in a field on the edge of the village.

Back at the inn, there's a smart terrace for lunch in the sun and a couple of open fires inside to keep things cosy. They serve their own ale, craft beers and well-priced wines, but you can just pop in for an espresso, too. Lovely rooms have big beds, pretty fabrics and smart TVs, perhaps timber frames or a wonky floor; bathrooms are a treat. As for the food, most is sourced within 20 miles. You'll find soups and sharing plates, burgers and fish and chips, or a three-course feast, perhaps smoked salmon, slow-cooked beef, marmalade Bakewell tart.

Rooms	2 doubles, 1 twin/double: £120-£160. Extra bed £10 p.p.p.n.
Meals	Lunch, 2-3 courses, £12-15. Dinner, 3 courses, about £25.
Closed	Never.

The Barrow House,
The Street, Egerton, TN27 9DJ

Tel	+44 (0)1233 756599
Email	digin@thebarrowhouse.co.uk
Web	www.thebarrowhouse.co.uk

The Kings Head

If you're searching for an award-winning foodie destination in an historic spot, you've struck lucky. Welcome to a grand old pub in very pretty Wye run by "a couple of down to earth boys from the North" (their words). Mark and Scott have created an up-to-the-minute village pub where you're as welcome to drop by for coffee and croissants as order a glass of Sicilian wine. Or a good meal... Stour Valley venison loin with pommes Maxim and remoulade and juniper jus hits the spot. This pub is a cool place to be – suave pendant lighting, purple feature wall – but not so cool that they don't keep dog biscuits behind the bar (handmade by the chef). So settle into a leather wing back chair, and soak up the vibe. There's a welcome for all, and if you're going to hole up in the countryside, you'd do well to do it here. Bedrooms upstairs are simple and uncluttered with a sunny feel; reclaimed and repainted furniture mixes with new; buttercup-coloured lamps and blankets add a touch of colour, there's robes to snuggle in, and bathrooms are stocked with nice toiletries and towels.

Rooms	5 doubles: £95-£105.
	1 family room for 3: £100-£120.
	1 single: £70-£90.
Meals	Lunch from £6. Dinner from £9.
	Sunday lunch from £12.
Closed	Rarely.

Tel	+44 (0)1233 812418
Email	info@kingsheadwye.com
Web	www.kingsheadwye.com

The Kings Head,
Church street, Wye, TN25 5BN

The Relish

It's not just the super-comfy interiors that make The Relish such a tempting port of call. There's a sense of generosity here: a drink on the house each night in the sitting room; tea and cakes on tap all day; free internet throughout. This is a grand 1850s merchant's house on the posh side of town – lovely old bricks and mortar, softly contemporary interiors. Laura and Rakesh took over recently and have already pulled out the paintbrushes, so wind up the cast-iron staircase to find bedrooms that make you smile. You get Hypnos beds with padded headboards, crisp white linen and pretty throws. There's a sense of space, a sofa if there's room, big mirrors and lovely bathrooms. Downstairs candles flicker on the mantelpieces above an open fire, the high-ceilinged dining room comes with stripped floors and padded benches and in summer you can decamp onto the terrace for breakfast, a communal garden stretching out beyond. You're one street back from Folkestone's cliff-top front for big sea views. Steps lead down to smart gardens, the promenade and waterside restaurants.

Rooms	9 doubles: £98-£150.
	1 single: £70-£75.
Meals	Restaurants nearby.
Closed	23-30 December.

The Relish,
4 Augusta Gardens,
Folkestone, CT20 2RR

Tel	+44 (0)1303 850952
Email	reservations@hotelrelish.co.uk
Web	www.hotelrelish.co.uk

The Dog at Wingham

Enjoy a locally-sourced steak served at a table set with fresh flowers in one of the oldest pubs in Kent. It's a 15th-century building on the main road in Wingham and offers a mix of old and new: a blazing fire in the ancient inglenook and stylish stools at the bar. Four creaky staircases lead to super-smart rooms, the most characterful in the old pub, and two more in the separate Doghouse. One room is on the ground floor with a private entrance; another has an extra bunk-bed room ideal for families. After a very good breakfast (brought to your room if you like), hop in the car to Sandwich. You can walk from the estuary quay to the wild shingle shore: a happy half hour for your dog. Three talented chefs have put this pub on the map: people travel miles for the modern British food. The whole place buzzes with fresh faced staff, overseen by young manager Marc. *Pets by arrangement.*

Rooms	4 doubles, 3 twin/doubles: £80-£260. 1 quadruple: £120-£300. Singles £64-£190. Dinner, B&B £75-£162 p.p.
Meals	Breakfast from £4-£10. Lunch & dinner, 2-3 courses, from £18-£22. Sunday lunch, 2-3 courses from £22-£26.
Closed	Never.

Tel	+44 (0)1227 720339
Email	info@thedog.co.uk
Web	www.thedog.co.uk

The Dog at Wingham,
Canterbury Road, Wingham, CT3 1BB

London

Artist Residence London, page 195

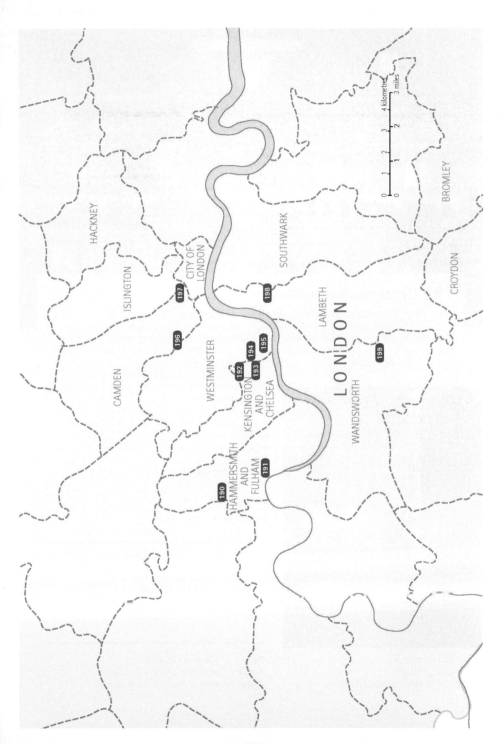

HACKNEY

ISLINGTON

CITY OF
LONDON

SOUTHWARK

CAMDEN

WESTMINSTER

LAMBETH

L O N D O N

KENSINGTON
AND
CHELSEA

WANDSWORTH

HAMMERSMITH
AND
FULHAM

BROMLEY

CROYDON

197

198

196

194 195

192 193

199

190

191

4 kilometres
3 miles

The Princess Victoria

Make yourself at home and while away an afternoon in one of the few remaining gin palaces in London. Beneath soaring ceilings, a fabulous collection of 120 gins takes centre stage, cossetted by staff who really know what they're talking about. The place buzzes, thanks to craft beers, seasonal ciders and a modern pub menu based on great ingredients. The beef is aged in-house and the pizzas are stone-baked. Eat in the bar or in the grand dining room, a home-from-home for gin lovers since 1829. Off here is a secret courtyard garden, a suntrap for cocktails. Given the location, the bedrooms are unexpectedly quiet. Enjoy rainhead showers, Nespresso machines and seamless air con. After a great (weekends only) brunch, take a bus to leafy Holland Park, or Portobello Market and Notting Hill. Your closest hub is Shepherd's Bush, a 20-minute walk.

Rooms	4 doubles, 1 twin/double: £89-£129.
Meals	Lunch from £9. Dinner from £11.50. Sunday lunch from £13.
Closed	Christmas & Boxing Day.

The Princess Victoria,
217 Uxbridge Road,
Shepherd's Bush, London, W12 9DH

Tel	+44 (0)20 8749 4466
Email	info@princessvictoria.co.uk
Web	www.princessvictoria.co.uk

Temple Lodge Club

Temple Lodge, once home to the painter Sir Frank Brangwyn, is sandwiched between a courtyard and a lushly landscaped garden. The peace is remarkable making it a very restful place – simple yet human and warmly comfortable, a nourishing experience. Michael and his team run it with quiet energy. You breakfast overlooking the garden, there are newspapers to browse, a library instead of TVs. Bedrooms are surprisingly stylish: pretty art, crisp linen, no clutter, a hint of country chic. They're exceptional value for money, too, so book well in advance. Some rooms have garden views, only a couple have their own bathrooms and loo; if you don't mind that, you'll be happy. The Thames passes by at the end of the road, the Riverside Studios is round the corner for theatre and film, and the Gate Vegetarian Restaurant is across the courtyard, a well-known eatery, its food so good even committed carnivores can't resist. It was also Brangwyn's studio, hence the artist's window. The house is a non-denominational Christian centre with two services a week, which you may take or leave as you choose.

Rooms	1 double; 2 doubles with separate bath/shower; 1 double, 2 twins sharing bath/shower: £77-£121. 5 singles: £59-£73. Extra bed £12-£14 p.p.p.n.
Meals	Continental breakfast included. Vegetarian restaurant across courtyard.
Closed	Never.

Tel	+44 (0)20 8748 8388
Email	booking@templelodgeclub.com
Web	www.templelodgeclub.com

Temple Lodge Club,
51 Queen Caroline Street,
Hammersmith, London, W6 9QL

The Levin Hotel

This is shopaholic heaven – Harrods at one end of the street, Harvey Nicks at the other. As for The Levin, it sits quietly on Basil Street, a peaceful retreat in the middle of Knightsbridge. Buffet breakfasts are served in the lobby; read a newspaper while you delve into freshly baked croissants, cheese, fruit, yogurt or nip next door to the Capital (their sister hotel) for a Full English. If you like seafood, book dinner here too; the kitchen is headed up by Nathan Outlaw. Bedrooms are spread over four floors with a lift to carry you up, though you may prefer to walk; a contemporary chandelier with an 18-metre drop fills the stairwell. As for the rooms, some are bigger, others smaller, but all have the same crisp style: bold colours, hand-stitched beds, marble bathrooms, books galore. Bigger rooms have sofas, all have white robes, crisp linen, Bose radios and flat-screen TVs. You get air conditioning and a handy smartphone, too. There's a full concierge service and Hyde Park is close. *Pets by arrangement.*

Rooms	3 doubles, 8 twin/doubles: £245-£479. 1 suite for 2: £395-£619. Extra bed/sofabed £45 p.p.p.n.
Meals	Lunch from £5.50. Dinner, 3 courses, about £30. Afternoon tea from £22.99.
Closed	Never.

The Levin Hotel,
28 Basil Street,
Knightsbridge, London, SW3 1AS

Tel	+44 (0)20 7589 6286
Email	reservations@thelevinhotel.co.uk
Web	www.thelevinhotel.co.uk

11 Cadogan Gardens

You're cared for here by super-friendly staff; it's smart but not stuffy and the location is great. A short walk takes you to gawp at the world's most expensive brands – Chanel, Tiffany's, Prada and Hermès – and even if you can't afford to buy anything you can always faire du *leche-vitrines* as the French say. Walk to view the pretty pastel-hued houses of Chelsea, visit the swinging King's Road, explore the Chelsea Physic Garden or the Saatchi Gallery. The brilliant Victoria and Albert museum is just over half a mile away as is the Natural History museum. Afternoon tea is a fancy affair but you can move swiftly on to chocolate cocktails inspired by Sir Hans Sloane, one of the first importers of cocoa from Jamaica. If you prefer to eat in, then the Hans Bar and Grill serves fresh modern British food conjured up by chef Adam England.

Rooms	25 doubles: £280-£350.
	25 suites for 2. £430-£4000.
	6 singles: £250. Extra bed available.
Meals	Starters from £7.50. Lunch from £15.
	Dinner, 3 courses, £45. Afternoon tea
	from £25.
Closed	Never.

Tel	+44 (0)20 7730 7000
Email	reservations@11cadogangardens.com
Web	www.11cadogangardens.com

11 Cadogan Gardens,
Chelsea, London, SW3 2RJ

Lime Tree Hotel

You'll be hard pressed to find better value in the centre of town. The Lime Tree – two elegant Georgian townhouses – stands less than a mile from Buckingham Palace, with Westminster, Sloane Square and Piccadilly all a short stroll. Add warm interiors, kind owners and a smart gastropub waiting round the corner and you've unearthed a London gem. The airy dining room serves a mean breakfast and is soon to turn into a café, with light meals served throughout the day. Rooms are smart without being lavish, all with mod cons. Expect warm colours, crisp linen, attractive wallpaper and excellent bathrooms (most have big showers). One on the ground floor has doors onto the garden; others on first floor have high ceilings; those at the top (a few stairs!) are cosy in the eaves; rooms at the back are the quietest. Charlotte and Matt will point you in the right direction, while there's a tiny sitting room for guide books and a computer for guests to use. The Thomas Cubitt pub – 50 paces from the door – serves great food. A handy base for the Chelsea Flower Show. *Minimum stay: 2 nights at weekends.*

Rooms	12 doubles, 4 twins: £155-£240.
	6 singles: £105-£180.
	3 triples: £200-£270.
Meals	Restaurants nearby.
Closed	Never.

Lime Tree Hotel,
135 Ebury Street,
Belgravia, London, SW1W 9QU

Tel	+44 (0)20 7730 8191
Email	info@limetreehotel.co.uk
Web	www.limetreehotel.co.uk

Artist Residence London

In the future, if a book is written about London hotels, they will divide it into two periods – before and after Artist Residence London. Because this gorgeous small hotel is a game changer, a new template of British cool, a space designed wholly to exercise your pleasure receptors. It proves resoundingly that small is more beautiful than big ever can be and while large hotels will try to copy it, they'll fail miserably, unable to match its intimacy, or the fantastic staff who look after you all the way. So what do you get? A small slice of heaven between Pimlico and the Kings Road. It's a phoenix from the ashes, a Thomas Cubitt pub recently rescued from neglect. The cellar bar, with pop art and exposed brick walls, must qualify as one of London's coolest; the sitting room has fat sofas in front of a roaring fire; the Cambridge Street Café offers lovely food in a stylish, relaxed setting. Bedrooms are flawless: cool art, chic fabrics, the best beds, power-showered bathrooms. Smaller rooms are divine, bigger rooms have sofas, the suites have free-standing baths. Battersea Park is close.

Rooms	8 doubles: £170-£280.
	2 suites for 2: £290-£425.
	Singles £150-£250.
Meals	Breakfast from £7. Lunch from £8.50.
	Dinner: starters from £9.50;
	mains from £16.
Closed	Never.

Tel	+44 (0)20 3019 8610
Email	london@artistresidence.co.uk
Web	www.artistresidence.co.uk/
	our-hotels/london/

Artist Residence London,
52 Cambridge Street,
Pimlico, London, SW1V 4QQ

The Grafton Arms Pub & Rooms

Smart décor and a buzzy vibe make this West End pub with rooms a great place for couples planning a city break. Sit out on the secret roof terrace with a cocktail or a guest ale, sample the pan-Asian menu, stay in one of the smart bedrooms upstairs. Central London is waiting to be delved into: Oxford Street, Bond Street and Selfridges are a 15-minute walk, Soho and theatres are about the same distance and teeming with great places to eat – try the French House on Dean Street. Once you've shopped and eaten take a walk through Regents Park and head back to your peaceful bedroom. Choose something to watch on Netflix, order a continental breakfast and free newspaper to be delivered in the morning.

Rooms	11 doubles: £145-£225.
Meals	Continental breakfast £12. Light bites from £4.50. Lunch & dinner from £8.50.
Closed	Rarely.

The Grafton Arms Pub & Rooms,
72 Grafton Way,
Fitzrovia, London, W1T 5DU

Tel	+44 (0)20 7387 7923
Email	info@graftonarms.co.uk
Web	www.pubandrooms.com

The Clerk & Well Pub & Rooms

On Clerkenwell Road, opposite Leather Lane Market, this old city pub has smart rooms above. Mingle with locals at the bar while you sample an ale or a cocktail then choose from the pan-Asian menu before heading out. Over the road the market throngs with office workers and tourists grabbing lunch – it's a street food paradise – try some falafel or a vegan burrito. Wander through the Hatton Garden jewellery quarter; St Pauls Cathedral and the British Museum are a 15-minute walk or you can be at the tube station in minutes. Back at base you can let yourself through the side door and up to your bedroom; all have Nespresso machines, mini fridges and TV, some have baths. Rooms at the front have thick fabric blinds and double glazing to shut out noise, while those at the back are completely quiet.

Rooms	8 doubles: £145-£225. Extra bed/sofabed £25 p.p.p.n.
Meals	Continental breakfast £12. Light bites from £4.50. Lunch & dinner from £8.50.
Closed	Never.

Tel	+44 (0)20 7837 8548
Email	info@theclerkandwell.co
Web	www.pubandrooms.com

The Clerk & Well Pub & Rooms,
156 Clerkenwell Road,
London, EC1R 5DU

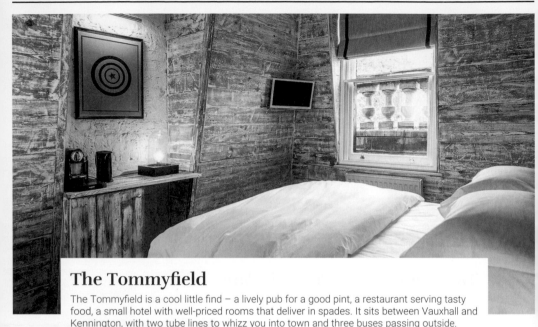

The Tommyfield

The Tommyfield is a cool little find – a lively pub for a good pint, a restaurant serving tasty food, a small hotel with well-priced rooms that deliver in spades. It sits between Vauxhall and Kennington, with two tube lines to whizz you into town and three buses passing outside. Inside, you find wooden floors, high ceilings and the odd ionic pillar. Lamps hang above the bar, where you can order a pint of Wandle, then dig into posh fish and chips. Leather banquettes run along big windows, an open kitchen is on display, a couple of booths are nicely private. Rooms are the big surprise, some with painted panelling, others with planked walls. You get pop art, good beds, coffee machines and flat-screen TVs. Excellent bathrooms have walk-in power showers, two have claw-foot baths. On weekdays a continental breakfast is left in your fridge, on weekends the full English is on tap below. As for the food – half-price for residents – pies, steaks and burgers sit alongside pumpkin ravioli, Chateaubriand and banoffee pie. Tuesday is quiz night, the Oval is close for the cricket.

Rooms	4 doubles, 2 twin/doubles: £109-£159. Cots available.
Meals	Continental breakfast included; cooked breakfast on weekends £6-£9. Lunch & dinner from £12.50. Sunday lunch from £13.50. Food half-price for residents.
Closed	Never.

The Tommyfield,
185 Kennington Lane,
Kennington, London, SE11 4EZ

Tel	+44 (0)20 7735 1061
Email	info@thetommyfield.co.uk
Web	www.thetommyfield.com

The Bedford

This huge 1930s, Grade II-listed building is one of London's most iconic venues. A pub, club, restaurant, live music and entertainment venue, now refurbished with pizazz, which has helped launch the careers of Ed Sheeran and KT Tunstall to name just two. Fifteen boutique bedrooms have all been individually designed: think roll top baths, opulent wallpaper and cool art. This place is full of surprises. Hotel manager, Robyn, is fun and energetic – she will check you in and give you a tour. You'll find a Nespresso coffee machine, fresh milk and juice in your room. In the week, breakfast is simply fruit and porridge – but there are plenty of good cafés nearby. At weekends tuck into the brunch menu which covers everything from granola and smashed avocado to a full English. Spanning five floors are convivial bars serving craft ales, artisan spirits and fine wines, events in a performance area dripping with chandeliers and a smart dining room serving pub classics, imaginative small plates and pizzas. Hop on the tube to get into central London in 15 minutes.

Rooms	15 doubles: £89-£149.
	Extra bed/sofabed no charge.
Meals	Dinner from £10.
Closed	Rarely.

Tel	+44 (0)20 3976 8007
Email	info@thebedford.com
Web	www.thebedford.com

The Bedford,
77 Bedford Hill,
Balham, London, SW12 9HD

East of England

The Brisley Bell, page 230

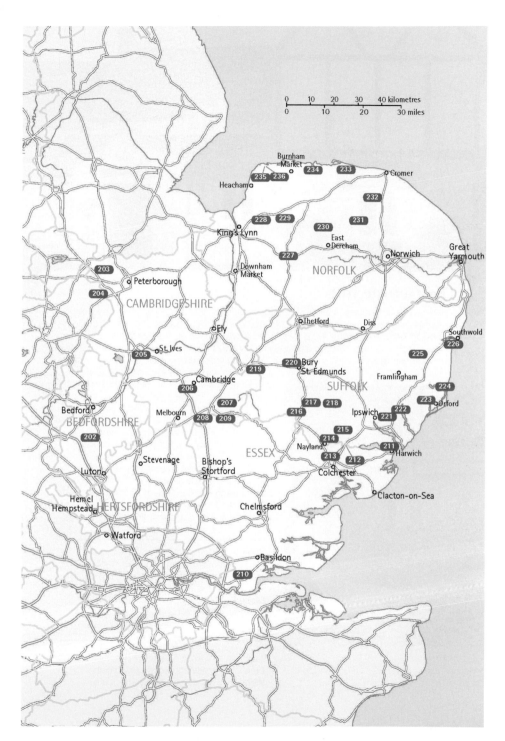

Burnham
Market
235 236 234 233 o Cromer
Heacham o
232
228 229 230 231
King's Lynn
East
Dereham
227 NORFOLK
Norwich
Great
Yarmouth
203
Peterborough o
204
Downham
Market
CAMBRIDGESHIRE
Thetford
Diss
Southwold
Ely
226
205 St Ives
225
219 220 Bury
St. Edmunds
Cambridge
Framlingham
224
206 SUFFOLK
223 Orford
207
217 218 222
Bedford o
216 Ipswich 221
BEDFORDSHIRE
Melbourn
208 209
215
202
214
Nayland
211
Stevenage o
213 212 Harwich
Luton o
Bishop's
Stortford
Colchester
Hemel
Hempstead HERTFORDSHIRE
Clacton-on-Sea
Watford o
Chelmsford
Basildon
210

0   10   20   30   40 kilometres
0   10   20   30 miles

The George Inn

A well-heeled pub in a large, leafy Bedfordshire village: this 16th-century building is encircled by ancient Maulden Wood and you're perfectly placed for yomping part (or all 40 miles!) of the Greensand Ridge Walk. Julian and Emma have always lived locally, they spotted that The George needed rescuing, snapped it up and lovingly transformed it into a smart, funky pub at the heart of its community. Lewis and his young, energetic team run the place with good humour.

The kitchen turns out hearty, wholesome lunches and evening meals, Sunday roasts, and pizza night is always busy. There's a gin bar, ales on tap, wines by the glass and you can choose to cosy up by a roaring wood-burner or dine in the conservatory; and tucked away in a separate annex, overlooked by charming St Mary's church, are seven boutique bedrooms. Jazzy feature wallpapers, fluffy throws and deep mattresses on solid oak beds make for a restful night and the gleaming en suite bathrooms have spoiling smellies. Best of all: there's no need to get dressed for breakfast because continental-style goodies are delivered to your door each morning.

Rooms	7 doubles: £100-£120. Children over 2 £15 per night.
Meals	Starters from £5. Lunch from £9.50. Mains from £9.50.
Closed	Rarely.

The George Inn,
6 George Street, Maulden,
Bedford, MK45 2DF

Tel	+44 (0)1525 841559
Email	info@thegeorgemaulden.com
Web	www.thegeorgemaulden.com

The White Hart

Wash up at the White Hart and mix with the locals drawn by the lovely lived-in farmhouse feel and the big, beamy bar. The ales are good too: Oakham Jeffrey Hudson, Tim Taylors, Grainstore's Red Kite. Farmers gather on Fridays, the cricket team drops by on Sundays; in summer life spills onto the terrace. Flags, floorboards and a crackling fire continue the rustic feel; railway signs, wooden pitch forks and hanging station lamps add colour. You can eat simply or more grandly, anything from a ploughman's to a three-course feast, with memorably good Sunday roasts full of flavour. Walk through rooms with lovely scrubbed tables to the orangery, a glass-gabled restaurant furnished with Lloyd Loom chairs. Bedrooms (some above the bar; the rest across the way) are simple and spotless, with crisp white linen and feather pillows, free WiFi and an honest price. One is airy and lovely, with period lounge chairs and views across the fields to the church; another has a four-poster bed. This forgotten slip of England – Stamford is five miles – is prettier than people imagine.

Rooms	10 doubles, 2 twins: £80-£130. Extra bed/sofabed £15 p.p.p.n.
Meals	Lunch, 2 courses, £14.95. Starters from £5.50. Mains from £10.50-£21.95. Sunday lunch, 2 courses, £19.90.
Closed	Rarely.

Tel	+44 (0)1780 740250
Email	info@whitehartufford.co.uk
Web	www.whitehartufford.co.uk

The White Hart,
Main Street, Ufford, Stamford, PE9 3BH

The Crown Inn

A thatched inn built of mellow stone that stands on the green in this pretty village. Paths lead out into open country and you can follow the river up to Fotheringhay, where Mary Queen of Scots lost her head. Back at the pub, warm interiors mix style and tradition to great effect. The bar has stone walls, ancient beams, flagstone floors and a roaring fire; in summer you can decant onto the terrace and sip a pint of Black Sheep while watching village life pass by. Back inside, a beautiful new restaurant has recently appeared with golden stone walls, pale olive panelling and some very good food, anything from glazed ham and local eggs to oxtail lasagne, saddle of venison, sticky toffee tart with toffee sauce. You can also eat in the sitting-room bar on smart armchairs in front of another fire. Stylish bedrooms – some in the main house, others off the courtyard – are all different. You'll find smart colours, chic wallpapers, excellent bathrooms and good art. The bar hosts quiz nights, live music and the odd game of rugby on the telly, while on May Day there's a hog roast for the village fête.

Rooms	6 doubles, 2 twin/doubles: £73-£210. Singles from £55. Sofabed £30 per child per night.
Meals	Lunch & dinner £5-£25; not Sun eve. Restaurant closed first week January.
Closed	Never.

The Crown Inn,
8 Duck Street, Elton,
Peterborough, PE8 6RQ

Tel	+44 (0)1832 280232
Email	inncrown@googlemail.com
Web	www.thecrowninn.org

The Old Bridge Hotel

The Old Bridge is one of those places that mixes old-fashioned hospitality with contemporary flair, a template of excellence for others to follow. It's a big hit with the locals, who come for delicious food and exceptional wines, and it inspired the founders of Hotel du Vin, who were amazed how busy it was. Ladies lunch, businessmen converse, kind staff weave through the throng. You can eat wherever you like: in the beautifully refurbished restaurant; on a sofa in the lounge; or sitting in a winged armchair in front of the fire in the bar. You feast on anything from homemade soup to rack of lamb (starters are available all day), while breakfast is served in a panelled morning room with Buddha in the fireplace. It's all the work of owners John and Julia Hoskins. Julia's interiors are dreamy, with style and comfort going hand in hand. Beautiful bedrooms have fresh colours, chic fabrics, crisp linen, padded bedheads. All have posh TVs and robes in excellent bathrooms, some of which overlook the river Ouse. John, a Master of Wine, has a wine shop in reception; you can taste before you buy (and you will).

Rooms	18 doubles, 1 twin, 3 four-posters: £145-£230. 2 singles: £95-£125 Dinner, B&B £104-£150 per person.
Meals	Lunch & dinner £5-£35.
Closed	Never.

Tel	+44 (0)1480 424300
Email	oldbridge@huntsbridge.co.uk
Web	www.huntsbridge.com

The Old Bridge Hotel,
1 High Street,
Huntingdon, PE29 3TQ

The Blue Ball Inn

The Blue Ball takes its name from one of the first hot air balloons, which landed nearby in the 1750s. Ideally placed, with Granchester Meadows for a front garden and views across the river to the spires of Cambridge's colleges, this pretty country pub is thriving under the care of Toby and Angela. Taking pride of place in a row of cottages, the Blue Ball's bright walls, bay window and flowing flower baskets is postcard-perfect. Inside, all is spotless, scrubbed and poised to welcome hungry locals, walkers, twitchers and tourists. Tuck into sausage casserole, vegetable tagine, or a bowl of hearty soup with a sandwich. At the back is a heated pavilion, shrine to the local cricket team, where you can while away a happy afternoon with a pint of cask ales. Upstairs: two pin-neat bedrooms with fresh flowers and local art, and a shared sitting room where you can enjoy a quiet drink while soaking up those fabulous views. Bathrooms sparkle. Breakfasts are generous, so fill your boots and then stroll across the Meadows to spend the day in Cambridge. *Minimum stay: 2 nights at weekends.*

Rooms	2 doubles: £120.
Meals	Starters from £4. Lunch from £9. Mains from £9.
Closed	Rarely.

The Blue Ball Inn,
Broadway, Grantchester,
Cambridge, CB3 9NQ

Tel	+44 (0)1223 846004
Email	info@blueballgrantchester.co.uk
Web	www.blueballgrantchester.co.uk

The Black Bull Inn

Buoyed by the success of the Red Lion at Hinxton, Alex has snapped up the 16th-century Black Bull. The beamed and timbered bar is spruced up, a new bar servery has been added, wooden floors gleam and there's a smart mix of old dining tables and leather sofas fronting the glowing log fire; so cosy up with a pint of Rusty Bucket on a winter evening. The ancient, high-raftered and adjoining barn has been restored and refurbished to perfection and is the place to sit and savour some cracking pub food; try the lamb shank with roasted garlic mash and rosemary jus, or the smoked haddock with tarragon foam. In the bar, tuck into roast beef and horseradish sandwiches or a plate of Suffolk ham, eggs and hand-cut chips. Comfortable rooms in the annexe, some overlooking the car park, sport oak floors and hand-made furniture, and huge duvets on king-size beds. Tiled bathrooms come with bath and shower. A peaceful bolthole with a sun-trap back garden, handy for Cambridge, country walks and the Newmarket Races. *Minimum stay: 2 nights at weekends in high season.*

Rooms	5 twin/doubles: £95-£149. Singles £90. Extra bed/sofabed £35 p p p.n.
Meals	Lunch & dinner from £12. Bar meals from £6. Sunday lunch £13.
Closed	Rarely.

Tel	+44 (0)1223 893844
Email	info@blackbull-balsham.co.uk
Web	www.blackbull-balsham.co.uk

The Black Bull Inn,
27 High Street, Balsham, CB21 4DJ

Red Lion Inn

In pretty, peaceful Hinxton, close to Cambridge, the rambling Red Lion is a popular stopover in an area deprived of good inns. And its secluded garden, replete with dovecote, arbour and patio, overlooks the church: a lovely spot for peaceful summer sipping. Another draw is the buzzy atmosphere Alex has instilled in the beamed bar with its deep green chesterfields, worn wooden boards, cosy log fire and ticking clock. Own label ale Red & Black and others from the local micro brewery add to the appeal, as do eclectic menus. Pop in for a beef and horseradish sandwich or linger over venison with blackberry jus or wild mushroom fettuccine; tuck into delicious roast Norfolk chicken on Sunday. Puddings are to die for: sticky toffee pudding with caramel sauce, lemon tart with mango coulis. Named after local beers and ciders, new-build rooms are comfortable and smart with a fresh, contemporary feel – lightwood furniture, wooden floors, crisp cotton on top-quality beds, fully tiled bathrooms. Breakfasts are a serious treat. *Minimum stay: 2 nights at weekends in high season.*

Rooms	3 doubles, 5 twin/doubles: £139-£159. Singles £99. Extra bed £39 p.p.p.n.
Meals	Lunch & dinner £11-£25. Bar meals £4.50-£10.50. Sunday lunch £12.
Closed	Rarely.

Red Lion Inn,
32 High Street, Hinxton, CB10 1QY

Tel	+44 (0)1799 530601
Email	info@redlionhinxton.co.uk
Web	www.redlionhinxton.co.uk

The Three Hills

Originally opened as an alehouse in 1847 this rural inn has been bought and refurbished with aplomb. It's the only pub in this tiny village of just over a hundred souls and doubles up as the village hall, the library and all-round buzzing hub. Food is taken seriously: classic British with a twist and sourced locally as much as possible – touchingly there is also a discount for the villagers. There's a warm buzz inside with muddy-booted walkers, lycra-clad cyclists and families with children who spill outside to the pretty garden on warm days – there's a pizza oven and barbecue in the garden for the summer months. Find a cosy spot by the roaring fire and choose a book from the library, eat in the light and airy Orangery overlooking the terrace, retreat to bedrooms (two upstairs) with soft wool throws and fresh flowers. It's great walking and cycling country so you can set off straight from the village but you're a short hop in the car from Cambridge, Ely and Newmarket for culture, cathedral and shopping.

Rooms	5 doubles, 1 twin: £130-£150.
Meals	Breakfast from £6. Lunch, 2 courses, £17. Starters from £6. Mains from £15.
Closed	Rarely. Pub closed Mondays.

Tel	+44 (0)1223 890500	The Three Hills,
Email	info@thethreehills.co.uk	Dean Road, Bartlow, CB21 4PW
Web	www.thethreehills.co.uk	

The Bell Hotel

A 600-year-old timber-framed coaching inn, as full of contented locals today as it was when pilgrims stopped on their way to Canterbury. Everything is a delight: hanging lanterns in the courtyard, stripped boards in the bar, superb staff in the restaurant, copious window boxes bursting with colour. It's a proper inn, warmly welcoming, with thick beams, country rugs, panelled walls and open fires. Stop for a pint of cask ale in the lively bar, then potter into the restaurant for top food, perhaps seared scallops with confit venison, grilled Dover sole, cherry parfait with chocolate brownie Alaska. Christine grew up here, John joined her years ago; both are respected in the trade, as is Joanne, Master Sommelier and manager of many years. An infectious warmth runs through this ever-popular inn. As for the bedrooms, go for the suites above – or a new room in the grand Georgian property up the high street: cosily inviting, individual, quite funky. In the morning, breakfast with the papers at elegant Hill House, where further bedrooms, snazzily refurbished, lie. Then head north into Constable country.

Rooms	15 doubles, 3 twins: £70-£100. 9 suites for 2: £120-£145. Singles £65-£140. Extra bed/sofabed £10-£20 p.p.p.n.
Meals	Lunch from £11.95. Bar meals from £8.95. Dinner, à la carte, £27.
Closed	Christmas Day & Boxing Day.

The Bell Hotel, High Road, Horndon-on-the-Hill, Stanford-le-Hope, SS17 8LD	**Tel** +44 (0)1375 642463 **Email** info@bell-inn.co.uk **Web** www.bell-inn.co.uk

The Pier at Harwich

They don't do things by halves at the Pier – a cool £1.5 million has recently been spent on a 21st-century makeover for this iconic coastal hotel. It sits on the harbourside with views of town and water, its front terrace a big draw in good weather. Inside, a cool new look captivates. A chic warehouse feel waits in the bar – stripped walls, hanging lamps, leather bar stools, big windows to frame the view. You get craft beers and cask ales, a gin library and prosecco cocktails, then small plates of Nordic design if you fancy a light bite. Hungry souls fly upstairs to the famous first-floor brasserie, where mirrored booths and leather banquettes now come as standard, and doors open onto a balcony, where you can tuck into your lobster Thermidor while gazing out onto the estuary. Bedrooms – some above, others next door in a former inn – have fancy bedheads, seaside colours, crisp white linen and super bathrooms; the suite, with its vast window, has a telescope with which to scan the high seas. Coastal walks and blue flag beaches wait, as does the Electric Palace, the second oldest cinema in Britain.

Rooms	10 doubles, 3 twins: £120-£170. 1 suite for 2: £200-£230. Singles from £95. Dinner, B&B from £100 p.p.
Meals	Lunch from £6.50. Sunday lunch from £19.50. Dinner à la carte £25-£40.
Closed	Never.

Tel	+44 (0)1255 241212
Email	pier@milsomhotels.com
Web	www.milsomhotels.com

The Pier at Harwich,
The Quay, Harwich, CO12 3HH

Maison Talbooth

The outdoor swimming pool is heated to 29°C every day, a chauffeur is on hand to whisk you down to the hotel's riverside restaurant, a grand piano waits in the sitting room, where guests gather for a legendary afternoon tea. They don't do things by halves at Maison Talbooth, a small-scale pleasure dome with long views across Constable country. The house, an old rectory, stands in three acres of manicured grounds; the pool house is a big draw with its open fire, honesty bar, beautiful art and treatment rooms. Interiors are equally impressive. There are no bedrooms, only suites, each divine; all pamper you rotten with flawless bathrooms, fabulous beds, cool colours and hi-tech excess. At dinner you're chauffeured to the family's restaurants (both within half a mile): Milsoms for bistro food served informally; Le Talbooth on the river Stour for more serious fare, perhaps poached lobster with orange and fennel, saddle of venison with plums and bitter chocolate, pineapple and coconut soufflé with piña colada ice cream. A great escape.

Rooms	12 suites for 4: £210-£420
	Singles from £170.
Meals	Dinner at Milsoms £25;
	at Le Talbooth £35-£50.
Closed	Never.

Maison Talbooth,
Stratford Road, Dedham,
Colchester, CO7 6HN

Tel	+44 (0)1206 322367
Email	maison@milsomhotels.com
Web	www.milsomhotels.com

The Sun Inn

This perennial favourite sits in an idyllic village made rich by mills in the 16th century. You're also in Constable country – the artist attended school in the village and often returned to paint the church. Best of all is the river – you can hire boats, grab a picnic from the inn, float down the sleepy Stour, then tie up on the bank for lunch al fresco. As for The Sun, you couldn't hope to wash up in a better spot. Inside, you find open fires, boarded floors, timber frames and an easy elegance. A panelled lounge comes with sofas and armchairs, the bar is made from a slab of local elm and the airy, beamed dining room offers fabulous food inspired by Italy, perhaps crab ravioli, squid with chilli and garlic, monkfish with truffle mash, chocolate mousse with Morello cherries. Bedrooms are gorgeous: creaking floorboards, timber-framed walls, a panelled four-poster. Those at the back are bigger and come in grand style, but all are lovely with crisp linen, local art and power showers in excellent bathrooms. There's afternoon tea on arrival if you book in advance and a garden for a pint in summer. *Pets by arrangement.*

Rooms	5 doubles, 1 twin/double, 1 four-poster: £120-£145. Dinner, B&B £100 £125 per person. Extra bed/sofabed £15 p.p.p.n. Singles from £90.
Meals	Lunch from £10.95. Dinner from £16.95.
Closed	Christmas.

Tel	+44 (0)1206 323351
Email	office@thesuninndedham.com
Web	www.thesuninndedham.com

The Sun Inn,
High Street, Dedham,
Colchester, CO7 6DF

The Crown

The Crown is all things to all men, a lovely country pub, a popular local restaurant, a small boutique hotel, a welcoming bolthole in Constable country. It sits in a pretty village with long views from its colourful terrace over the Box Valley, not a bad spot for a glass of Pimm's after a day exploring the area. It dates to 1560 and has old beams and timber frames, though interiors have youthful good looks: warm colours, tongue-and-groove panelling, terracotta-tiled floors, a fancy wine cellar behind a wall of glass. You'll find rugs and settles, the daily papers, leather armchairs in front of a wood-burner. Four ales wait at the bar, 30 wines come by the glass and there's seasonal food that will make you smile, perhaps confit duck leg ravioli, pan-roasted cod with chorizo and crayfish, popcorn panna cotta. Airy bedrooms are quietly hidden away at the bottom of the garden – excellent beds, lovely linen, a dash of colour and super bathrooms. All have armchairs or sofas, three have French windows that open onto private terraces with fine views. A great place to eat, sleep and potter.

Rooms	10 doubles: £145-£250.
	1 suite for 2: £225-£295.
	Singles from £110.
	Extra bed/sofabed £20-£30 p.p.p.n.
Meals	Lunch & dinner £5-£30.
Closed	25-26 December.

The Crown,
Park Street, Stoke-by-Nayland,
Colchester, CO6 4SE

Tel	+44 (0)1206 262001
Email	info@crowninn.net
Web	www.crowninn.net

Marquis Hotel

There are surprises around every corner at this 250-year-old building brought lavishly back to life: an archway leads to a pretty courtyard, huge views are revealed over lawns, terrace and the river Brett beyond; a wine cellar doubles up as an intimate dining space. All the bedrooms have their own style – the big Cornwallis suite with floor to ceiling windows for that vista and even the smallest has a sumptuous roll top with a view – all have Nespresso machines and fresh milk in the mini fridges. Wander to the TV room, or the upstairs bar or find a bench in the manicured gardens from where you can stroll along the river. Breakfast on homemade waffles, eggs all ways, avocados and apple juice from the owners' orchards. Sunday roasts are popular and the dinner menu changes with the seasons. Food is sourced locally and prepared with much care: oysters from Colchester, crab from Cromer, Suffolk cheese. Views from the dining room are mesmerising but you can eat on the terrace in summer.

Rooms	9 twin/doubles: £165-£242.
	1 suite for 2: £280-£310.
	Extra beds & cots available
Meals	Starters from £9. Mains from £19.
	Desserts from £7.
	Sunday lunch from £10.
Closed	Never.

Tel	+44 (0)1473 377977
Email	gm@themarquissuffolk.co.uk
Web	www.themarquissuffolk.co.uk

Marquis Hotel,
Upper Street, Layham, IP7 5JZ

The Black Lion

This elegant inn is a valued part of Long Melford life, with locals propping up the bar and families booked in for Sunday lunch in the popular restaurant. Whether you're honeymooners or a holidaying clan, there's a bedroom to suit you (ten to choose from), and the Black Lion team look after you very well. You can even bring your well-behaved dog. Foodies will be in their element: local produce is the star here, from full Suffolk breakfasts, light lunches and pub classics to afternoon teas and à la carte dinners. Gin, beers and wines are often locally sourced too. Take over the conservatory if you come with a group. A five-minute walk into the village reveals a main street lined with cafés, restaurants and shops, with a definite emphasis on antiques and interiors. Cult TV series *Lovejoy* was filmed in the area for good reason. The Tudor splendour of Melford Hall, just a hundred yards away, is open to the public most days and hosts regular Elizabethan pageants.

Rooms	7 doubles: £89-£145.
	1 suite for 2: £165-£195.
	2 family rooms for 4: £99-£175.
Meals	Lunch from £8. Dinner from £14.
	Sunday lunch, 2 courses, £20.
Closed	Never.

The Black Lion,
The Green, Long Melford, CO10 9DN

Tel	+44 (0)1787 312356
Email	gm@theblacklionhotel.com
Web	www.theblacklionhotel.com

The Great House

The ingredients here are simple. Take a medieval wool town trapped in aspic, add a 15th-century merchant's house that overlooks the square, then whisk up the best food in Suffolk and you have one of the loveliest restaurants with rooms in the land. It sits opposite the Guildhall, its Georgian façade giving way to original interiors, where timber frames and old beams mix with light colours and varnished wood floors. A Suffolk institution for 30 years, it is French to its core, with a cheese board to beat all others. You eat in the airy dining room with an ancient fireplace in one corner, perhaps crab and prawn ravioli followed by guinea fowl roulade with black tiger prawn mousse, then grapefruit and champagne Baba with marjoram cream. Bedrooms are just as good: timber frames, wonky floors, beautiful beds, a sofa is there's room. You'll find decanters of sherry, coffee machines, flat-screen TVs, robes in chic bathrooms. Four are huge, one has a regal four-poster, another a 14th-century fireplace in its bathroom. There's a courtyard for breakfast in the sun, too. *Minimum stay: 2 nights at weekends.*

Rooms	4 doubles, 1 twin/double: £105-£239. Singles from £105. Dinner, B&B from £119 p.p. Extra bed £15-£20 p.p.p.n.
Meals	Breakfast £12-£17. Lunch £25; not Mon/Tue. Dinner £36.50; not Sun/Mon. À la carte only Sat night.
Closed	January & 2 weeks in October.

Tel	+44 (0)1787 247431
Email	info@greathouse.co.uk
Web	www.greathouse.co.uk

The Great House,
Market Place, Lavenham, CO10 9QZ

The Bildeston Crown

Chris and Hayley ran the Crown for ten years, upped sticks to head a few miles north, then got an offer they couldn't refuse and now the place is theirs. Their home is this beautifully preserved 15th-century inn. All the lovely old bits survive – timber frames, sagging beams, an ancient inglenook with a roaring fire – but interiors have an elegant, contemporary style with bold colours, stripped floorboards, comfy sofas and big art on the walls. Farmers drop in to chew the cud, walkers come to defrost in front of the fire while knocking back a pint of local ale, and the world and his wife come from near and far for Chris' delicious local food, perhaps truffled arancini with English asparagus, pheasant and foie gras Wellington, then an After Eight soufflé with chocolate ice cream. Stylish rooms have comfy beds, wonky floors, lots of colour and art. One has a fake Canaletto hanging above a claw-foot bath, another has a four-poster bed, all have robes in good bathrooms and flat-screen TVs. Don't miss Bury St Edmunds, a market town steeped in history. Medieval Lavenham is close, too.

Rooms	11 doubles, 1 twin: £100-£175. Dinner, B&B from £87.50 p.p. Singles from £70.
Meals	Lunch from £6.50. Bar meals from £14. Dinner, 3 course, £30-£40. Sunday lunch from £17. Afternoon tea £15.
Closed	Never.

The Bildeston Crown,
104 High Street, Bildeston, IP7 7EB

Tel	+44 (0)1449 740510
Email	reception@thebildestoncrown.com
Web	www.thebildestoncrown.com

The Packhorse Inn

The rise of the cool country inn continues apace and the Packhorse is a prime example, a beautifully renovated pub rescued from neglect. It's a small-scale pleasure dome – stylish interiors, ambrosial food, beautiful bedrooms and bathrooms – yet it remains a village local with a bar that welcomes all. The downstairs is open plan with a fire that burns on both sides and the odd armchair to take the strain. You'll find varnished floorboards, lots of art, lamps hanging above a cool bar. Chic bedrooms are scattered about. Coach house rooms have a warm rustic elegance, those in the inn are a little fancier, a couple with baths in the room; all have fantastic bathrooms. Irresistible food waits below, maybe truffled goat's cheese with quince and figs, Suffolk venison and kidney pudding, plum tarte tatin with fruit-cake ice-cream. There's a terrace for good weather, and a private dining room that can turn into a meeting room. This is prime horse-racing country: Newmarket is three miles west, the peerless Frankel is at stud nearby. Cambridge and Bury St Edmunds are close.

Rooms	6 doubles, 2 twin/doubles: £100-£175. Singles from £85. Extra beds for children £10.
Meals	Lunch from £6. Dinner, 3 courses, about £35
Closed	Rarely.

Tel	+44 (0)1638 751818
Email	info@thepackhorseinn.com
Web	www.thepackhorseinn.com

The Packhorse Inn,
Bridge Street, Moulton,
Newmarket, CB8 8SP

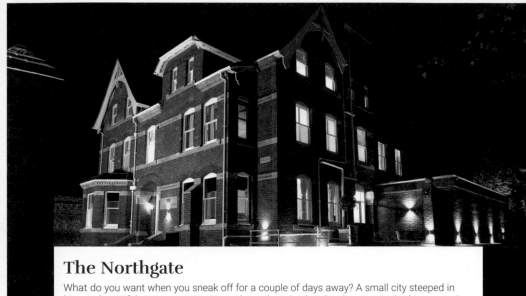

The Northgate

What do you want when you sneak off for a couple of days away? A small city steeped in history, beautiful country waiting beyond, a welcoming hotel with attractive bedrooms and excellent food? The Northgate offers all that and more. It's small and sits 500 metres from Abbey Gardens, the crown jewel of medieval Bury St Edmunds. Downstairs, the cocktail bar doubles as a sitting room, doors open onto a terrace for lunch in the sun, a well-kept garden waits beyond.

Bedrooms above have a contemporary country-house feel: cool colours, smart wood furniture, pretty throws on beds that come with cool bedheads. Bathrooms are just as good: some have walk-in showers, two have freestanding baths in the room, all are excellent. As for the food, it's on tap all day: breakfast, elevenses, lunch, afternoon tea, then a delicious dinner, perhaps mackerel with apple and parsnip, rump of mutton with water chestnuts, an irresistible banana soufflé. Cambridge and Newmarket are close.

Rooms	7 doubles, 1 twin/double: £155-£225. 1 family room for 4: £280. Extra beds £15 p.p.p.n.
Meals	Lunch from £6. Dinner, 3 courses, about £35; 9-course tasting menu £75.
Closed	Never.

The Northgate,
13-14 Northgate Street,
Bury St Edmunds, IP33 1HP

Tel	+44 (0)1284 339604
Email	info@thenorthgate.com
Web	www.thenorthgate.com

Kesgrave Hall

This Georgian mansion sits in 38 acres of woodland and gardens, sound-proofing it from the outside world. It was home to US airmen during WWII, but the locals have reclaimed it as their own now and they come for the easy style, the excellent service, the delicious food and the informal vibe. The emphasis here is firmly on the food, so it's almost a restaurant with rooms, albeit quite a grand one. Inside, you find wellington boots in the entrance hall, high ceilings in the big sitting room, stripped boards in the humming bistro and doors that open onto a terrace in summer. Colourful bedrooms have lots of style. One is huge and comes with a free-standing bath and a faux leopard-skin sofa. The others might not be quite as wild, but they're lovely nonetheless, some cosy in the eaves, others in beautifully refurbished outbuildings. Expect warm colours, crisp linen, good lighting and fancy bathrooms. Back downstairs, tasty food flies from the kitchen, perhaps smoked haddock fishcakes, a char-grilled steak, a delicious coffee cheesecake with Tia Maria ice cream. Suffolk's magical coast waits.

Rooms	10 doubles, 7 twin/doubles: £130-£230. 6 suites for 2: £275-£300.
Meals	Breakfast £10-£16. Lunch & dinner, 3 courses, £25-£30.
Closed	Never.

Tel	+44 (0)1473 333741	Kesgrave Hall,
Email	reception@kesgravehall.com	Hall Road, Kesgrave, Ipswich, IP5 2PU
Web	www.milsomhotels.com	

The Crown at Woodbridge

This cute little hotel in the middle of Woodbridge slopes downhill to the river, its rainbow of pastel colours making it a landmark in town. Inside, open-plan interiors flood with light courtesy of a glass ceiling. A Windermere skiff hangs above the bar, you find painted panelling, comfy sofas, slate floors and a wood-burner to keep things cosy. An airy restaurant comes in pale olive with leather banquettes, wooden floors and contemporary art, a fine spot for some tasty local food, perhaps seared scallops with Suffolk chorizo, slow braised pork with glazed carrots, white chocolate and passion fruit cheese cake. Breakfast is just as good; expect poached fruits, flagons of juice, smoked kippers, the best sausages in Suffolk. Bedrooms above vary in size, but all have the same feel: off-white colours, duck-down duvets, padded headboards, Hypnos beds. You'll find panels of entwined willow, pitchforks hanging on the wall, robes and power showers in sparkling bathrooms. Don't miss Sutton Hoo, the Aldeburgh food festival or Rendlesham Forest, the UK's equivalent of Area 51. *Minimum stay: 2 nights at weekends.*

Rooms	8 twin/doubles: £110-£180.
	2 family rooms for 4: £140-£200.
	Extra beds/sofabeds £25 p.p.
Meals	Lunch & dinner £6-£30.
	Sunday lunch from £12.50.
Closed	Never.

The Crown at Woodbridge,
Thoroughfare, Woodbridge, IP12 1AD

Tel	+44 (0)1394 384242
Email	info@thecrownatwoodbridge.co.uk
Web	www.thecrownatwoodbridge.co.uk

The Crown & Castle

A great place to wash up for a few lazy days. Orford is hard to beat, a sleepy Suffolk village blissfully marooned at the end of the road. River, beach and forest wait, as does the Crown & Castle, a welcoming English hostelry where the art of hospitality is practised with unstinting flair. The inn stands in the shadow of Orford's 12th-century castle. Uncluttered interiors have a warm, airy feel with stripped floorboards, open fires, wonderful art and flickering candles at night. Chic bedrooms have Vi-Spring beds, fancy bathrooms, lovely fabrics, the odd armchair. Four in the main house have watery views, the suite is huge, the garden rooms big and light, the courtyard rooms a real delight. Wellington boots wait at the back door, so pull on a pair and explore Rendlesham Forest or hop on a boat and chug over to Orfordness. Ambrosial food awaits your return, perhaps potted brown shrimps, a faultless steak and kidney pie, crushed pistachio meringue with a chocolate ice-cream sundae. Sutton Hoo is close. Dogs are very welcome. *Minimum stay: 2 nights at weekends. Children over 8 welcome.*

Rooms	18 doubles, 2 twins: £90-£250.
	1 suite for 2: £150-£163.
	Dinner, B&B from £100 per person.
Meals	Lunch from £8.50.
	À la carte dinner around £35.
Closed	Rarely.

Tel	+44 (0)1394 450205
Email	info@crownandcastle.co.uk
Web	www.crownandcastle.co.uk

The Crown & Castle,
Orford, IP12 2LJ

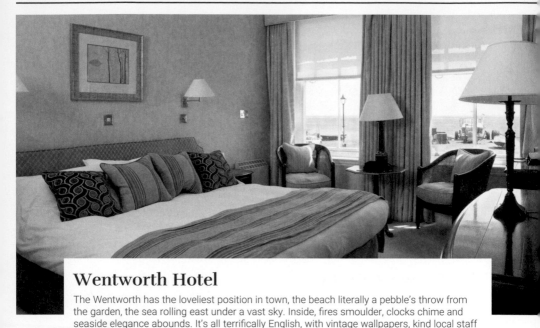

Wentworth Hotel

The Wentworth has the loveliest position in town, the beach literally a pebble's throw from the garden, the sea rolling east under a vast sky. Inside, fires smoulder, clocks chime and seaside elegance abounds. It's all terrifically English, with vintage wallpapers, kind local staff and an elegant bar that opens onto a terrace garden. The restaurant looks out to sea, spilling onto a sunken terrace in summer for views of passing boats. Proper English fare is the order of the day: stilton soup, breast of guinea fowl, lemon posset with raspberries and shortbread. The hotel has been in the same family since 1920 and old-fashioned values mix harmoniously with interiors that are refreshed often to keep things sparkling. Airy bedrooms are deeply comfy, those at the front have sea views (and binoculars). Expect warm colours, smart fabrics, and good beds; all have stylish bathrooms, too. You'll find sofas galore in the sitting rooms, but you may want to spurn them to walk by the sea. Joyce Grenfell was a regular. The Snape Maltings are close. *Minimum stay: 2 nights at weekends.*

Rooms	7 doubles, 24 twin/doubles: £140-£220.
	4 singles: £85-£119.
	Dinner, B&B from £83 p.p.
Meals	Lunch from £5.
	Dinner, 2-3 courses, £21-£26.50.
Closed	Never.

Wentworth Hotel,
Wentworth Road, Aldeburgh, IP15 5BD

Tel	+44 (0)1728 452312
Email	stay@wentworth-aldeburgh.com
Web	www.wentworth-aldeburgh.com

Sibton White Horse

The heart of this thriving village local is 16th-century and the bar is steeped in charm: old pews, a huge inglenook, horse brasses and a roaring fire. Peek through the window panel into the cellar to see the reclaimed Roman floor. Ale drinkers will note the gleaming brass beer engines of Adnams and Woodfordes, and there are guest beers, a long wine list and 26 gins. Food is seasonal, local and very good: meat from the next village and veg from the kitchen garden. On sunny days you can spill onto the lawns for Friday barbecues or Shakespeare plays, festivals of music or beer. Return to thoroughly modern annexe bedrooms furnished in old and new pine with views to open countryside, and wake to generous breakfasts of fresh fruit, homemade muesli, full English (even veggie) or Lowestoft smoked kippers. You're 20 minutes from Aldeburgh and charming Southwold for pints of prawns and chilly dips in the North Sea.

Rooms	5 twin/doubles: £80-£105.
Meals	Lunch from £7.50. Dinner from £13.25.
	Sunday lunch £14.25.
Closed	Christmas.

Tel	+44 (0)1728 660337	Sibton White Horse,
Email	info@sibtonwhitehorseinn.co.uk	Halesworth Road, Sibton,
Web	www.sibtonwhitehorseinn.co.uk	Saxmundham, IP17 2JJ

The Anchor

This is a cool little seaside inn where relaxed informality reigns; kids are welcome, staff are friendly, dogs fall asleep in the bar. You're 500 yards from the sea with a terrace that fills with locals in summer and lawns that run off towards the water. Inside, beautiful simplicity abounds – Cape Cod meets English country local. You get books everywhere, beautiful art, roaring fires, a happy vibe. The big draw is Sophie's lovely food. Game and venison come from local estates, fish and seafood from nearby waters, samphire and sea kale are foraged along the coast. Bedrooms fit the mood perfectly. Those in the house are warm and homely; garden rooms are big and airy with sofas inside and terraces that overlook nearby dunes. Don't miss dinner, perhaps fish soup, game ravioli, chocolate fondant with caramel ice cream. You wash it all down with Mark's legendary collection of bottled beers and fancy wines. There are festivals by the score – don't miss Latitude or Folk East. Starry skies amaze. Unmissable. *Minimum stay: 2 nights at weekend & in high season. Pets by arrangement.*

Rooms	10 doubles: £105-£165. Singles £85-£100. Extra bed £20-£30 p.p.p.n.
Meals	Lunch from £5.25. Sunday lunch, 2 courses, £20. Dinner, 3 courses, about £30.
Closed	Rarely.

The Anchor,
Main Street, Walberswick,
Southwold, IP18 6UA

Tel	+44 (0)1502 722112
Email	info@anchoratwalberswick.com
Web	www.anchoratwalberswick.com

Strattons

You arrive to find an exquisite Queen Anne villa that wouldn't look out of place in France, then you step inside and discover a contemporary art gallery with rooms. Strattons is a treasure trove of beautiful things. It is in constant flux, too – the new café/deli overflows with delicious treats and comes with a roof terrace, not a bad spot for afternoon tea. Back inside, you find august busts, contemporary chandeliers, stylish sofas. Bedrooms are equally creative: a carved four-poster in priestly red, Botticelli's angels hovering on a wall, bedside lights that hang from the ceiling. Some have double-ended baths in the room, others a roof terrace with sun loungers. You breakfast in the deli on irresistible delights: natural yoghurt and muesli, sweet-smelling bacon rolls, the full cooked works. Head off to the Brecks for walks through its magical forest or spin up to King's Lynn to explore its Hanseatic architecture. A very good dinner awaits your return, perhaps Norfolk asparagus with wild garlic, pan fried sea trout and King's Lynn brown shrimp, followed by banana parfait. *Minimum stay: 2 nights at weekends. Pets by arrangement.*

Rooms	6 doubles, 1 twin/double: £99-£244.
	5 suites for 2: £131-£254.
	2 apartments for 2: £154-£244.
	Extra bed £10-£45 p.p.p.n.
Meals	Lunch from £6, Sunday lunch from £14.
	Dinner, 3 courses, £30-£35.
Closed	1 week over Christmas.

Tel	+44 (0)1760 723845
Email	enquiries@strattonshotel.com
Web	www.strattonshotel.com

Strattons,
4 Ash Close, Swaffham, PE37 7NH

Congham Hall

This is a beautiful Georgian merchant's house set in 30 acres of parkland. It's also a cool little spa hotel with an indoor pool and treatment rooms. Outside, three gardeners grow flowers for the house, vegetables for the kitchen and keep the gardens looking serene. Inside, country house interiors have an elegant contemporary feel. There's an open fire in the sitting room, a chic bar with low-hanging lampshades, then an airy dining room for excellent local food, perhaps crayfish salad, slow-cooked chicken, hot chocolate fondant with banana ice cream. After which you'll need to atone, so roast away in the sauna before a dip in the pool; there are sunbeds and a hot tub on the decked terrace, too. Refurbished rooms are gorgeous. House rooms have beautiful fabrics and excellent beds. The suite has a balcony for breakfast, all have robes in striking bathrooms (one is entered through cupboard doors). Courtyard rooms are big and airy and open onto the kitchen garden. Children are welcome and have their own menu. Sandringham is close. There's tennis and croquet, too. *Minimum stay: 2 nights at weekends.*

Congham Hall,
Grimston, King's Lynn, PE32 1AH

Rooms	25 twin/doubles: £135-£260. 1 suite for 2: £275. Extra beds: children under 12 free.
Meals	Breakfast £8-£15. Lunch from £5. Dinner, 3 courses, about £35. Afternoon tea from £8.75. Sunday lunch, 3 courses, £27.50.
Closed	Rarely.

Tel	+44 (0)1485 600250
Email	info@conghamhallhotel.co.uk
Web	www.conghamhallhotel.co.uk

The Dabbling Duck

Join the locals propped around the bar with a real ale or their own brand gin, or book a table to sample gourmet pub food. If you sit in the garden on Friday and Saturday evenings in summer you can have pizza from the wood-fired oven. Bedrooms have home-made biscuits; dogs are welcome and there's a communal hallway with books and a sofa. A varied breakfast menu is served at separate tables in the high-ceilinged Library: duck egg waffles; Mexican breakfast with smashed avocado, beans and salsa; full English with sausages and bacon from the local butcher. The Peddars Way walking and cycling route runs past the back of the pub, and you're ten minute's drive from Sandringham, Castle Rising and Houghton Hall and Gardens. The coast at Hunstanton and bird-rich salt marshes are 18 miles away. *Pets by arrangement.*

Rooms	8 twin/doubles: £100-£130
	Singles £75-£130
	Dinner, B&B £70-£85 per person.
	Extra bed/sofabed £15-£40 p.p.p.n.
Meals	Lunch from £5.75. Bar meals from £5.
	Dinner from £10.
Closed	Never.

Tel	+44 (0)1485 520827
Email	info@thedabblingduck.co.uk
Web	www.thedabblingduck.co.uk

The Dabbling Duck,
11 Abbey Road, Great Massingham,
King's Lynn, PE32 2HN

The Brisley Bell

Amelia and Marcus have transformed a derelict 17th-century pub overlooking the village common into a handsome inn with two stylish dining rooms, a book-lined garden room and a cosy snug with an open fire for winter. Sit at the friendly bar or in one of the many nooks and crannies. Bedrooms are in the converted barns set around a courtyard in the garden; find some homemade shortbread as a welcome. Breakfast is in the Garden Room or outside on the terrace – you can opt for continental or anything you like cooked to order. You'll want to stay for lunch and dinner too – the French chef's hearty pub fare attracts plenty of locals. Settle in the snug or out in the garden with a good book and a coffee, or chat in the bar over a hand-drawn local ale. The nearest town is Dereham, six miles away; Norwich is 20 miles, and the many attractions of the north Norfolk coast about the same. *Pets by arrangement.*

Rooms	4 doubles, 2 twin/doubles: £95-£185. Z-bed £25 per night.
Meals	Lunch/dinner from £13.95. Sunday lunch from £14.75.
Closed	Rarely.

The Brisley Bell,
The Green, Brisley, NR20 5DW

Tel	+44 (0)1362 705024
Email	welcome@thebrisleybell.co.uk
Web	www.thebrisleybell.co.uk

The Dial House

Don't miss afternoon tea. Scones fresh from the oven are served on triple-tiered stands, and mismatched tea pots add to the fun. There's a buzz about this place from the moment you step in. Staff are happy, friendly and keen, and a delightful eccentricity prevails. The Queen Anne building dominates the market square of Reepham – sit on the terrace and watch the world go by. Back inside, a blackboard announces cookery workshops and spa treatments, and a listed staircase leads to bedrooms above.

Like much of Norfolk, Reepham is a place of curiosities. Discover its secret lanes, and its two churches built a few feet apart, or set off with a hamper to the Norfolk Broads, perhaps in a chauffeur-driven limousine – which can all be organised for you. Return to an elegant Norfolk-sourced meal, served beneath a vintage chandelier. *Pets by arrangement.*

Rooms	8 doubles: £130-£225. Singles £130-£190.
Meals	Light lunches from £4. Hot sandwiches from £8. Afternoon tea £18. Dinner: starters from £7; mains from £14.
Closed	Never.

Tel	+44 (0)1603 879900
Email	info@thedialhouse.org.uk
Web	www.thedialhouse.org.uk

The Dial House,
Reepham, NR10 4JJ

Saracens Head

Lost in the lanes of deepest Norfolk, an inn that's hard to match. Outside, Georgian red-brick walls stand to attention at the front, but nip round the back and find them at ease in a beautiful courtyard where you can knock back a pint of Wherry in the evening sun before slipping inside to eat. Tim and Janie upped sticks from the Alps, unable to resist the allure of this lovely old inn. A sympathetic refurbishment has worked its magic, but the spirit remains the same: this is a country-house pub with lovely staff who go the extra mile. Downstairs the bar hums with happy locals who come for Norfolk ales and good French wines, while the food in the restaurant is as good as ever: Norfolk pheasant and rabbit terrine, wild duck or Cromer crab, treacle tart and caramel ice-cream. Upstairs, there's a sitting room on the landing, then six pretty bedrooms. All have smart carpets, wooden furniture, comfy beds and sparkling bathrooms. There's masses to do: ancient Norwich, the coast at Cromer, golf on the cliffs at Sheringham, Blickling Hall, a Jacobean pile. Don't miss Sunday lunch.

Rooms	5 twin/doubles: £110-£130.1 family room for 4: £110-£160. Singles £75. Extra bed/sofabed £25 p.p.p.n.
Meals	Lunch from £6.50. Dinner, 3 courses, £25-£35.
Closed	Rarely.

Saracens Head,
Wolterton, NR11 7LZ

Tel	+44 (0)1263 768909
Email	info@saracenshead-norfolk.co.uk
Web	www.saracenshead-norfolk.co.uk

The Blakeney Hotel

The view here is matchless, a clean sweep across the salt marshes up to Blakeney Point. The estuary passes five paces from the front door and you can watch the boats slide by from a sun-trapping terrace, a convivial bar, a stylish restaurant and a beautiful first-floor sitting room that comes with binoculars to follow the local wildlife. Bedrooms have a contemporary country-house style: chic fabrics, cool colours, antique furniture, white linen on beautiful beds, sparkling bathrooms with posh oils. Many have views to the front, a couple have balconies, too. Elsewhere, you'll find three open fires, a bar for light lunches and local ales, an elegant drawing room where you can play Scrabble, read the papers, or dig into afternoon tea. There's an indoor pool with a gym, a steam room and a sauna, then glass doors onto the garden; you'll also find a games' room for children. Outside, paths lead down to the marshes, there are seals to spot, birds to watch, links golf at Sheringham and Cromer, a point to point at Fakenham. Sandringham is close, too. Dogs and children are very welcome. *Minimum stay: 2 nights at weekends.*

Rooms	19 doubles, 37 twin/doubles: £268-£424. 8 singles: £134-£212. Prices include dinner.
Meals	Lunch from £9.50. Dinner included; non-residents, 3 courses, £32.
Closed	Never.

Tel	+44 (0)1263 740797
Email	reception@blakeneyhotel.co.uk
Web	www.blakeneyhotel.co.uk

The Blakeney Hotel,
The Quay, Blakeney, Holt, NR25 7NE

The Globe Inn at Wells-next-the-Sea

It's as English as England can be – a beautiful inn on a Georgian green. Potter down to the water and find a sandy beach for family fun, then a small harbour, where day boats land their catch on the quay. As for the Globe, it's an inn for all seasons. Outside, there's a sun-trapping terrace at the front, a flower-filled courtyard where you can eat in summer, try a pizza from the wood-fired oven. Inside, wood-burners sit at both ends of the bar, there are sofas and armchairs, games for rainy days, then local ales and excellent wines with which to wash down delicious local food. You eat in an airy restaurant with local art on the walls, perhaps clam linguini with chilli and garlic, dressed Wells crab or a rib-eye steak, then chocolate mousse with pistachio ice cream. Rooms upstairs and in the courtyard wing have the comfiest beds in the land. Those at the front have views of the green. Rooms connect for families, dogs are very welcome, boat trips can be arranged. Sandringham is up the road and there's a hut on Wells beach that can be hired for the day. *Minimum stay: 2 nights at weekends. Pets by arrangement.*

Rooms	10 doubles, 5 twin/doubles: £110-£190. 3 suites for 2: £190-£250. 1 single: £60-£100. Extra bed/sofabed £30 p.p.p.n.
Meals	Lunch from £6. Dinner, 3 courses, £25-£30.
Closed	Rarely.

The Globe Inn at Wells-next-the-Sea,
The Buttlands,
Wells-next-the-Sea, NR23 1EU

Tel	+44 (0)1328 710206
Email	hello@theglobeatwells.co.uk
Web	www.theglobeatwells.co.uk

The Lifeboat Inn

You're in heaven here, under the big skies of Norfolk's north coast with its sweeping salt marshes, nature reserves and sandy beaches. The Lifeboat sails a smooth and stylish path with glowing fires, scrumptious seafood and the comfiest of rooms. Tucked down a hidden lane in pretty Thornham, the inn's darkly-beamed bar conjures a smugglers retreat, while the conservatory and restaurant are light, bright and contemporary. Settle by a crackling fire with a pint of Woodforde's Wherry and plan a day's bird- or seal-spotting. In summer, the sun-trap courtyard beckons, or book one of two cedar wood pavilions for private dining. Wherever you settle, the menu will tempt you with seasonal specials, cream teas, hearty sandwiches and children's treats. Our Brancaster mussels were the tastiest we've eaten. Bedrooms (most are upstairs, one is on the ground floor) are wonderfully comfy with colour schemes that reflect the long landscape views. Bathrooms sparkle, and breakfasts are a treat. *Minimum stay: 2 nights at weekends*.

Rooms	13 doubles: £145-£225. Dinner, B&B £145-£215 per person. Extra bed/sofabed £25 p.p.p.n.
Meals	Starters from £6.25. Lunch from £6.50. Dinner from £9.95.
Closed	Never.

Tel	+44 (0)1485 512229
Email	info@chequersinnthornham.com
Web	www.lifeboatinnthornham.com

The Lifeboat Inn,
Ship Lane, Thornham, PE36 6LT

The Chequers Inn

Cheerful Chequers, beloved by locals and visitors alike, is thriving under the new care of Agellus. General Manager Ewen takes the helm and all is smooth sailing – with some of the best seafood you'll find in this lovely part of the world. Thornham is a pretty little village nestled along the coast, close to spectacular scenery and nature reserves, where Chequers gleams with its whitewashed walls and red pantiles. Inside, the fireplace glows and crackles, fresh flowers sit on scrubbed tables and the menu beckons. Our tempura of Brancaster mussels with tartar espuma and chilli vinegar (part of their Norfolk tapas range) was bursting with delicate flavours, but you might try slow-cooked crispy belly of pork with cider potato fondant, black cabbage, black pudding bonbon and grain mustard velouté. Pizzas are a treat too (crispy duck caught our eye) and there's private dining in the all-weather Pavilions outside. Both Sandringham and Holkham Hall are close. *Minimum stay: 2 nights at weekends.*

Rooms	11 doubles: £120-£195. Extra bed/sofabed £25 p.p.p.n.
Meals	Breakfast from £15. Tapas from £3.95. Lunch from £8.95. Mains from £13.95.
Closed	Rarely.

The Chequers Inn,
High Street, Thornham, PE36 6LY

Tel	+44 (0)1485 512229
Email	info@chequersinnthornham.com
Web	www.chequersinnthornham.com

East Midlands

The Olive Branch, page 241

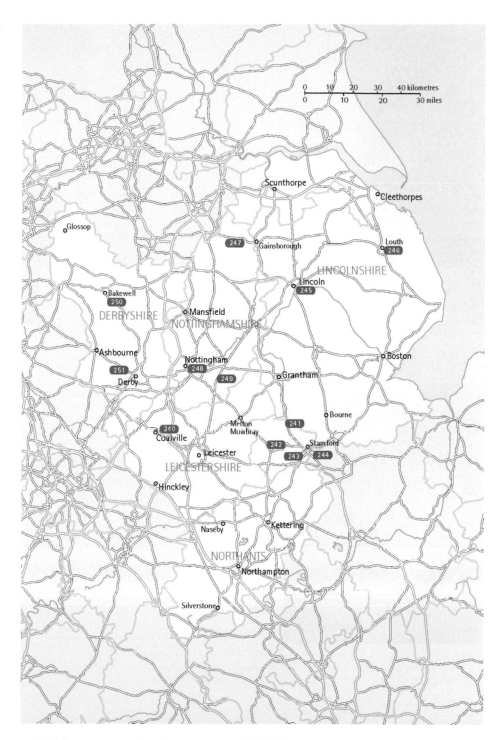

Abbots Oak Manor

Sarah and Anthony have brought this listed house back from the brink with style and a real passion for the place. The old bones: dark beams, stone mullion windows and ornate carvings, flatter the contemporary luxury of the interiors. The sophisticated bedrooms have a calm, light-grey colour scheme, excellent mattresses on kingsize beds; one has a fireplace, the suite can fit an extra two guests, all have Nespresso machines. The bathrooms are fabulous: double-ended tap-free baths with music at the touch of a button, and great showers. Seriously good food – as seasonal, foraged and local as possible – is served on vintage china in the chandeliered dining room; perhaps rump and belly of lamb with wilted baby gem lettuce followed by jasmine mousse with cherry soup and lavender biscuits. There's a smörgåsbord of craft gins to sample at the bar and the grounds are being beautifully restored. Marvellous.

Rooms	5 doubles: £145-£225. 1 suite for 2: £225. Extra beds £50 including breakfast.
Meals	Dinner £30. Children's dinner £15. Pubs/restaurants 2 miles.
Closed	Rarely.

Abbots Oak Manor,
Warren Hills Road, Abbots Oak,
Coalville, LE67 4UY

Tel	+44 (0)1530 833952
Email	info@abbotsoak.co.uk
Web	www.abbotsoak.co.uk

The Olive Branch

Start the evening with a local, seasonal, hedgerow cocktail – try a crab-apple bellini. Move onto dinner: the menu changes each day. All the produce is lovingly sourced – eggs from the hens, veg from the garden, local meat and fish – then cooked with passion by Sean and his team. Set off for Stamford (ten miles), a town rich in history, notable for its medieval Sheep Market, All Saints church (climb the bell-tower), and numerous side streets to get lost down. The town's prosperity is linked still to Burghley House, the finest Elizabethan house in England. Take a pub picnic to its lawns. As for the pub, it's 400 years old and an absolute gem. It stands at the end of a tree-lined avenue, next to a beautiful stone barn (the pub's dining room). Bedrooms lie in Beech House across the lane, three with private terraces. Everyone's welcome, from children to dogs.

Rooms	5 doubles: £120-£210.
	1 family room for 4: £250-£270.
	Singles from £97.50. Extra beds £30.
Meals	Lunch from £8.50. Dinner, 3 courses,
	£28.50-£40. Sunday lunch from £24.50.
Closed	Rarely.

Tel	+44 (0)1780 410355
Email	info@theolivebranchpub.com
Web	www.theolivebranchpub.com

The Olive Branch,
Main Street, Clipsham,
Oakham, LE15 7SH

Hambleton Hall Hotel & Restaurant

Hambleton is matchless, one of the seven wonders of English country-house hotels. It sits on a tiny peninsular that juts into Rutland Water. You can sail on it, cycle round it, or watch terns and osprey commute across it. Back at the house the undisputed wonders of Hambleton wait: sofas by the fire in the panelled hall, a pillared bar in red for cocktails, a Michelin star in the elegant dining room. French windows in the sitting room – beautiful art, fresh flowers, the daily papers – open onto fine gardens. Expect clipped lawns and gravel paths, a formal parterre garden that bursts with summer colour and a walled swimming pool with views over parkland to the water. Bedrooms are flawless: hand-stitched Italian linen, mirrored armoires, Roberts radios and marble bathrooms. Stefa's eye for fabrics, some of which coat the walls, is impeccable; the Pavilion, a two-bedroom suite, has its own terrace. Polish the day off with ambrosial food, perhaps beetroot terrine with horseradish sorbet, venison with Asian pear, passion fruit soufflé with banana sorbet. Barnsdale Gardens are close. *Minimum stay: 2 nights at weekends.*

Rooms	15 twin/doubles: £295-£775.
	1 suite for 4: £550-£775.
	Singles £210-£225.
Meals	Lunch from £31.50. Sunday lunch £60.
	Dinner, 3 courses, £78.
	Tasting menu £95.
Closed	Never.

Hambleton Hall Hotel & Restaurant, Ketton Road, Hambleton, Oakham, LE15 8TH	**Tel** +44 (0)1572 756991
	Email hotel@hambletonhall.com
	Web www.hambletonhall.com

The Bull & Swan at Burghley

A magical renovation, an ancient inn that stands a short walk from the middle of glorious Stamford, part of the Burghley estate. Step inside to discover varnished wood floors, golden stone walls, and fires smouldering all over the place. At the bar venison Scotch eggs are impossible to resist, as are a raft of local ales and splendid wines. Regal oils adorn the walls, leather-backed settles take the strain, and you eat wherever you want – in the kitchen garden with a delicious pizza and a film on Thursdays and Sundays! As for beautiful bedrooms, they come in country-house style with huge beds, fabulous linen, warm colours and super-funky bathrooms. Most are big, all are delightful, two interconnect for families, and mattresses are divine. Back downstairs, delicious food waits, perhaps duck terrine, crispy pork belly, rhubarb crumble. And don't miss Burghley, a five-minute stroll, one of Britain's finest houses.

Rooms	7 doubles, 2 twins: £100-£170. Singles £90-£150.
Meals	Lunch from £5.50. Dinner from £12.95. Sunday lunch from £15.95.
Closed	Never.

Tel	+44 (0)1780 766412
Email	enquiries@thebullandswan.co.uk
Web	www.thebullandswan.co.uk

The Bull & Swan at Burghley,
St Martins, Stamford, PE9 2LJ

The William Cecil

This attractive townhouse hotel stands yards from the gates of the Burghley estate. Inside, interiors offer a pleasing mix of English quirkiness and splendour. Downstairs, informality reigns. There are armchairs in front of the fire in the bar, smart wicker tables in the conservatory, doors onto a lovely terrace in summer, then hanging lamps and half-panelling in the colourful restaurant. The food is fresh and local with seasonal delights that include game from the estate. You might find pan fried stonebass with pak choi and curried Thai green broth, king prawn & sundried tomato linguine, salted caramel tart with peanut butter powder and candied peanuts. You can walk it all off through historic Stamford or spin over to Burghley for one of the finest Elizabethan houses in the realm. Come back to country-house bedrooms that mix eclectic Rajasthan furniture with a little English decorum. You'll find beautiful art, a wall of paper, perhaps a day bed or a ceiling rose. Some have views onto the estate, all have good bathrooms, the best with roll top tubs and vast walk-in showers.

Rooms	20 doubles, 7 twin/doubles: £100-£180.
Meals	Lunch, 2 courses, from £15.95.
	Dinner, 3 courses, from £27.50.
	Sunday lunch, 3 courses, from £28.50.
Closed	Never.

The William Cecil,
St Martins, Stamford, PE9 2LJ

Tel	+44 (0)1780 750070
Email	enquiries@thewilliamcecil.co.uk
Web	www.thewilliamcecil.co.uk

Washingborough Hall

In its day Lincoln was one of the most important cities in England. Its castle was built by William the Conqueror in 1068 and holds one of the four original copies of the Magna Carta; its cathedral dates to 1090 and remains one of the finest in Europe. All of which makes it a great city to visit, and if you want to beat a peaceful retreat into the country at the end of the day, this is the place to stay. It sits two miles east of Lincoln in a small village on the river Witham – footpaths by the water lead back into town. As for this Georgian rectory, you'll find smart lawns to the front, then a big welcome within – Edward and Lucy go out of their way to make your stay special. There's a wood-burner in the hall, a breakfast room with garden views, a sitting-room bar for afternoon tea, then a light-filled orangery restaurant. Stylish bedrooms offer unstinting comforts. Rooms at the front are bigger and have the view, all have good beds, bold wallpapers, excellent bathrooms, a sofa if there's room. As for the food, there's posh fish and chips in the bar or sea bass with spring greens in the orangery.

Rooms	12 doubles, 3 twin/doubles, 2 four-posters: £85-£175. 1 suite for 2: £175-£195. 2 singles: £65-£85.
Meals	Lunch from £5.50. Dinner, 3 courses, £25-£35. Sunday lunch from £18.50.
Closed	Never.

Tel	+44 (0)1522 790340	Washingborough Hall,
Email	enquiries@washingboroughhall.com	Church Hill, Washingborough, LN4 1BE
Web	www.washingboroughhall.com	

The Masons Arms Hotel

Feel very welcome here in newly smartened bedrooms – some facing the bustling market, others the church. Each has an espresso machine, snuggly bathrobes and a spotless black and white bathroom. Take over the whole place and throw a bash in the ballroom or just come for the weekend to read in the library and potter around the markets. Stay in for suppers of classic pub food sourced locally – smoked haddock chowder, steak frites – followed by gin and whisky cocktails at the Habits Bar upstairs, open on weekends. Breakfast is a full English, eggs anyway you like or perhaps granola or porridge. Bring your appetite for afternoon tea: the usual scones-and-sandwiches, plus miniature soup cups, puddings and prosecco. Drive half an hour east to stroll Mablethorpe and Anderby Creek's sandy beaches or make for the Donna Nook Nature Reserve to spot the resident seal colony.

Rooms	4 doubles, 6 twin/doubles: £70-£120. Singles £69-£95. Dinner, B&B £110-£130 per person.
Meals	Dinner £30. Restaurant 2-minute walk.
Closed	25-26 December.

The Masons Arms Hotel,
Cornmarket, Louth, LN11 9PY

Tel	+44 (0)1507 621200
Email	reception@the-masons-arms.com
Web	the-masons-arms.com

The Blacksmiths

With its smartly renovated interiors and happy team, the Blacksmiths has a top-notch reputation for the quality of its local, seasonal food. Expect to be tempted by the likes of pan-fried pigeon breast with courgette, black pudding and smoked almonds, lamb with summer vegetables, spelt, pea and mint risotto; finish with warm honey cake with Clayworth honey and buttermilk ice cream or orange and whisky bread and butter pudding with crème anglaise. There are pub classics too: the perennial favourite prawn cocktail, fish and chips or wild mushroom pithivier. Cosy up in front of the log-burner in the stone-floored bar, dine at reclaimed wooden tables in the award-winning restaurant or sip a pint of real ale in the walled garden. There's a great selection of wines, too. Why not come for the weekend and book one of the stylish bedrooms in the barn; all have comfy beds and quirky, spotless bathrooms with Cowshed smellies. For a longer stay, take the airy studio apartment with its revolving TV and fire, perfect for a family. Fashionable, poised, self-assured, re-invigorated: The Blacksmiths is designed to please.

Rooms	1 double, 2 twin/doubles: £120-£170. 1 studio for 4: £160-£200.
Meals	Starters from £5.50. Mains from £12.95. À la carte menu available.
Closed	Mondays.

Tel	+44 (0)1777 818171
Email	enquiries@blacksmithsclayworth.com
Web	www.blacksmithsclayworth.com

The Blacksmiths,
Town Street, Clayworth,
Retford, DN22 9AD

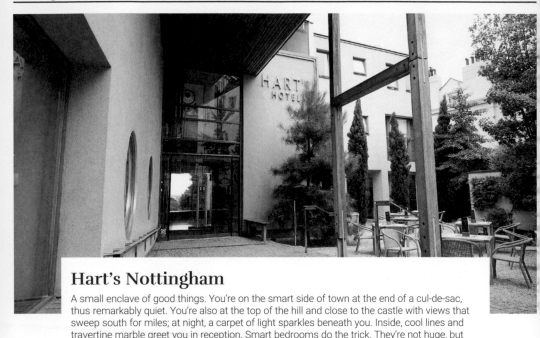

Hart's Nottingham

A small enclave of good things. You're on the smart side of town at the end of a cul-de-sac, thus remarkably quiet. You're also at the top of the hill and close to the castle with views that sweep south for miles; at night, a carpet of light sparkles beneath you. Inside, cool lines and travertine marble greet you in reception. Smart bedrooms do the trick. They're not huge, but come with all the trimmings: wide-screen TVs, Bose sound systems, super little bathrooms, king-size beds wrapped in crisp white cotton. Those on the ground floor open onto the garden, each with a terrace where you can breakfast in good weather; rooms on higher floors have better views (six overlook the courtyard). There is a cool little bar, the hub of the hotel, and Hart's Kitchen which serves breakfast and light bites, and offers excellent food: perhaps wild mushroom arancini, sea bream with lemon and hazelnut, quince soufflé with vanilla ice cream. There's lots to explore: the Lace Market, the city caves, Trent Bridge for the cricket (the England team stay here). There's a private car park for hotel guests, too.

Rooms	29 doubles: £139-£189. 2 suites for 2: £279. 1 family room for 4: £149-£206.
Meals	Continental breakfast £10; full English £15. Lunch, 2 courses £22. Dinner, 3 courses £32. Sunday lunch, 3 courses, £29.50.
Closed	Never.

Hart's Nottingham,
Standard Hill, Park Row,
Nottingham, NG1 6GN

Tel	+44 (0)115 988 1900
Email	reception@hartshotel.co.uk
Web	www.hartsnottingham.co.uk

Langar Hall

Langar Hall is one of the loveliest places in this book, reason enough to come to Nottinghamshire. It sits at the top of a hardly noticeable hill in glorious parkland, bang next door to the church. The Skirving family arrived 160 years ago, building on the site of Admiral Lord Howe's burned-down home. Much of what fills the house arrived then and it's easy to feel intoxicated by statues and busts in the pillared dining room, ancient tomes overflowing from bookshelves, an eclectic collection of art. Lila – Imogen's granddaughter – is now in charge, and very much following in her grandmother's footsteps; Langar remains a quirky country house with charming staff and a touch of bohemian flair. Bedrooms are lovely, some resplendent with antiques, others with beautiful wallpapers or a grand four-poster. As for dinner, it's a big treat, perhaps wild turbot with mussels and dill, Belvoir pheasant with cider and thyme, rhubarb soufflé with ginger beer sorbet. There's a cocktail bar, a conservatory, a flower-filled terrace for afternoon tea in summer, then beautiful gardens that delight. One of a kind.

Rooms	7 doubles, 2 twins, 1 four poster: £130-£225. 1 suite for 2: £160-£225. 1 chalet for 2: £125. Singles £110-£180.
Meals	Lunch £18.50-£23.50. Dinner £30-£50. Sunday lunch £39.50.
Closed	Never.

Tel	+44 (0)1949 860559	Langar Hall,
Email	info@langarhall.co.uk	Church Lane, Langar,
Web	www.langarhall.com	Nottingham, NG13 9HG

The Peacock at Rowsley

The Peacock sits between two fine houses, Haddon Hall and Chatsworth House. You can follow rivers up to each – the Derwent to Chatsworth, the Wye to the Hall – both a stroll through beautiful parkland. As for the hotel, it was built in 1652 and was home to the steward of Haddon. Inside, old and new mix gracefully: mullioned windows, hessian rugs, aristocratic art, then striking colours that give a contemporary feel. You'll find Mouseman tables and chairs in the restaurant, where French windows open onto the terrace. Elsewhere, a fire smoulders in the bar, the daily papers wait in the sitting room, the garden lawn runs down to the river. Stylish bedrooms have crisp linen, good beds, Farrow & Ball colours, the odd antique; one has a bed from Belvoir Castle. Good food waits in the restaurant, with meat and game from the estate, perhaps venison terrine, roast partridge, Bakewell Tart with buttermilk ice cream. There's afternoon tea in the garden in summer and you can fish both rivers, with day tickets available. Guests also receive a discount on entry to Haddon Hall. *Minimum stay: 2 nights at weekends.*

Rooms	10 doubles, 2 four-posters: £165-£310. 1 suite for 2: £250-£310. 2 singles: £130-£145. Dinner, B&B £142-£195 p.p.
Meals	Lunch from £4.50. Sunday lunch £22.50-£29.50. Dinner £60.
Closed	Rarely.

The Peacock at Rowsley,
Bakewell Road, Rowsley,
Matlock, DE4 2EB

Tel	+44 (0)1629 733518
Email	reception@thepeacockatrowsley.com
Web	www.thepeacockatrowsley.com

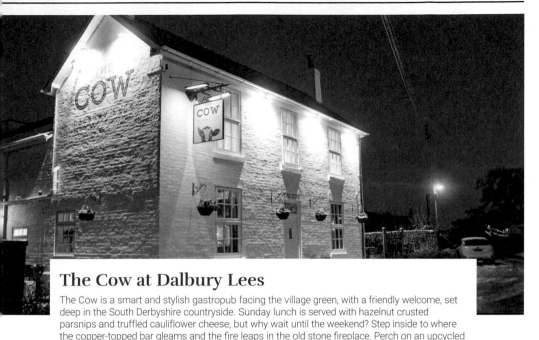

The Cow at Dalbury Lees

The Cow is a smart and stylish gastropub facing the village green, with a friendly welcome, set deep in the South Derbyshire countryside. Sunday lunch is served with hazelnut crusted parsnips and truffled cauliflower cheese, but why wait until the weekend? Step inside to where the copper-topped bar gleams and the fire leaps in the old stone fireplace. Perch on an upcycled milk churn to down a pint of local ale and choose from the imaginative menu with daily specials. Perhaps chilli and smoked paprika dusted pork scratchings with spiced apple compote scrumped from Lisa's garden, followed by slow-cooked oxtail with broad beans, peas and baby carrots. Leave room for clootie dumpling soufflé. Upstairs, the bedrooms have padded headboards, plump cushions, gleaming linens, hi-tech touches and a warm glow from clever lighting. Bathrooms sparkle, and have attractive stone basins. Breakfast will set you up for a day of exploring the Dales; tuck into poached Finnan haddock or a three egg omelette. You're in Derbyshire's Golden Triangle so take time to admire the little villages and vast views.

Rooms	12 doubles: £150-£238.
Meals	Starters £5.50. Lunch & dinner £11.
Closed	Never.

Tel	+44 (0)1332 824297
Email	enquiries@cowdalbury.com
Web	www.cowdalbury.com

The Cow at Dalbury Lees,
The Green, Dalbury Lees,
Ashbourne, DE6 5BE

West Midlands

The Lion & Pheasant, page 275

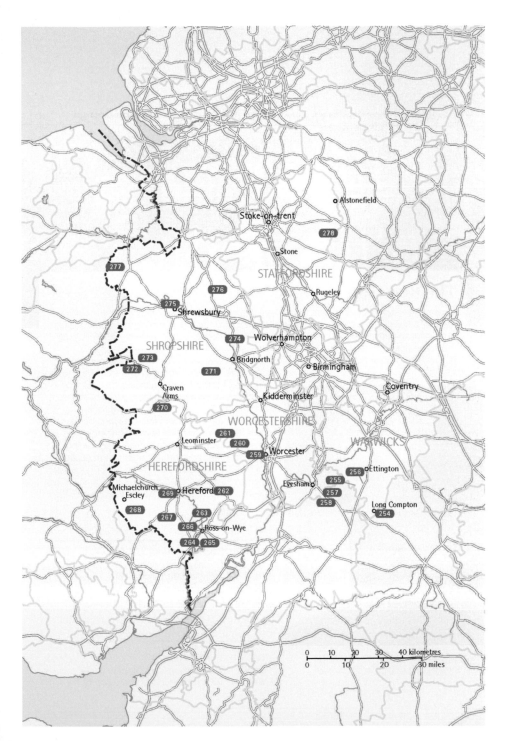

Alstonefield

Stoke-on-trent

278

Stone

STAFFORDSHIRE

Rugeley

277

276

275
Shrewsbury

274
Wolverhampton

SHROPSHIRE

273
272

271
Bridgnorth

Birmingham

Coventry

Craven
Arms

270

Kidderminster

WORCESTERSHIRE

WARWICKS

261
260
Leominster

259
Worcester

256
Ettington

Evesham

255

HEREFORDSHIRE

Michaelchurch
Escley
269
Hereford 262

257

258

Long Compton
254

268

267

263

266
Ross-on-Wye

264 265

0   10   20   30   40 kilometres
0   10   20   30 miles

253

The Red Lion

Dogs are welcome in this ancient warren of a pub where canine sketches adorn the walls; the pub's own pup – is often around. Enter to a mouthwatering aroma of imaginative dishes from chef/co-patron Sarah Keightley. Crispy-battered cod and chips with caper berries and mushy peas are served on *The Red Lion Times*, and pork tenderloin comes wrapped in pancetta with apple purée and black pudding. A meltingly warm pear and ginger pudding with toffee sauce rounds it all off nicely. Easy to find, this characterful pub has benefited from a wonderful refurb and there's space for everyone, from the pool room to the restaurant to the beautiful flagged bar with fire and wood-burning stove. There are five bedrooms too, the quietest at the back, which reflect the unfussy approach: natural colours; comfort and attention to quality make up for their size, though the King Room has an ante chamber should anyone snore! It is cheerful, hospitable, and breakfasts are worth waking up for.

Rooms	2 doubles, 1 twin: £95-£130. 1 family room for 4: £115-£150. 1 single: £90. Singles £60.
Meals	Lunch & dinner £15-£20.
Closed	Christmas.

The Red Lion,
Main Street, Long Compton, CV36 5JS

Tel	+44 (0)1608 684221
Email	info@redlion-longcompton.co.uk
Web	www.redlion-longcompton.co.uk

The Howard Arms

The Howard stands on Ilmington Green, eight miles south of Stratford-upon-Avon. It was built at roughly the same time as Shakespeare wrote *King Lear* and little has changed since. It's a lovely country inn and comes with original fixtures and fittings: polished flagstones, heavy beams, mellow stone walls, a crackling fire. Outside, roses ramble on golden stone walls, while a pretty garden waits at the back. Good food comes as standard, perhaps ham hock terrine with homemade piccalilli, marinated duck breast, apple tarte tatin with mascarpone cream; there's fish and chips, too. Elsewhere, you find oils on walls, books on shelves, settles in alcoves, beautiful bay windows. A colourful dining room floods with light courtesy of fine arched windows that overlook the green. Bedrooms in the main house have a charming old-world feel, garden rooms are more contemporary with excellent bathrooms. You can walk across fields to Chipping Campden; Simon de Montfort once owned this land. The village church dates to the 11th century and has Thompson mice within. *Minimum stay: 2 nights on weekdays.*

Rooms	4 doubles, 4 twins: £120-£160. Singles £90. Extra bed/sofabed £25 p.p.p.n.
Meals	Lunch & bar meals from £14. Dinner, 3 courses, from £30.
Closed	Rarely

Tel	+44 (0)1608 682226
Email	info@howardarms.com
Web	www.howardarms.com

The Howard Arms,
Lower Green, Ilmington, CV36 4LT

The Fuzzy Duck

In the rolling folds of the Cotswold countryside is this 18th-century coaching inn, polished to perfection by Tania, Adrian and their team. Beautiful fireplaces and gleaming tables, fine china and big sprays of wild flowers tell a tale of comfort and luxury, while the smiling staff are rightly proud of this gem of a pub. You dine like kings and queens in the sparkling bar, or in the clever conversion at the back, overlooking grounds that are part-orchard, part-walled-

garden. Try Cotswold chicken breast with slow-cooked chorizo and white bean stew, or a splendid ploughman's with warm Scotch quail's egg. For pudding, try the zingy lemon posset, or treacle tart with orange scented milk ice. If you over-indulge, borrow wellies in your size for a bracing walk then back to your beautiful bed above the bar; rooms are sound-proofed and two have double loft beds (up very vertical ladders) for families. Best of all, the generous team has provided indulgent treats: lovely slippers; a nightcap tipple – come prepared to be spoiled.

Rooms	2 doubles: £110-£140. 2 family rooms for 4: £160-£200.
Meals	Starters from £4.50. Mains from £9.95.
Closed	Never.

The Fuzzy Duck,
Ilmington Road, Armscote,
Stratford-upon-Avon, CV37 8DD

Tel	+44 (0)1608 682 635
Email	info@fuzzyduckarmscote.com
Web	www.fuzzyduckarmscote.com

The Fish Hotel

Come for Scandi chic on a smart estate with some perfectly well-priced rooms. It's like summer camp, only for adults – a place designed for fun. Expect a striking simplicity with airy colours, white linen, padded bedheads, robes in sparkling bathrooms. Rooms are scattered about in pretty buildings on the hill, the suites altogether fancier with claw-foot baths in the room, huge beds, maybe a sofa or a wood-burner, too. They spiral around a central lodge, where you can eat, drink and be merry. If the style is coolly contemporary, then the feel is cosy and informal, with lovely staff on hand to help. The big bar is the hub: sofas galore, cool colours, walls of glass that open onto a terrace, a funky wood-burner for winter nights. There's a games room for pool and table football and 400 acres of countryside to explore from the door. Deer roam the hill, there's a nature trail and maps for joggers. As for the food, you can eat in the bar, the restaurant, or out on the terrace in good weather.

Rooms	10 doubles, 33 twin/doubles: £150-£255.
	4 suites for 2: £230-£275.
Meals	Lunch from £5.
	Dinner, 3 courses, £25-£35.
Closed	Never.

Tel	+44 (0)1386 858000
Email	reservations@thefishhotel.co.uk
Web	www.thefishhotel.co.uk

The Fish Hotel,
Farncombe Estate,
Broadway, WR12 7LH

The Lygon Arms Hotel

This hotel has a guest book signed by Pierce Brosnan and Kylie Minogue but you, your children, and the dog will be welcomed with equal grace. There's much to do in a huge choice of drawing rooms and good food and drinks are served in several different areas, all lively and bustling. This isn't an old-fashioned hushed sort of place: staff wear a uniform but there's a light-hearted feel and they are über efficient without being in the least fawning. Children can go to Kids Club, you can wind down in the spa and there's even a warm water tap for hosing down your dog. And across the road there are three acres to explore. Broadway has two museums, a fantastic deli and lots of independent – rather expensive – shops, but you're on holiday. Walk to Broadway Tower in half an hour, hop on a steam train or hire bikes. Return for drinks in the atmospheric cocktail bar before dinner. *Minimum stay: 2 nights at weekends. Parking on-site.*

Rooms	27 doubles, 31 twin/doubles: £225-£280. 26 suites for 4: £360. Extra bed/sofabed £25-£65 p.p.p.n.
Meals	Lunch from £9. Dinner from £15. Afternoon tea from £10.
Closed	Never.

The Lygon Arms Hotel,
High Street, Broadway, WR12 7DU

Tel	+44 (0)1386 852255
Email	reservations@lygonarmshotel.co.uk
Web	www.lygonarmshotel.co.uk

The Cardinal's Hat

Wines to suit Spanish charcuterie, luscious local ciders, and a small terrace out back; welcome to the oldest pub in Worcester. Most of it is 18th-century – fine brickwork, sash windows – but it originates from the 14th and stands on a street of Tudor houses close to the cathedral. Step in to find an oak-planked bar and a carpeted 'snug' from whose easy chairs and leaded windows you can watch the world go by. The most atmospheric room is at the back, where dark wood panelling glows in the candlelight and the burner roars in the fireplace. As for the food, they keep it simple and authentic: hot pork pies, smoked kippers on toast, platters of fine local cheeses. Accompaniments include spicy chutneys, quince jellies, and ever-changing ales... how about Hobson's Old Prickly? Then it's up to one of the best bedrooms in Worcestershire. Immerse yourself in a world of soft carpets, polished antiques, glam wallpapers, and bathrooms that are state of the art (one with a tub in the room itself). Continental breakfast is delivered to your door, but there's full English at Mac & Jac's across the street.

Rooms	6 doubles: £80-£125.
Meals	Bar snacks from £4.30. Platters from £8.95.
Closed	Rarely.

Tel	+44 (0)1905 724006	The Cardinal's Hat,
Email	info@the-cardinals-hat.co.uk	31 Friar Street, Worcester, WR1 2NA
Web	www.the-cardinals-hat.co.uk	

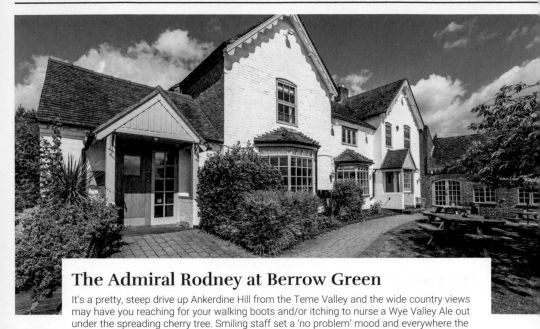

The Admiral Rodney at Berrow Green

It's a pretty, steep drive up Ankerdine Hill from the Teme Valley and the wide country views may have you reaching for your walking boots and/or itching to nurse a Wye Valley Ale out under the spreading cherry tree. Smiling staff set a 'no problem' mood and everywhere the attention to detail makes you feel properly looked after; you'd trust them with your wedding party; immaculate bedrooms are well sound-proofed; winter fires burn brightly. The inn's 21st-century renovations sit well with its 17th-century origins and the barn, with its lofty beams and nautical nods to the Admiral, is where you dine on beautifully cooked, mostly local, food. The stops are pulled out for breakfast too: porridge with whisky and brown sugar, gently poached haddock and egg. Everything is fresh and seasonal.

Rooms	6 doubles, 1 twin: £80-£160.
Meals	Lunch from £10. Dinner from £15.
Closed	One week in January.

The Admiral Rodney at Berrow Green,
Berrow Green, Worcester, WR6 6PL

Tel	+44 (0)1905 886181
Email	info@admiral-rodney.co.uk
Web	www.admiral-rodney.co.uk

The Baiting House at Upper Sapey

A lovely old pub that has upped its game hugely (sound-proofed bedrooms, fine dining) yet still has a proper bar and an authentic snug for snoozing over the daily papers. Staff are fresh-faced, well-trained and cheery. Outside, there's a terraced beer garden, and a wood fired pizza cabin that does a roaring trade in the summer. Head chef Charles Bradley conjures memorable dishes from carefully sourced food: breakfasts are posh but not small and if you're planning to walk all day just the ticket; lunchtime pub classics have been given a tasty twist; evening menus are a tour de force. Sample one of the forty gins, a hand-pumped ale from the Wye Valley Brewery or something from the thoughtful wine list. Choose between subtly luxurious bedrooms with plush bathrooms in the main building or the annexe.

Rooms	5 doubles, 1 twin: £75-£150. Singles £70-£150.
Meals	Lunch from £10. Dinner, 3 courses, from £25.
Closed	One week in January.

Tel	+44 (0)1886 853201
Email	info@baitinghouse.co.uk
Web	www.baitinghouse.co.uk

The Baiting House at Upper Sapey,
Upper Sapey, WR6 6XT

The Verzon

This English auberge has a cute rustic style and serves some seriously good food. It sits on the Hereford to Ledbury road and is owned by William and Kate Chase, farmers who turn their potatoes and apples into Chase vodka and gin. Not that this is the limit of their world. They also rear cattle and pigs and have a vineyard in the Lubéron. The Verzon exists to bring it all together – a gin and tonic on the terrace in summer, then a lovely dinner washed down by French wines. Most of the food is sourced within 30 miles, perhaps a hoppy Hereford rarebit, a perfect Chase steak, an ambrosial pecan tart with espresso mousse. Interiors mix old and new playfully, with timber frames and Union-Jack sofas in the bar, then a white marble fireplace in the theatrical dining room. Bedrooms have warm colours, crisp linen and robes in fine bathrooms. Two have baths in the room, those at the back have views over fields to the Malvern Hills. Local ales and a roaring fire wait in the bar, while the Chase distillery is up the road, with tours easily arranged. Don't miss Hereford cathedral for the Mappa Mundi.

Rooms	4 twin/doubles: £90-£140. 3 suites for 2: £160-£180. 1 single: £80. Extra beds £15.
Meals	Lunch from £12. Sunday lunch £22-£27. Afternoon tea from £15. Dinner, 3 courses, £30-£40.
Closed	Never.

The Verzon,
Hereford Road, Trumpet,
Ledbury, HR8 2PZ

Tel	+44 (0)1531 670381
Email	info@verzonhouse.com
Web	www.verzonhouse.com

Wilton Court Restaurant with Rooms

This Grade-II listed house dates to 1510 and looks across the lane to the river Wye: herons dive, otters swim, kingfishers nest. Roses ramble outside, happy guests potter within. This is a small hotel with pretty rooms, good food and owners that care. Bedrooms upstairs come in different shapes and sizes, but all have style. Those at the front have watery views, William Morris wallpaper, lots of space, perhaps a four-poster. A couple of rooms are small (as is their price), but, along with several others, have recently been refurbished. Expect lots of colour, white bathrooms, and sofas in the bigger rooms. Downstairs there's a bar for pre-dinner drinks, a wood-burner in the panelled library, then a conservatory restaurant for tasty food, perhaps Shropshire blue cheese soufflé, Herefordshire beef with savoy cabbage, caramel panna cotta with vanilla ice cream. Berries from a Grade-I listed mulberry tree in the garden are turned into sorbets and pies. You can cross the lane to a second garden for drinks by the river in summer. Ross is a five-minute stroll. *Minimum stay: 2 nights at weekends.*

Rooms	4 doubles, 5 twin/doubles, 1 four-poster: £135-£185. 1 family room for 4: £165 £205. Singles £110-£160.
Meals	Lunch: snacks from £6.95; 2-3 courses, £17.50-£22.50. Dinner, à la carte £35 £40.
Closed	1-22 January & rarely.

Tel	+44 (0)1989 562569	Wilton Court Restaurant with Rooms,
Email	info@wiltoncourthotel.com	Wilton Lane, Wilton,
Web	www.wiltoncourthotel.com	Ross-on-Wye, HR9 6AQ

The Bridge House

Kevin and Kathryn left high-flying jobs to cook, clean, polish and shine; they couldn't be happier. Their new home is this attractive 17th-century merchant's house with the best view in town. Lawns run down to the river Wye, then views shoot up the other side to St Mary's church. Inside, you find original elm floors and painted beamed ceilings, but the feel is contemporary, with cool colours, beautiful armchairs and antler chandeliers in the sitting room. Bedrooms have an easy elegance: comfy beds, crisp linen, pretty art, the odd timber frame. Five have the view, two have a claw-foot bath, others have power showers, a couple on high can be taken together. Breakfast is delicious, with doors in the sun room that fold back to drink in the view. Walk in the hills, kayak on the Wye, cycle in the Forest of Dean. Come home to an honesty bar in the sitting room and three terraces in the gorgeous garden, where colourful beds flourish. Wilton Castle, a 12th-century ruin, stands across the field; Hereford is close for the Mappa Mundi; good local restaurants wait. Dogs are welcome. *Minimum stay: 2 nights at weekends.*

Rooms	6 doubles, 2 twin/doubles: £95-£130. Singles £80.
Meals	Restaurants within walking distance.
Closed	16-27 December, 2 January – 1 February.

The Bridge House,
Wilton, Ross-on-Wye, HR9 6AA

Tel	+44 (0)1989 562655
Email	info@bridgehouserossonwye.co.uk
Web	www.bridgehouserossonwye.co.uk

Orles Barn Hotel & Restaurant

Roxy and Matt look after you beautifully. She's the smiley host that greets you; he's busy cooking delicious meals. They live in one part of the attractive 17th century red-brick building with their young family; the four guest rooms are on the first floor. Bright and airy, all are large, two are huge with free-standing baths for long soaks. The food here is a focal point and you eat in the informal dining room with views to the Forest of Dean. Breakfast on the full works or something lighter like omelette with smoked haddock and hollandaise. The lunch and dinner menus are short but interesting; perhaps Moroccan lamb in filo pastry paired with a good red wine. There are plenty of comfy spots to sit – choose a book or a board-game on rainy afternoons or Netflix in the bedrooms. The front garden and lawn at the back are peaceful and look over wooded hills and you can walk into Ross-on-Wye in 30 minutes – a small market town with a selection of independent shops.

Rooms	4 doubles: £100-£145.
Meals	Lunch, 2-3 courses £14.95-£19.95.
	Starters from £5.95.
	Mains from £14.95.
	Sunday lunch, 2 courses, £21.95.
Closed	24-27 December & 1-3 January.

Tel	+44 (0)1989218081
Email	orlesbarnhotel@gmail.com
Web	www.orlesbarnhotel.co.uk

Orles Barn Hotel & Restaurant,
Wilton, Ross-on-Wye, HR9 6AE

Brooks Country House

Led Zeppelin used to stay here when recording at studios on a nearby farm, and there's still a bit of a rock-star feel to the place. A big house in the country, a swimming pool in the kitchen garden and its own vineyard that produces wine for the restaurant... The house once stood in 1,000 acres, it now has a mere 12, but the land beyond is owned by the National Trust and you can walk straight out, skirt a copse and find yourself at a 14th-century church. As for the hotel – smart, but relaxed, with down-to-earth Andrew and Carla at the helm. Expect an open fire in the sitting room, wood floors in the restaurant and cowhide rugs in a bar that opens onto a sun-trapping garden. Nicely priced rooms are scattered about, some grander, others smaller, all with good beds, warm colours and lovely bathrooms; and there's an apartment for four in the grounds if you want to look after yourselves. As for the food, it's earthy stuff; homemade soups, a local rib-eye, a sinful chocolate tart. Hard to beat. *Minimum stay: 2 nights at weekends. Pets by arrangement.*

Rooms	14 twin/doubles, 6 four-posters: £79-£169. 2 suites for 2: £99-£169. 1 apartment for 4: £133-£250. 3 trucks for 2: £99-£139. Singles £89-£119.
Meals	Dinner £18-£24 (not Sundays). Sunday dinner £19-£23.
Closed	Never.

Brooks Country House, Pengethley Park, Ross-on-Wye, HR9 6LL	**Tel** +44 (0)1989 730211 **Email** info@brookscountryhouse.com **Web** www.brookscountryhouse.com

The Kilpeck Inn

Kilpeck – known for its Norman church – has a second string to its bow: a super little country inn with a facelift. It stands on the edge of the village overlooking beautiful fields, ten miles south of Hereford. Outside, smart white walls sparkle in the sun. Inside: old stone, slate floors and a warm contemporary feel. Find darts in the locals' bar, alongside the daily papers and a smouldering fire, and original beams, candle lanterns and painted panelling in the airy restaurant. Dig into the sort of food you'd hope to find in a country inn: River Exe mussels in a cider and sage cream sauce with hand cut chips; shepherd's pie, green beans, redcurrant and red wine jus. Rooms are above, crisp and comfortable. Named after local rivers, all have countryside views, plus pocket sprung mattresses, Egyptian cotton sheets and cloud-soft duvets. Bathrooms are spotless and sparkling. It's as local as possible and seriously green, what with low food miles, hi-spec insulation and a rainwater tank. Walkers rejoice: the Black Mountains and Offa's Dyke are close.

Rooms	3 doubles, 1 twin: £80-£110.
Meals	Lunch & bar meals from £5.95.
	Dinner £9.95-£17.95; not Sun eves.
	Sunday lunch, 3 courses, £15.95.
Closed	Rarely.

Tel	+44 (0)1981 570464
Email	booking@kilpeckinn.com
Web	www.kilpeckinn.com

The Kilpeck Inn,
Kilpeck, HR2 9DN

The Bridge Inn

Getting here is half the fun, in the wilds of Herefordshire (but it could be tricky in the dark). In a pretty spot down by the river, beneath the Black Hill of Bruce Chatwin fame, the 16th-century Bridge started life as a house, achingly lovely on its river side with willows weeping down the footbridge. Walkers descend, so do dogs, and families and shooting parties, and Glyn is the nicest host. Inside, hops hang from dark beams and the wood-burner belts out the heat, there are solid wooden pews, scrubbed pine tables and small bar stools on the other side. It's properly pubby yet there's an organic and fine wine menu. Eat in one of two dining areas; our pints of Butty Bach slipped down nicely and our food – hake with seafood stew, and barbecue brisket – was very, very good. Stay the night? We would! Four super country bedrooms lie in the farmhouse a minute away, with antiques, deep window seats, and a dark panelled sitting room below. In summer you can camp in the field above the pub or – for romantics – in a super yurt with decking and a vintage interior up a wooded path.

Rooms	2 doubles, 2 twin/doubles: £95-£110. Hay Festival price for 2 per night: £165.
Meals	Lunch £8-£22. Dinner £12-£22.
Closed	Rarely.

The Bridge Inn,
Michaelchurch Escley,
Hereford, HR2 0JW

Tel	+44 (0)1981 510646
Email	enquiries@thebridgeinnmichaelchurch.co.uk
Web	www.thebridgeinnmichaelchurch.co.uk

Castle House

Hereford's loveliest hotel stands 200 paces from the city's magnificent 11th-century cathedral, home to the Mappa Mundi. It's English to its core with a beautiful garden that overlooks what remains of the castle moat – in summer you eat here watching ducks glide by. Inside, the lap of luxury: a fine staircase, painted panelling, a delicious restaurant. Big bedrooms are lavish. Those in the main house are more traditional (the top-floor suite runs all the way along the front of the house); those in the townhouse (a 30-second stroll) are distinctly 21st century. All have a smart country-house feel with beautiful fabrics, super beds, excellent bathrooms with L'Occitane essential oils. Seriously good food, much grown on the owner's nearby farm, waits in the restaurant, perhaps Wye Valley asparagus and smoked salmon or fillet of Hereford beef followed by cardamom custard crème brûlée. Walk it off along the river Wye, which runs through the park behind. Hereford has lots to offer: Laskett Gardens, the racecourse, independent shops, Evensong in the cathedral.

Rooms	4 doubles: £155-£200.
	16 suites for 2: £225-£260.
	4 singles: £140.
	Dinner, B&B from £100 per person.
Meals	Lunch from £5. Sunday lunch from £18.50. Dinner, 3 courses, about £35.
Closed	Never.

Tel	+44 (0)1432 356321
Email	info@castlehse.co.uk
Web	www.castlehse.co.uk

Castle House,
Castle Street, Hereford, HR1 2NW

Old Downton Lodge

Hidden down a winding single track, discover buildings surrounded by the pristine countryside of the Downton Estate where pheasants strut, hills roll and woodlands sprawl along distant ridges. Will and Pippa will look after you in great style: breakfast includes homemade granola and muesli, fresh fruit, porridge with local honey, home smoked salmon, waffles, bacon and maple syrup. There's a lovely sitting room in the old stables with a roaring fire and a dining room in an 11th-century barn; in summer, head to the courtyard to eat (incredibly well), drink and make merry. You'll sleep in converted barns that mix timber frames, stone walls, flagged floors and oak furniture. Walks lead from the lodge, and you can follow the river Teme up to Downton Gorge for ferns, otters, Roman baths and bluebells in spring. The nearest village, Leintwardine, is a ten-minute drive and has three pubs – The Lion offers a friendly welcome and good food. It's a 12-minute drive to Ludlow's medieval town centre and ruined Norman castle.

Rooms	5 doubles, 2 twins, 2 four-posters: £155-£295. Singles £145-£295.
Meals	Dinner, 3-9 courses, from £50.
Closed	Christmas.

Old Downton Lodge,
Downton-on-the-Rock,
Ludlow, SY8 2HU

Tel	+44 (0)1568 771826
Email	bookings@olddowntonlodge.com
Web	www.olddowntonlodge.com

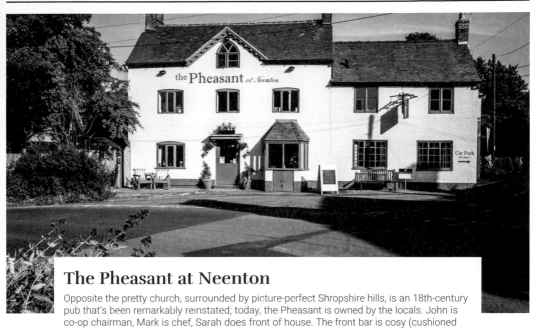

The Pheasant at Neenton

Opposite the pretty church, surrounded by picture-perfect Shropshire hills, is an 18th-century pub that's been remarkably reinstated; today, the Pheasant is owned by the locals. John is co-op chairman, Mark is chef, Sarah does front of house. The front bar is cosy (cushioned leather sofa and chairs, wood-burner in the chimney breast, rugs strewn on the tiled floor), the second bar is painted a deep chestnut, and the dining room is in an oak-framed extension at the back, its windows filling it with light. There's an orchard in the beer garden providing fruits for the kitchen, they tune their menus to the seasons and they seek out local suppliers (including lamb from the field next door). The beers include Hobson's and other Shropshire breweries, the wines are from Bibendum, and if you want to stay the night, you can. Three bedrooms, reached via an external stair, are spotless, spanking new, and decorated in restful colours (whites, greys, olive greens). Bathrooms are immaculate with tip-top showers, and we hear the breakfasts are fabulous.

Rooms	2 doubles, 1 twin/double: £90-£110. Dinner, B&B £65-£75 per person.
Meals	Starters from £6.50. Dinner from £10.95. Sunday lunch, 1-3 courses, £13.95-£19.95.
Closed	Rarely.

Tel	+44 (0)1746 787955
Email	info@pheasantatneenton.co.uk
Web	www.pheasantatneenton.co.uk

The Pheasant at Neenton,
Neenton, Bridgnorth, WV16 6RJ

The Castle Hotel

This thriving medieval market town sits amid some of the loveliest country in the land, a launch pad for walkers and cyclists alike, with Offa's Dyke, Long Mynd and the Kerry Ridgeway all close. After a day in the hills, roll back to this quirky hotel for a night of gentle carousing. You'll find heaps of country comforts: hearty food, impeccable ales, super rooms with honest prices. Downstairs, there's a coal fire in the pretty snug, oak panelling in the breakfast room, and Millie the short-haired dachshund who patrols the corridors with aplomb. Stylish bedrooms upstairs have all been refurbished. Expect good beds, warm colours, flat-screen TVs, an armchair if there's room. Some are up in the eaves, several have views of the Shropshire hills, two have baths in the room. Back downstairs you find the sort of food you'd want after a day in the hills, perhaps hot garlic prawns, beef and ale pie, sticky toffee pudding. Don't miss the hugely popular real ale festival in July, the beer drinker's equivalent of Glastonbury. The garden terrace, with long country views, is a fine spot for a sundowner.

Rooms	9 doubles, 1 twin: £95-£150. 2 family rooms for 4: £130-£155. Singles from £75. Dinner, B&B from £82.50 p.p. Extra beds for children £20.
Meals	Lunch from £4.50. Dinner, 3 courses, about £25.
Closed	Rarely.

The Castle Hotel,
Bishops Castle, SY9 5BN

Tel	+44 (0)1588 638403
Email	stay@thecastlehotelbishopscastle.co.uk
Web	www.thecastlehotelbishopscastle.co.uk

The Coach House

The drive here from any direction is virtually traffic free and the south Shropshire hills will have soothed any 'getting away' stress, so you'll be even more happy to arrive at this nurturing Inn. It opened first as a B&B but due to popular demand from the villagers morphed into a pop-up pub, then a restaurant with rooms. It juggles all these balls in a light, relaxed manner. Delicious smells come from the kitchen where Head Chef Harry Bullock's artistry concentrates on seasonal menus sourced as locally as possible.

Start your day with The Shropshire Breakfast which includes Wenlock Edge Farm sausages and black pudding – there are tasty non-meat choices too with wilted spinach and farm mushrooms. This is prime walking country so set off on one of the many walking paths that are close to the village, spot castles and birds, or cycle on hushed roads. Return for a pint of Salopian or Monty's, or a quiet read in the upstairs reading room. Dinner will be superb, bedrooms are all different but top class, service is on wheels. If you don't feel relaxed here you probably never will be.

Rooms	4 doubles, 2 twin/doubles; 1 double with separate bathroom: £89-£119. 1 suite for 2. £149-£169.
Meals	Lunch from £15. Dinner from £35. Bar menu, from £10.
Closed	Christmas. January. 2 weeks in June. 1 week in October.

Tel	+44 (0)1588 650846
Email	info@coachhousenorbury.com
Web	www.coachhousenorbury.com

The Coach House,
Norbury, Bishop's Castle, SY9 5DX

The Hundred House Hotel

The Phillips family has been at the helm for 25 years and Henry is an innkeeper with humour. As for the inn, having begun its life in the 14th century, it rambles charmingly inside as well as out. Enter a world of blazing log fires, soft brick walls, oak panelling and quarry-tiled floors. Dried flowers hang from beams, herbs sit in vases, and blackboard menus trumpet Hundred House fish pie, roast rack of Shropshire lamb and double chocolate mousse with orange anglaise. You are surrounded by Sylvia's wild and wonderful collage art hanging on the walls, and the fun continues in riotously patterned and floral bedrooms upstairs. Just go easy on the ale before you open the door: some have a swing hanging from the oak beams with a vibrant velvet seat. Lounge on antique beds – large, comfortable and wrapped in lavender-scented sheets. Wander out with a pint from the Ironbridge Brewery and share a quiet moment with a few stone lions in the beautiful garden, a flight of fancy full of herbaceous plants and over a hundred herbs – a summer treat. You can tie the knot in the restored Tithe Barn.

Rooms	8 doubles, 1 twin/double: £79-£140. Singles from £55.
Meals	Lunch from £4.95. Bar meals from £9.95. Mains from £17.95. Sunday lunch, 2 courses, £19.95.
Closed	Rarely.

The Hundred House Hotel,
Bridgnorth Road,
Norton, Shifnal, TF11 9EE

Tel	+44 (0)1952 580240
Email	reservations@hundredhouse.co.uk
Web	www.hundredhouse.co.uk

The Lion & Pheasant

The hotel has had a full makeover inside and out, but the foundations date back to the 16th century. There's a welcoming bar serving great cocktails and numerous gins, and a big open fire in the dining area. The warren of bedrooms above are packed with character and atmosphere; find slipper bath tubs, cavernous walk-in showers and perhaps views of the stone bridge and river. Food is very good: breakfasts are continental or hot, brunch goes on until midday so late risers can happily chomp bacon or sausage sarnies before heading out for the day; lunch and dinner menus are seasonal and change throughout the week and service is relaxed and friendly. Explore the Stretton Hills and Long Mynd on foot, go canoeing and fishing on the river Severn. Return for afternoon tea in the café bar, then flickering candles and Wye Valley ales on tap – the smart Georgian building shines after dark. You're central in town, for shopping, dining and the historic abbey.

Rooms	20 doubles, 1 twin: £119-£190. 4 suites for 3: £130-£230. 1 single: £109-£149. Dinner, B&B £179 per person. Extra bed/sofabed £30 p.p.p.n.
Meals	Lunch from £8. Starters from £7. Dinner from £16.
Closed	Christmas Day.

Tel	+44 (0)1743 231658
Email	info@lionandpheasant.co.uk
Web	www.lionandpheasant.co.uk

The Lion & Pheasant,
50 Wyle Cop, Shrewsbury, SY1 1XJ

Meeson Hall

Sitting in eight acres of lawns and woodland with open country all around, this lovely country house dates back to 1640 and is a treasure trove of beautiful things – the Jacobean chimney piece in the dining room is one of the finest in the land. Guests have the run of the ground floor: a grandly panelled hall with a crackling fire, an airy drawing room for afternoon tea and a library filled with original art. You eat communally in the splendid dining room, merrily digging into Mark's lovely home cooking – perhaps pâté with redcurrant jelly, a Barnsley chop with a red wine jus, followed by bread and butter pudding. Bedrooms come in smart country-house style: warm colours, smartly dressed beds, antique furniture, fresh flowers. There are sofas, silver teapots, perhaps a chandelier, then robes and the odd claw-foot bath in wallpapered bathrooms. Outside, bluebells run riot in spring. All of this would be blossom in the wind without Adrian and Mark, who go out of their way to make your stay here special. Ironbridge, birthplace of the Industrial Revolution, is close. *Over 16s welcome.*

Rooms	4 doubles: £165-£195. 1 suite for 4: £180-£320. Singles from £145.
Meals	Lunch from £15. Dinner, 3 courses, £42.50. Afternoon tea £15. Sunday lunch £35.
Closed	Rarely.

Meeson Hall,
Meeson, TF6 6PG

Tel	+44 (0)1952 541262
Email	enquiries@meesonhall.co.uk
Web	www.meesonhall.co.uk

Pen-y-Dyffryn Country Hotel

In a blissful valley lost to the world, a small country house that sparkles on the side of a peaceful hill. This is one of those lovely places where guests return again and again, mostly due to Audrey and Miles, who run a very happy ship. Outside, fields tumble down to a stream that marks the border with Wales. Daffodils erupt in spring, the lawns are scattered with deckchairs in summer, paths lead into the hills for fine walking. Lovely interiors are just the ticket: Laura Ashley wallpaper and an open fire in the quirky bar; colourful art and super food in the pretty restaurant; the daily papers and the odd chaise longue in the sitting room. Bedrooms hit the spot. Most have the view, one has a French sleigh bed, a couple have jacuzzi baths for two. Four lovely rooms outside are dog-friendly and have their own patios. You get warm colours, crisp linen, pretty fabrics and sparkling bathrooms. After a day in the hills come back for a good dinner, perhaps wild mushroom risotto, pan-fried wood pigeon, hot chocolate fondant. Offa's Dyke and Powis Castle are close. *Minimum stay: 2 nights at weekends.*

Rooms	8 doubles, 4 twins: £120-£190. Singles £90-£99. Dinner, B&B £99-£136 per person. Extra bed £35 p.p.p.n.
Meals	Light lunch by arrangement. Dinner £30-£37
Closed	Rarely.

Tel	+44 (0)1691 653700
Email	stay@peny.co.uk
Web	www.peny.co.uk

Pen-y-Dyffryn Country Hotel,
Rhydycroesau, Oswestry, SY10 7JD

The Duncombe Arms

Walnut House stands alone just behind the Duncombe Arms and has views of Dove Valley and the Derbyshire Hills in the distance. Find homemade biscuits, tea and coffee in your room, plus comfy armchairs, magazines to flick through and original artworks on the walls. Huge breakfasts in the pub feature top quality ingredients sourced from local farms – lunch and dinner are a treat too. Sip a pint of Duncombe Ale, specially brewed for the pub, or try one of the 40 craft gins; you can play dominoes in front of the fire, chat to the friendly locals (this place gets busy in summer) or sit out on the garden in fine weather. A range of activities and spectacular scenery in the Peak District National Park are within half an hour's drive, as are water sports on Carsington Water. English Heritage houses such as Chatsworth, Haddon Hall and Hardwick Hall are within an hour's drive.

Rooms	10 doubles: £160.
	2 suites for 2: £190.
Meals	Starters £5-£12. Mains £15-£25.
	Sunday lunch, 3 courses, £28.50.
Closed	Rarely.

The Duncombe Arms,
Ellastone, DE6 2GZ

Tel	+44 (0)1335 324275
Email	hello@duncombearms.co.uk
Web	www.duncombearms.co.uk/

North West

Borrowdale Gates, page 305

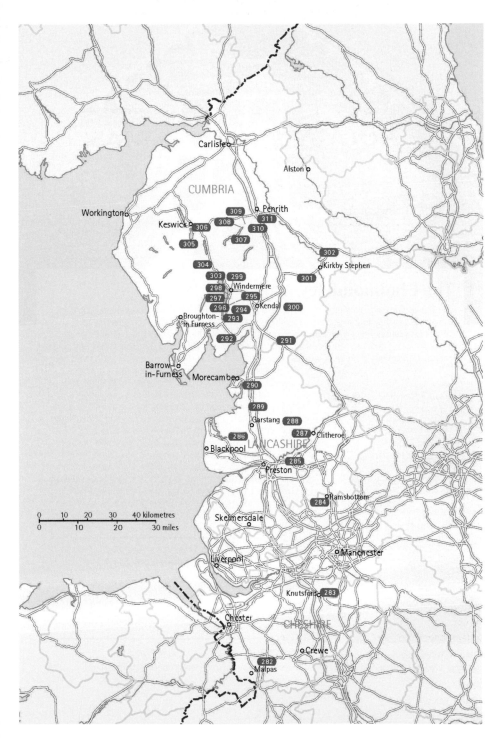

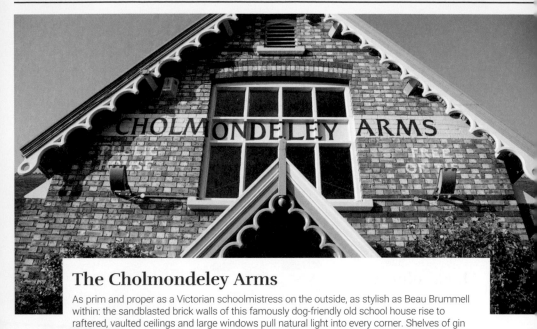

The Cholmondeley Arms

As prim and proper as a Victorian schoolmistress on the outside, as stylish as Beau Brummell within: the sandblasted brick walls of this famously dog-friendly old school house rise to raftered, vaulted ceilings and large windows pull natural light into every corner. Shelves of gin hover above fat radiators, cartoons and photos nestle amongst old sporting paraphernalia, and oriental rugs sprawl beneath an auction lot of tables, pews and chairs. The glorious carved oak bar dominates the main hall and apart from the malted charms of Cholmondeley Best Bitter and other local cask ales; a staggering 366 varieties of ruinously good gin to discover, with the aid of a well-thumbed guide or one of the charming staff. Study the menus on antique blackboards or opt for sharing a seafood trawler board followed by their legendary steak and kidney pie. Rooms in the old headmaster's house behind are calm and civilised with all the comfort you need. There's an annual Gin Fest, and Juniper Berry Music Festival in July. Weddings can be held in the grounds. Seldom has going back to school been this much fun.

Rooms	5 doubles, 1 twin: £60-£110.
Meals	Lunch & dinner from £11.95.
	Sunday lunch £14.95.
Closed	Rarely.

The Cholmondeley Arms,
Wrenbury Road, Cholmondeley,
Malpas, SY14 8HN

Tel	+44 (0)1829 720300
Email	info@cholmondeleyarms.co.uk
Web	www.cholmondeleyarms.co.uk

The Roebuck

From the cobbled pavement planted with trees to the split-level terrace that catches the sun, you'll believe you're in a French valley rather than an English village whose lucky residents now have a third offering from the Cheshire Cat team. The Roebuck dates back to 1708. Rustic shutters, shipped from France along with the beds, sit prettily on the pink-brick masonry. Café tables, wine-red leather settles, mirrors, candles and a host of wine bottles make a colourful backdrop for tasty lunches and dinners with a Mediterranean flavour: Amalfi lemon risotto with crab, mascarpone and baby basil. Sample local craft beers and ciders, or let the wine list tempt you. Six double bedrooms, two on the ground floor, four upstairs, are full of colour, warmth and texture: embroidered brocades, leather armchairs, even funky pony skins. All have sparkling bathrooms and the best (Bobal) has a woodburner between the bed and bath. Romantics can get hitched here; the Roebuck has a wedding license and can be booked exclusively for 55 guests.

Rooms	6 doubles: £130-£200.
Meals	Lunch & dinner from £8.95.
	Sunday lunch £16.
Closed	Rarely.

Tel	+44 (0)1565 873939
Email	info@roebuckinnmobberley.co.uk
Web	roebuckinnmobberley.co.uk

The Roebuck,
Mill Lane, Mobberley,
Knutsford, WA16 7HX

The Eagle & Child

A passionate desire to do something different, an exceptional eye for detail and a clear vision from the start, to create a community pub with top-quality food, has been key to the Eagle's soaring success. Menus focus on Lancashire's food heritage, with classic local recipes and ingredients given a modern twist, such as the award winning 'Double Bomber' pie made with Lancashire Bomb cheese and curd, and Thwaites Lancaster Bomber braised onions. Glen has a background in community regeneration and a commitment to training and employing disadvantaged young people; the service here is faultless. The 'Incredible Edible' beer garden is a great space for drinking and dining while the fabulous orangery has floor to ceiling views that showcase the splendid views. Bedrooms are a delightful surprise, brimming with character and comfort. The three doubles have superb wet rooms, while the two suites come with Juliette balconies and baths with showers. Each room is named after an owl and features strikingly bespoke artwork and murals. An absolute delight.

Rooms	3 doubles: £75-£100.
	2 suites for 2: £150.
	Extra bed/sofabed £15 p.p.p.n.
Meals	Starters from £4.25. Lunch from £5.95.
	Mains from £12.95.
Closed	Never.

The Eagle & Child,
3 Whalley Road,
Ramsbottom, BL0 0DL

Tel	+44 (0)1706 824477
Email	glen@eagle-and-child.com
Web	www.eagle-and-child.com

The Millstone, Mellor

Modern meets traditional – in a handsome 18th-century coaching inn in a pretty village on the edge of the Ribble valley. There's a welcoming glow in the bar, with its oak beams and panelling, so get cosy by the roaring fire with a pint of local Thwaites Bitter and a crispy duck spring roll. Or eat in the stylish dining room with warm wood-panelled walls. Local ingredients are carefully sourced and the food is wholesome and unpretentious. Tuck into the likes of ham hock and Lancashire cheese croquette with chilli tomato chutney followed by Bowland steak, kidney and Wainwright ale pudding with mushy peas, fat chips and a jug of gravy. Or share a fishmonger's board of smoked Scottish salmon, crab bonbon, Thwaites battered haddock, crayfish... and freshly baked bread. Leave room for blackberry, rum and honey cheesecake with raspberry curd. Bedrooms ooze comfort: sumptuous fabrics and luxurious linen, digital radios and plasma TVs, high-spec bathrooms, umbrellas for wet days. No wonder it's popular.

Rooms	23 twin/doubles: £75-£125. Singles £75-£125.
Meals	Lunch & dinner £8.95-£16.95.
Closed	Never.

Tel	+44 (0)1254 813333
Email	relax@millstonehotel.co.uk
Web	www.themillstonemellor.co.uk

The Millstone, Mellor,
Church Lane, Mellor,
Blackburn, BB2 7JR

The Cartford Inn

This quirky inn is full of its own delights, not least its stylish interiors, fabulous food and helpful staff. This might explain why it was named Best Inn in Britain in 2016, a richly deserved award. Julie and Patrick love their world and can't stop spending money on it. Recently they opened a gorgeous deli on the terrace and they've built two gob-smacking suites on stilts overlooking the river. It's a mecca for locals, who come to eat, drink and gossip. Outside, views stretch across to the Trough of Bowland. Inside, delicious food waits, perhaps fresh crab gnocchi, roasted Lytham poussin, Ovaltine panna cotta with dark chocolate mousse. The bar, with its cool art and roaring fire, is a great place to linger over a pint of local ale, but a courtyard garden will draw you out in good weather. Bedrooms have style in spades: gilded sleigh beds, signature wallpapers, river views, perhaps a roll-top bath in the room; the penthouse has a rooftop terrace, too. You can follow the river on a two-mile circular walk. Don't miss Blackpool, a proper northern town. Brilliant.

Rooms	11 doubles: £130-£230. 2 suites for 2: £230-£250. 2 family rooms for 3-4: £150. Singles £80-£150.
Meals	Lunch from £8.50; not Monday. Dinner, 3 courses, £25-£35.
Closed	25-26 December.

The Cartford Inn,
Cartford Lane, Little Eccleston,
Preston, PR3 0YP

Tel	+44 (0)1995 670166
Email	info@thecartfordinn.co.uk
Web	www.thecartfordinn.co.uk

Red Pump Inn

Down meandering lanes in the lovely Ribble valley is a handsome roadside inn with a south-facing terrace tumbled with flowers. In the cosy snug bar: flag floors, crackling fires, oak settles and tables, and shuttered windows with green views. Changing cask ales might include Bowland Hen Harrier and Moorhouse's Pride of Pendle, while Jonathan hand-picks wines and malt whiskies. For lunch there are two rooms to choose from: one cosy with mustard walls, the other with bare oak tables and settles by the wood-burner.

In the evening, sit in the large, beamed, candlelit restaurant and tuck in to something from the chargrill steaks are to die for. The menu is warming, hearty and rich, and meat comes from Ginger Pig. Try lamb's kidneys with spinach and bacon, home cured salmon with caper and lemon dressing, slow roast pork belly and bean cassoulet. The bedrooms have Fran's design flair with French antique beds, wonderfully comfy mattresses and super wet room showers; hearty Irish breakfasts with white pudding. Clitheroe Castle and the Forest of Bowland are nearby. *Pets by arrangement.*

Rooms	8 twin/doubles: £95-£150.
	Dinner, B&B £65-£75 per person.
Meals	Bar snacks from £2.50.
	Lunch & dinner £8.95-£24.
Closed	4 December – 15 January.

Tel	+44 (0)1254 826227	Red Pump Inn,
Email	enquiries@theredpumpinn.co.uk	Clitheroe Road, Bashall Eaves,
Web	www.theredpumpinn.co.uk	Clitheroe, BB7 3DA

The Inn at Whitewell

It is almost impossible to imagine a day when a better inn will grace the English landscape. Everything here is perfect. The inn sits just above the river Hodder, and doors in the bar lead onto a terrace where guests can enjoy five-mile views across parkland to rising fells. Inside, fires roar, newspapers wait, there are beams, sofas, maps and copies of *Wisden*. Bedrooms, some in the Coach House, are exemplary and come with real luxury, perhaps a peat fire, a lavish four-poster, a fabulous Victorian power shower. All have beautiful fabrics, top linen and gadgets galore; many have the marvellous view – you can fall asleep to the sound of the river. There are bar meals for those who want to watch their weight (the Whitewell fish pie is rightly famous) or a restaurant for splendid food, so dig into seared scallops, Bowland lamb, a plate of local cheese (the Queen once popped in for lunch). Elsewhere, a wine shop in reception, seven miles of private fishing and countryside as good as any in the land. Dogs and children are very welcome. Magnificent.

Rooms	17 doubles, 5 twin/doubles: £137-£270. 1 suite for 2: £235-£270. Singles £99-£218.
Meals	Bar meals from £8. Dinner £25-£35.
Closed	Never.

The Inn at Whitewell,
Dunsop Road, Whitewell,
Clitheroe, BB7 3AT

Tel	+44 (0)1200 448222
Email	reception@innatwhitewell.com
Web	www.innatwhitewell.com

The Fleece Inn

A handsome grey stone building which sits on a crossroads in green farmland with the Bowland Fells to the east. The place was much in decline until local businessman Marcus took it on with the aim of making it into the sort of inn he admires – one with outstanding service, great food and attractive surroundings. All is fresh and welcoming inside with gleaming furniture, fresh flowers in jugs, blazing fires on cooler days and a cheery vibe; there's even a shop. Chef Ian Manning creates honest dishes without fuss: rack of Pilling Marsh lamb, halibut with a velouté sauce, scallops in pancetta with black pudding fritters. There's Black Sheep bitter or a choice of three other local beers, a specialist gin, malt whisky, and sensible wine menu from a Clitheroe merchant. On sunny days spill outside to the garden, well-tended and with a good play area. Choose to stay and you'll sleep well in quiet bedrooms with fine wool carpets, flat screen TVs, pretty fabrics for curtains and headboards, the best beds; bathrooms are new and glossy. Breakfast will set you up for hearty walking from the door.

Rooms	8 doubles: £90-£115.
	1 family room for 4: £115.
Meals	Lunch from £5.95; 2 courses, £11.95.
	Starters from £5.25. Mains from £9.95.
Closed	Mondays,

Tel	+44 (0)1524 791233
Email	admin@fleeceinn.co.uk
Web	www.fleeceinn.co.uk

The Fleece Inn,
Dolphinholme, Lancaster, LA2 9AQ

Toll House Inn

This grand old city pub-hotel is bound to impress: high ceilings, stained-glass windows, huge Art Deco lights (yes, the originals) and ornate plasterwork abounds. And the elegant dining room with its vintage mismatch of furniture and gleaming parquet is a pleasing space from which to ponder a varied menu; locally potted shrimps, Lancashire hotpot, and steak and ale pudding all appeal. In the bar, sandwiches are packed with the likes of Lancashire cheese and chutney. Well-kept Thwaites cask beers await, and there's a selection of wines by the glass. Contemporary bedrooms of different shapes and sizes pick up on the period mood, and are comfortable and quiet, with drenching showers and triple-glazed windows, plasma TVs, snowy white linen; one has a beautiful listed wardrobe! Breakfast is full Lancashire – the works, and delicious. In short, a lovely friendly pub-hotel, and a fine place for a spot of retail therapy, slap in the heart of historic Lancaster.

Rooms	28 doubles: £70-£105. Singles from £64.
Meals	Breakfast £8.95. Lunch from £6.95. Bar meals from £5.95. Dinner from £8.95. Sunday lunch, 2 courses, £11.95.
Closed	Rarely.

Toll House Inn,
Penny Street, Lancaster, LA1 1XT

Tel	+44 (0)1524 599900
Email	relax@tollhouseinnlancaster.co.uk
Web	www.tollhouseinn.co.uk

The Sun Inn

This fine old inn sits between the Dales and the Lakes in an ancient market town, one of the prettiest in the north. It backs onto St Mary's churchyard, where wild flowers flourish, and on the far side you'll find 'the fairest view in England' to quote John Ruskin. Herons fish the river, lambs graze the fells beyond, a vast sky hangs above. Turner came to paint it in 1825 and benches wait for those who want to linger. As for the Sun, it does what all good inns do, it looks after you in style. It dates to 1670 and started life as a butcher's.

Inside, there's lots of pretty old stuff – stone walls, rosewood panelling, wood-burners working overtime – then warm colours, fresh flowers and the daily papers. You'll find leather banquettes, local art and dining chairs from Cunard's Mauretania, so eat in style, perhaps goat's cheese with honey, hogget with onion jam, banana parfait with chocolate sorbet. Bedrooms have good beds, smart fabrics, spotless bathrooms. Parking permits come with your room and can be used far and wide. Market day is Thursday, dogs are welcome, don't miss Sunday lunch. *Minimum stay: 2 nights at weekends.*

Rooms	9 doubles, 2 twin/doubles: £135-£189. Dinner, B&B from £90 p.p. Singles from £85. Extra beds £20.
Meals	Lunch from £6; not Mondays. Dinner, £21-£34. Sunday lunch from £14.50.
Closed	Never.

Tel	+44 (0)15242 71965	The Sun Inn,
Email	email@sun-inn.info	6 Market Street, Kirkby Lonsdale,
Web	www.sun-inn.info	Carnforth, LA6 2AU

Aynsome Manor Hotel

A small country house with a big heart. It may not be the grandest place in the book but the welcome is genuine, the peace is intoxicating and the value unmistakable. From the front, a long sweep across open meadows leads south to Cartmel and its priory, a view that has changed little in 800 years. The house, a mere pup by comparison, dates to 1512. Step in to find red armchairs, a grandfather clock and a coal fire in the hall. There's a small bar for a dram at the front and a cantilever staircase with cupola dome that sweeps you up to a first-floor drawing room, where panelled windows frame the view. Downstairs, you eat under a wildly ornate ceiling with Georgian colours and old portraits on the walls. You get lovely country cooking, too: French onion soup, roast leg of Cumbrian lamb, rich chocolate mousse served with white chocolate sauce. Bedrooms are simple, spotless, cosy and colourful. Some have views over the fields, one may be haunted, all have good bathrooms. Staff are lovely, nothing is too much trouble, kippers at breakfast are a treat. Windermere and Coniston are close.

Rooms	5 doubles, 7 twins: £90-£160. 1 family room for 4: £90-£160. Singles £85-£145. Dinner, B&B £75-£97 per person. Extra bed £45-£55 p.p.p.n.
Meals	Packed lunches by arrangement £9.50. Dinner, 4 courses, £33.
Closed	Christmas & 2-30 January.

Aynsome Manor Hotel, Aynsome Lane, Cartmel, Grange-over-Sands, Cumbria, LA11 6HH	**Tel** +44 (0)15395 36653 **Email** aynsomemanor@btconnect.com **Web** www.aynsomemanorhotel.co.uk

The Masons Arms

The Masons is a Lakeland institution, an ancient inn lost in blissful country. You're on the side of a hill with 15-mile views across a quilt of fields to Scout Scar. In summer, pub life decants onto a beautiful terrace – a sitting room in the sun – where window boxes and flowerbeds tumble with colour. The inn dates to the 16th century and is impossibly pretty. The bar is gorgeous, with low ceilings, wavy beams, flagged floors and roaring fires, then splendid local ales to quench your thirst. Rustic elegance upstairs comes courtesy of stripped floors, country rugs and red walls in the first-floor dining room, so grab a window seat for fabulous views and dig into local fare, perhaps cheese soufflé, haunch of venison, toffee and banana sundae. Rooms (in the main house) and cottages (off the courtyard, great for families) are a steal. All have comfort and style in spades. You'll find lovely beds, pretty fabrics and super bathrooms; several have terraces, too. As befitting a community local, events are often on the calendar: live music, a food market, even the odd busker. Cartmel Priory is close. *Minimum stay: 2 nights at weekends.*

Rooms	5 apartments for 2: £95-£140. 1 self-catering cottage for 4, 1 self-catering cottage for 6: £130-£185. .
Meals	Breakfast & lunch from £4.95. Bar meals from £9.95. Dinner, 3 courses, £25-£30. Sunday lunch from £12.95.
Closed	Never.

Tel	+44 (0)15395 68486
Email	info@masonsarmsstrawberrybank.co.uk
Web	www.masonsarmsstrawberrybank.co.uk

The Masons Arms,
Strawberry Bank, Cartmell Fell,
Grange-over-Sands, LA11 6NW

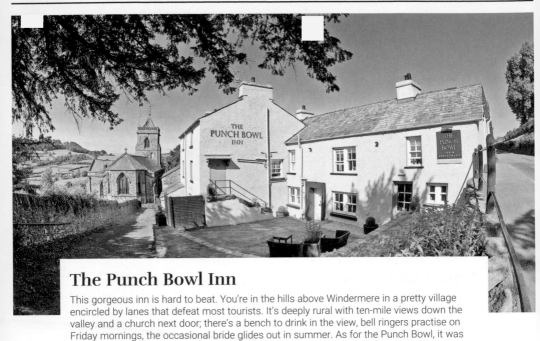

The Punch Bowl Inn

This gorgeous inn is hard to beat. You're in the hills above Windermere in a pretty village encircled by lanes that defeat most tourists. It's deeply rural with ten-mile views down the valley and a church next door; there's a bench to drink in the view, bell ringers practise on Friday mornings, the occasional bride glides out in summer. As for the Punch Bowl, it was rescued from neglect, renovated beautifully, and now sparkles, a stylish mix of old and new.

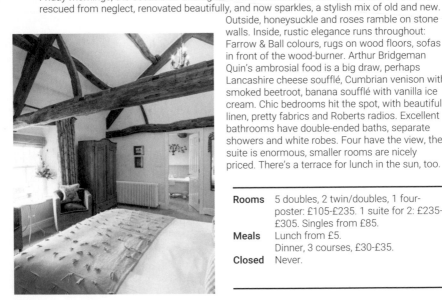

Outside, honeysuckle and roses ramble on stone walls. Inside, rustic elegance runs throughout: Farrow & Ball colours, rugs on wood floors, sofas in front of the wood-burner. Arthur Bridgeman Quin's ambrosial food is a big draw, perhaps Lancashire cheese soufflé, Cumbrian venison with smoked beetroot, banana soufflé with vanilla ice cream. Chic bedrooms hit the spot, with beautiful linen, pretty fabrics and Roberts radios. Excellent bathrooms have double-ended baths, separate showers and white robes. Four have the view, the suite is enormous, smaller rooms are nicely priced. There's a terrace for lunch in the sun, too.

Rooms	5 doubles, 2 twin/doubles, 1 four-poster: £105-£235. 1 suite for 2: £235-£305. Singles from £85.
Meals	Lunch from £5. Dinner, 3 courses, £30-£35.
Closed	Never.

The Punch Bowl Inn,
Crosthwaite, Kendal, LA8 8HR

Tel	+44 (0)15395 68237
Email	info@the-punchbowl.co.uk
Web	www.the-punchbowl.co.uk

Gilpin Lake House & Spa

Every now and then you bump into a hotel that knocks your socks off. Gilpin Lake House is an extraordinary place – a tiny spa hotel with only six rooms, luxury and intimacy entwined. It sits away from the crowds, lost in the hills, surrounded by acres of peaceful woodland. A swimming pool in the house opens onto a terrace, where you can flop on loungers and gaze down on the lake. Elsewhere, beautiful gardens, a rowing boat, and a second hot tub overlooking fells. There's a treatment room in a cabin that sits above the lake, then a snug boathouse with a deck on the water. As for the house, you'll find sofas in front of a wood-burner in the sitting room, then lake views, books galore and beautiful art. Spoiling rooms have fabulous beds, sofas, beautiful fabrics, bathrooms that don't hold back. Breakfast is served wherever you want: your room, the terrace, the conservatory. There's a chauffeur to whizz you up to their sister hotel for dinner (included in the price). Come with friends and take the whole place. Out of this world. *Minimum stay: 2 nights at weekends, 3 at bank holidays & Easter. Children over 7 welcome.*

Rooms	6 twin/doubles: £495-£605. Price includes dinner for two at Gilpin Hotel, chauffeur included!
Meals	Dinner included; non-residents £70. Sunday lunch, £35. Tasting menu, £90. Afternoon tea from £22.50.
Closed	Never.

Tel	+44 (0)15394 88818
Email	hotel@thegilpin.co.uk
Web	www.thegilpin.co.uk/lake-house

Gilpin Lake House & Spa,
Crook, Windermere, LA8 8LN

Gilpin Hotel

Gilpin is one of the loveliest places to stay in the country, simple as that. It's a family affair and delivers at every turn, its staff delightful, its Michelin-starred food divine, its interiors a treasure trove of beautiful things. It is one of those rare places that never stands still and recent additions include five stunning spa chalets above a small lake and a second restaurant serving pan-Asian food. Despite all this, it remains an English country-house hotel. A cool elegance flows throughout with smouldering fires, Zoffany wallpapers, gilded mirrors, flowers everywhere. An elegant sitting room runs into a chic bar, where doors open onto a terrace for Pimm's in the sun; magnolia trees, cherry blossom and a copper beech wait in the 20-acre garden. Bedrooms are divine: crisp linen, smart fabrics, robes in beautiful bathrooms. The garden suites have hot tubs, the spa suites have saunas, too. As for the food, it's all whisked up by Hrishikesh Desai (who won Chefs On Trial to land his job), perhaps chilli-glazed lobster, spring lamb with masala sauce, Yorkshire rhubarb with Bergamot panna cotta. *Minimum stay: 2 nights at weekends.*

Rooms	8 doubles, 12 twin/doubles: £365-£715. 11 suites for 2: £545-£715. Special rates for three or more nights.
Meals	Dinner included; non-residents £70. Sunday lunch, £35. Tasting menu, £90. Afternoon tea from £22.50.
Closed	Never.

Tel	+44 (0)15394 88818
Email	hotel@thegilpin.co.uk
Web	www.thegilpin.co.uk

Gilpin Hotel,
Crook Road, Bowness-on-Windermere,
Windermere, LA23 3NE

Linthwaite House

The hotel sits perched on a hill with views over Windermere, woods and peaks. Smartly-dressed staff greet you as you park your car and take you through newly-planted gardens to the front door of this Arts and Crafts house. Service is on wheels here. Chef Ritu Dalmia is in charge of the kitchen and her passion for Italian food is evident, only made better by such good local ingredients. Visit the Lakes Library to plan your days: boat trips, steam trains, walks near and far, visits to Cartmel, Hilltop or Grasmere. You don't really need to lift a finger, it can all be organised for you. There are mountain bikes to borrow, wellies to put on; fishing can be sorted either in the hotel's own tarn or further away – one-to-one fly fishing lessons too. The gardens will be stunning when they have become more established and the terrace is a dreamy place to sit with a drink. This is an indulgent sort of place that people like to return to year after year.

Rooms	30 twin/doubles: £306-£454.
	6 suites for 2. £492-£684.
Meals	Lunch, 3 courses, from £24.95.
	Dinner, 3 courses à la carte, £58.
Closed	Rarely.

Tel	+44 (0)15394 88600
Email	stay@linthwaitehouse.com
Web	www.linthwaitehouse.com

Linthwaite House,
Crook Road, Bowness-on-Windermere,
Windermere, LA23 3JA

Dome House

Dome House featured on Grand Designs in 2011 and is architecturally intriguing, with quirky interiors and floor-to-ceiling windows of coloured glass. It's set on a hill above Bowness and has stunning views down to Lake Windermere. Phil and Joyce live in a private apartment in the house and are very warm and welcoming. Breakfast hampers are delivered to your room at a time of your choosing: yoghurt, granola, berries, charcuterie, cheese, bread and pastries – you'll find tea and coffee already in your room, along with some chocolates and Brambleberry gin. The big, open-plan sitting room on the top floor has a dining table and kitchen plus a wood-burner and board games, and the large indoor heated swimming pool opens out onto the garden. Walk for 5-10 minutes downhill for the nearest good restaurants and pubs in town – your hosts' can help you organise a trip in your own private chartered yacht.

Rooms	2 doubles: £200-£250.
	1 suite for 2: £250-£300.
Meals	Continental breakfast included.
	Pubs/restaurants 10-minute walk.
Closed	Christmas, 3-31 January.

Dome House,
Brantfell Road,
Bowness on Windermere, LA23 3AE

Tel	+44 (0)7957 073251 (mobile)
Email	stay@domehouselakes.co.uk
Web	www.domehouselakes.co.uk

Cedar Manor Hotel

A small country house on the edge of Windermere with good prices, pretty interiors and delicious food. Jonathan and Caroline love it here and are incredibly proud of the world they've created. There's a smart terrace at the front, a comfy sitting room, and some seriously fancy bathrooms. This 19th-century Victorian-Gothic house was once home to a retired vicar, hence the ecclesiastic windows. Outside, an ancient Himalayan cedar shades the lawn. Inside, cool colours and an easy style flow throughout. The big sitting room doubles as the bar and comes in browns and creams with sofas and local art. Bedrooms – some warmly traditional, others nicely contemporary – have Zoffany fabrics and flat-screen TVs; the bathroom in the coach-house suite is out of this world. You eat in a pretty dining room or on the terrace in good weather, perhaps smoked haddock and Morecambe Bay shrimp mousseline, local lamb with dauphinoise potatoes, and the Lakeland classic – sticky toffee pudding to finish. The brand-new Windermere Jetty Museum is on your doorstep. *Minimum stay: 2 nights at weekends.*

Rooms	7 doubles, 1 twin: £145-£245.
	2 suites for 2: £245-£395.
	Singles £125-£455.
Meals	Dinner £35-£45.
Closed	Rarely.

Tel	+44 (0)15394 43192
Email	info@cedarmanor.co.uk
Web	www.cedarmanor.co.uk

Cedar Manor Hotel,
Ambleside Road,
Windermere, LA23 1AX

The Black Bull

This smartly refurbished 17th-century coaching inn has an easy-going atmosphere, lots of bedrooms, a suntrap picnic area and walks in the Yorkshire Dales on the doorstep. Off the main street so it's a stroll to all the town's attractions including heaps of bookshops, a weekly farmers' market, restaurants, antiques and a fabulous tea room above a boutique gift shop. Nina and James are very hands-on and passionate about provenance – from Herdwick

blankets to locally roasted artisan coffee. Nina bakes the breakfast bread and pastries, they do their own smoking and curing and there's a little kitchen garden at the back. Choose from any kind of breakfast, including vegan, sample inventive cooking by the fire in the cosy bar; the airy restaurant with floor-to-ceiling windows looks out onto the street. Sedbergh is one of the UK's three book towns – even the bus shelter has a selection. The Dales Way footpath leaves from your door and you can reach the Howgill Fells in ten minutes; Kendal and Windermere are just under half-an-hour's drive away.

Rooms	14 doubles, 2 twin/doubles: £99-£165. 1 suite for 2: £185.
Meals	Starters from £6.50. Mains from £12.95.
Closed	Never.

The Black Bull,
44 Main Street, Sedbergh, LA10 5BL

Tel	+44 (0)1539 620264
Email	bookings@theblackbullsedbergh.co.uk
Web	www.theblackbullsedbergh.co.uk

The Black Swan

A lovely small inn in the middle of a pretty village that's surrounded by blistering country. It's all things to all men – a smart restaurant, a lively bar, pretty rooms – and very dog-friendly. A stream runs through the big garden, where you can eat in good weather; free-range hens live in one corner. Inside, chic country interiors fit the mood perfectly. You get fresh flowers, tartan carpets, games and books galore. There's a bar for local ales, a sitting-room bar with an open fire, but the hub of the hotel is the bar in the middle, where village life gathers. You can eat wherever you want – there's an airy restaurant, too – so dig into delicious country fare, with meat from the hills around you, perhaps a tasty home-made soup, Galloway beef and root vegetable stew, sticky toffee pudding with vanilla ice cream. Pretty bedrooms are fantastic for the money. Expect warm colours, beautiful linen, smart furniture, super bathrooms; one suite has a wood-burner. Stunning walking waits, the Lakes and Dales are close, children and dogs are welcome. A very happy place.

Rooms	5 doubles, 1 twin/double: £85-£115. 4 suites for 2: £120-£145. 6 annexes for 2: £105-£150. Singles £75-£140. 3 double bell tents available.
Meals	Lunch from £4.50 Dinner, 3 courses, £25-£30.
Closed	Never.

Tel	+44 (0)15396 23204
Email	enquiries@blackswanhotel.com
Web	www.blackswanhotel.com

The Black Swan,
Ravenstonedale,
Kirkby Stephen, CA17 4NG

Augill Castle

Augill is a one-off, a folly castle in beautiful country. It may look grand, but it's anything but – Simon and Wendy run their home with a rod of pure sponge. It's wonderfully informal and children love it. There are no uniforms, no rules, you just come to kick off your shoes and relax. You can do this in various places: on sofas in front of the fire in the hall; by a grand piano in the music room; in the honesty bar that opens onto a terrace; or in the cinema in the old potting shed. Breakfast is served in a vast dining room under a fine, ornate ceiling – local bacon, eggs from resident hens, homemade breads and jams. Elsewhere, panelled walls, roaring fires, books, art and antiques. Colourful bedrooms are all different. Some are enormous, one has a wardrobe in the turret, you'll find big bathrooms, bold colours and vintage luggage. Cottages are good for families and there's lots for children to do – dressing up boxes, five acres of gardens, a treehouse and playground, too. The Dales and the Lakes are close, but sybarites may just want to stay put. You can come to get married, too. *Minimum stay: 2 nights at weekends.*

Rooms	3 doubles, 4 four-posters: £160-£220. 1 suite for 2, 1 suite for 4: £200-£320. 3 cottages for 4: £220-£300. Singles from £100.
Meals	Dinner £25-£30. Supper platters £15. Afternoon tea £18. Children's high tea £10.
Closed	Never.

Augill Castle,
South Stainmore,
Kirkby Stephen, CA17 4DE

Tel	+44 (0)17683 41937
Email	enquiries@stayinacastle.com
Web	www.stayinacastle.com

Rothay Manor Hotel

This tranquil 1820s country house has retained much of its original character, and is surrounded by mature gardens with no immediate neighbours so feels private. Jamie and Jenna run the place along with their team of friendly staff. Bedrooms are comfortable and generous in size, and all include seating areas – one room has a hot tub. This is the kind of place where dogs aren't just tolerated but welcomed, and there are several dog-friendly rooms with wooden floors and private garden areas. Settle next to a roaring fire in the lounge with a good book and a drink from the bar, head to the Brathay Lounge for a light lunch or casual dinner, or treat yourself to a lavish afternoon tea or a tasting menu in the fine dining restaurant. Ambleside is a 10-minute walk for a wide selection of shops, restaurants and art galleries, and Lake Windermere is just a short stroll further. *Minimum stay: 2 nights at weekends.*

Rooms	16 twin/doubles: £155-£375.
	2 suites for 2: £260-£350.
	1 single: £155.
Meals	Dinner, 3 courses, £55. 5-course tasting menu, £65. Afternoon tea, £21.50.
Closed	Start of January.

Tel	+44 (0)1539 433605
Email	hotel@rothaymanor.co.uk
Web	www.rothaymanor.co.uk

Rothay Manor Hotel,
Rothay Road, Ambleside, LA22 0EH

Lancrigg

There's nothing stuffy about this rambling old house on a hillside bang in the middle of the Lake District. A friendly informality pervades the place, so everyone will feel completely at home, from families with young ones to lone walkers. You can drink and snack in the cosy and stylish Poet's Bar, once the old library, or get down to more serious eating in the dining room. This is where the hotel's chef creates imaginative feasts, inspired by vintage recipes, using the very best of local, seasonal ingredients. Simon and his friendly staff look after you well. While the kids run wild in the woodland playground, relax in the sitting room by the fire, drink in those outstanding views, and tell yourself you're going to go for a bracing walk soon. Wordsworth found this house an inspiring place to stay, and so will you. *Minimum stay: 2 nights at weekends.*

Rooms	5 doubles, 3 twins: £79-£220. 2 family rooms for 4: £79-£220. Extra bed/sofabed £30-£45 p.p.p.n.
Meals	Breakfast £8-£12. Lunch from £12.95. Dinner à la carte, 4 courses, £39.95.
Closed	15 January to early February.

Lancrigg,
Easedale Road,
Grasmere, LA22 9QN

Tel	+44 (0)1539 435317
Email	info@lancrigg.co.uk
Web	www.lancrigg.co.uk

Borrowdale Gates

If you want deep peace, spectacular landscapes and a slice of luxury in a stylish hotel, you'll find it here. This is Borrowdale, an unchanged corner of the rural idyll, "the loveliest square mile in Lakeland" to quote Alfred Wainwright. High peaks encircle you, sheep graze the fields, the river Derwent potters past. The view from the top of High Seat is one of the best in the Lakes, with Derwentwater sparkling under a vast sky. Lowland walking is equally impressive: long or short, high or low, Borrowdale delivers. At the end of the day roll back to this lovely hotel. Big windows downstairs frame majestic views. You get binoculars, the daily papers, afternoon tea in front of roaring fires or out on the terrace in summer. Bedrooms are great value for money, with warm colours, super beds and smart bathrooms. Some open onto terraces, several have small balconies, all have the view. As for the restaurant, a wall of glass looks out over the village and beyond, a fine spot for a good meal, perhaps hand-dived scallops, fell-bred lamb, lemon tart with cassis sorbet.

Rooms	18 twin/doubles: £214-£288. 3 suites for 2: £262-£318. 4 singles: £106-£116. All prices include dinner.
Meals	Light lunch from £8. Dinner included; non-residents £35.50-£44. Afternoon tea from £16.50. Sunday lunch £27.50.
Closed	3-24 January.

Tel	+44 (0)17687 77204	Borrowdale Gates,
Email	hotel@borrowdale-gates.com	Grange-in-Borrowdale,
Web	www.borrowdale-gates.com	Keswick, CA12 5UQ

The Royal Oak at Keswick

Step off a pedestrianised high street, into a cosily traditional haunt. This much-loved inn beside Keswick's old Moot Hall, with its old dark quarry tiles, long narrow bar, swish wallpapers and comfy seating attracts a diverse crowd: walkers, holiday makers, families, suits. Now it's pulling in diners too, with accessible menus and local supplies. The crispy duck spring rolls are delicious for kids, although they might be tempted by smaller portions of the hearty mains such as sausage and mash with cider apple chutney. Arrive early and pick a seat by a fire, then order homemade fish pie with parsley mash and mop up bread (winter doesn't get cosier than this); leave room for pear and apple crumble. Most of Thwaites' cask ales are available, and well-kept. The wines are good, the landlord is interested, the staff are obliging, and there's always a water bowl for a walker's dog. There are delightful bedrooms too; all welcome dogs, and the largest are fabulous for families. They even have parking passes for further up the street – a boon in popular Keswick.

Rooms	19 doubles: £70-£140.
Meals	Starters from £4.95. Mains from £8.95.
Closed	Never.

The Royal Oak at Keswick,
Main Street, Keswick, CA12 5HZ

Tel	+44 (0)1768 773135
Email	relax@royaloakkeswick.co.uk
Web	www.royaloakkeswick.co.uk

Howtown Hotel

Welcome to Howtown, a world lost in time on a lane that goes nowhere on the quiet side of Ullswater. The position here is heavenly – water, mountain, field and sky – one of the best in the Lakes. The house sits in its own hamlet, dates to 1640, and has been welcoming guests for 117 years, a licensed farmhouse that has passed though five generations of the same family, who still run sheep and cattle on 400 acres of Lakeland fell. Inside, the past lives on: a panelled bar, William Morris wallpaper, smouldering coal fires, wall clocks and lots of brass. Homely bedrooms upstairs have simple pleasures: good beds, sheets and blankets, toile throws, fabulous views. Most are en suite, three have bathrooms one step across the landing. Dinner is old-school – you're summoned by a gong – then served at oak tables with a beautiful dresser at one end of the dining room. The food is a joy, perhaps Stilton soufflé, loin of venison, steamed marmalade pudding; there's a walkers' café and a locals' bar, too. David has an amphibious car for the odd lake cruise. Walks start from the front door. Matchless. *No email – phone enquiries only.*

Rooms	8 doubles; 3 twin/doubles with separate bathrooms: £112-£208 incl. dinner. 1 single sharing shower: £112 incl. dinner. 2 cottages for 5, 2 for 7: £420-£800.
Meals	Lunch from £4.50. Packed lunch £8.50. Dinner incl. Sunday lunch £20.
Closed	10 November to mid-March.

Tel	+44 (0)17684 86514
Web	www.howtown-hotel.co.uk

Howtown Hotel,
Ullswater, Penrith, CA10 2ND

Another Place – The Lake

This is a fantastic contemporary renovation of a Lakeland country house hotel. It sits on Ullswater in 18 beautiful acres that roll down to the lake shore. Both hotel and water offer lots to do. You can paddle board on the lake, jump in for a swim, or set off to explore in a kayak. If that sounds too energetic, head back to the hotel for sofas to sink into and an indoor 20-metre pool where walls of glass frame the view and adults reign after 6pm. The main building dates to 1714 and comes with ornate ceilings, marble fireplaces, the odd panelled wall. You'll find an airy restaurant for super food, then sofas and banquettes in The Living Space, a child-friendly place to stop and eat, play games by the fire in the library, or slip onto the sun-trapping terrace where views shoot across the lake to mountains soaring beyond. There's a gym, a hot tub, a sauna and treatment rooms, and forest school for kids. Rooms have fine beds, the best linen, robes in smart bathrooms. Most have the view, some have baths that look the right way. There's a kitchen garden, a croquet lawn, and wellies at the front door, too.

Rooms	28 twin/doubles: £180-£205.
	6 suites for 2, 6 suites for 5: £285-£385.
	Singles from £120. Extra bed from £40.
Meals	Lunch from £7. Dinner, 3 courses, £40.
Closed	Never.

Another Place – The Lake,
Watermillock, Penrith, CA11 0LP

Tel	+44 (0)1768 486442
Email	life@another.place
Web	www.another.place/the-lake

The Crown Inn

In the middle of Pooley Bridge, behind its smartly traditional façade, the Crown Inn has had a thoroughly stylish makeover. The indoor spaces have a contemporary country inn feel: a mix of upholstered wall seating, stable-style stalls and separate chairs and tables; wooden floors and plaid carpeting; open fires and wood-burning stoves; subtle lighting and the dramatic statement of a glazed rear wall separating the dining room from the great outdoors. Decked ground and first floor terraces (with heated, sheltered 'pods')

make the absolute most of lovely river views backed by woodland and high fells – Ullswater Steamers ply from a pier a few hundred metres away. There's a whole range of drinks, including Thwaites cask ales of course. Family-friendly and modern bistro-style dishes, like grilled sea bass and lamb shank with puy lentils, are served by attentive staff; it's an efficiently-run, busy place. And upstairs (no lift), in different shapes and sizes to fit the old building, are the good-looking, comfortable bedrooms, with chic rustic touches in traditional materials and fabrics – and pristine bathrooms.

Rooms	12 double, 1 twin: £50–£149. 1 suite for 4; 3 family rooms for 4: £93-£174. Dogs £15. Ground floor accessible room available.
Meals	Light bites from £3. Starters from £5. Lunch from £6.50. Mains from £10.
Closed	Rarely.

Tel	+44 (0)1768 425869
Email	relax@crowninnpooleybridge.co.uk
Web	www.crownpooleybridge.co.uk

The Crown Inn,
Pooley Bridge, Penrith, CA10 2NP

Askham Hall

Askham is a dream, one of the loveliest houses in the Lakes. It's a Grade I-listed manor house with a 12th-century peel tower, but grand as it is, Charlie grew up here and it retrains the feel of home, making it a delightfully informal base. Expect contemporary art and open fires, a beautiful drawing room with an honesty bar, a small spa with an outdoor pool, then a café for lunch and gardens that open to the public. The hall sits in 40 acres of prime Cumbrian grazing land with paths that follow a river into glorious parkland. It's all part of the Lowther estate, where Charlie rears his own meat for Richard Swale's kitchen. As for the food, it's out of this world, ambrosial stuff that makes you want to move in permanently. You might find Askham pork cheek and barbecued hock, rough fell lamb with wild garlic risotto, Yorkshire rhubarb tart with brown butter ice cream; a kitchen garden and two polytunnels provide much for the table. Chic bedrooms have a cool country-house style (Prince Philip loved his). Some are vast, one has a tented bathroom, others have views to Knipe Scar. One of the best.

Rooms	11 twin/doubles: £150-£260. 4 suites for 2: £250-£320. Extra bed/sofabed £35 p.p.p.n.
Meals	Lunch from £9. Dinner, 3 courses, £50; 5-course tasting menu £65.
Closed	Sundays and Mondays. January and early February.

Askham Hall,
Askham, CA10 2PF

Tel	+44 (0)1931 712350
Email	enquiries@askhamhall.co.uk
Web	www.askhamhall.co.uk

George and Dragon

Charlie Lowther has found a new head chef, award-winning Gareth Webster, who does perfect justice to the slow-grow breeds of beef, pork and lamb produced on the Lowther Estate – and you'll find lovely wines to match. Ales and cheeses are local, berries and mushrooms are foraged, vegetables are home-grown. Our twice-baked cheese soufflé with a hint of spinach was divine. As for the long low coaching inn, it's been beautifully restored by craftsmen using wood, slate and stone, and painted in colours in tune with the period. Bare wooden tables, comfy sofas, intimate alcoves and crackling fires make this a delightful place to dine and unwind; old prints and archive images tell stories of the 800-year-old estate's history. Outside is plenty of seating and a lawned play area beneath fruit trees. Upstairs are bedrooms of varying sizes (some small, some large and some above the bar), perfectly decorated in classic country style. Carpeting is Cumbrian wool, beds are new, ornaments come with Lowther history, showers are walk-in, baths (there are two) are roll top, and breakfast is fresh and delicious.

Rooms	11 twin/doubles: £100-£160. Singles £85-£119. Extra bed/sofabed £25 p.p.p.n.
Meals	Lunch & dinner from £12. Sunday lunch from £12.95.
Closed	26 December.

Tel	+44 (0)1768 865381	George and Dragon,
Email	enquiries@georgeanddragonclifton.co.uk	Clifton, Penrith, CA10 2ER
Web	www.georgeanddragonclifton.co.uk	

Yorkshire

The Talbot Malton, page 331

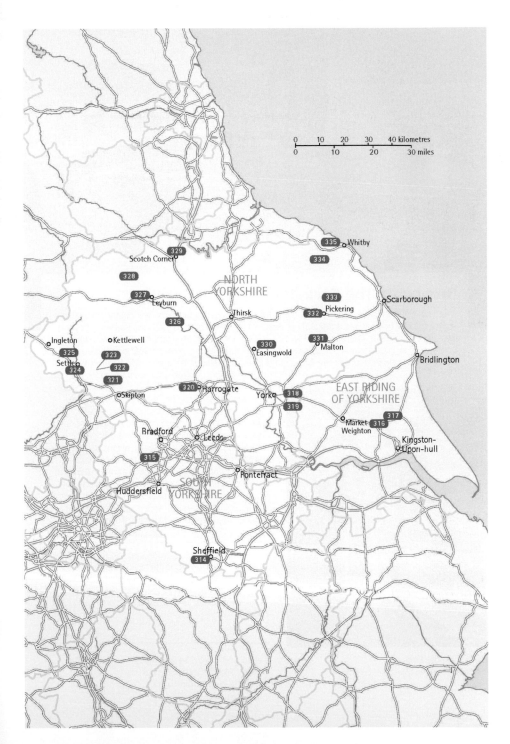

0   10   20   30   40 kilometres
0   10   20   30 miles

335 Whitby
334

NORTH
YORKSHIRE

329
Scotch Corner

328

327 Leyburn   333   Scarborough
326   Thirsk   332 Pickering

Ingleton   Kettlewell   331 Malton
325   330
323   Easingwold   Bridlington
Settle   322
324   EAST RIDING
321   OF YORKSHIRE
Skipton   320 Harrogate   York 318
319
316 317
Bradford   Leeds   Market   Kingston-
Weighton   Upon-hull
315
Pontefract
Huddersfield   SOUTH
YORKSHIRE

Sheffield
314

Brocco on the Park

Sheffield is a friendly city, an arty hub that's full of surprises, a fact ably demonstrated by this stunning small hotel. It sits amid leafy streets, with a smart park to the front, then hills beyond that ripple over to the Peak District. Picasso stayed here when he attended the World Peace Conference in 1950, though things have changed a little since – a recent refit has turned this into a small-scale pleasure dome. Downstairs, there's a Scandi feel in the café/kitchen, with joggers and dog walkers swapping the park for delicious smoothies or a slice of cake. Bedrooms are divine, as good as they look. Expect the best white linen, smart neutral colours, the coolest bathrooms with robes and organic oils. A vast window in one room opens to frame the view; another has a free-standing bath; all are named after birds, their colours reflected in the fabrics. Back downstairs, tasty food waits at night, perhaps cauliflower and pistachio fritters, rib-eye steak with wild mushrooms, spiced plum crumble with vanilla ice cream. Don't miss the Millennium Gallery, the Winter Garden or the cool streets around you.

Rooms	6 doubles, 2 twin/doubles: £110-£240. Extra bed/sofabed £35 p.p.p.n.
Meals	Breakfasts from £7. Lunch from £7. Dinner from £12. Sunday lunch from £16.
Closed	Rarely.

Brocco on the Park,
92 Brocco Bank, Sheffield, S11 8RS

Tel	+44 (0)114 266 1233
Email	hello@brocco.co.uk
Web	www.brocco.co.uk

The Shibden Mill Inn

The rambling and beautifully renovated old corn mill is hidden in a tranquil wooded valley overlooking Red Beck, just minutes from the hustle and bustle of Halifax; at night, the peaceful stream-side terrace is floodlit and heated, for idyllic summer drinking. An unstuffy integrity lies at the heart of Simon Heaton's welcoming inn, from the front-of-house warmth to the pubby bar where locals gather for a natter over a pint of Shibden Bitter. From the modern British kitchen innovative dishes flow: sumac pork fillet with fondant potato, turnip, peach and red wine jus; curried monkfish tail with sauté potatoes, peas and lobster sauce; mango and passion fruit cannelloni with white chocolate mousse, almond and chocolate crumb. There are beams and timbers, roaring log fires and stone-flagged floors, deep sofas and soothing colours in the cosy, candlelit bar and dining rooms, and the wine list is impressive. Refurbished bedrooms are comfortable, individual and decorated with warmth and style, with big beds, bold colours, Roberts radios and smart tiled bathrooms.

Rooms	10 doubles: £95-£186.
	1 suite for 2: £202-£238.
Meals	Lunch & dinner from £14.
	Sunday lunch £15.
Closed	Rarely.

Tel	+44 (0)1422 365840	The Shibden Mill Inn,
Email	enquiries@shibdenmillinn.com	Shibden Mill Fold,
Web	www.shibdenmillinn.com	Shibden, Halifax, HX3 7UL

Beverley Arms

This 17th-century coaching inn was once the grande dame of Beverley and has now been rescued from the doldrums. It's a buzzing place full of ladies who lunch, deeply efficient staff and excellent food from fine dining to a home cooked pie and good local ale at the bar. There are plenty of places to unwind – lounges with comfy seating areas and blazing fires, a restaurant in the conservatory, a terrace with a fire pit, and two bars – one for champagne, the other cosy and overlooking lovely St Mary's church. Discover homemade biscuits on the tea tray in your room, and the full Yorkshire breakfasts include black pudding – late risers can choose from the brunch menu. Eat in at the all-day restaurant or walk down the road for Michelin-starred dining at The Westwood. You're also two minutes from the Market Square and lots of good shops. Explore the 15th-century North Bar gate and the fine Gothic church of Beverley Minster. *Minimum stay: 2 nights stay on some weekends. Check when booking.*

Rooms	38 twin/doubles: £100-£200.
Meals	Lunch from £8. Dinner from £12.
Closed	Never.

Beverley Arms,
25 N Bar Within, Beverley, HU17 8DD

Tel	+44 (0)1482 296999
Email	relax@beverleyarms.co.uk
Web	www.thwaites.co.uk/hotels-and-inns/inns/beverley-arms-at-beverley/

Tickton Grange

This fine Georgian manor house surrounded by four acres of formal gardens, parklands and fields was once the home of wealthy landowners – King Edward VIII used to play cards here – and is now a family-run country house hotel. Feel pampered by meticulous attention to detail: dinner that looks like a work of art served on specially commissioned and hand-painted Royal Crown Derby china; drinks afterwards in the stylish library; dressing gowns, slippers and eye masks in your room, plus handmade truffles on your pillow. Start the day with breakfast – scrambled eggs and local-cured salmon, croissants, freshly squeezed juices and specially blended coffee. Visit Beverley or Hull, join the Hockney trail, take a trip to the coast and return to stroll the grounds and enjoy an afternoon tea that could put the Ritz to shame – dainty cakes and scones with champagne or a G&T – the bar has 45 varieties.

Rooms	17 doubles, 1 twin/double, 1 twin: £120-£150. 2 suites for 2: £200.
Meals	Lunch from £9.95. Dinner, 2-3 courses, £35-£45
Closed	Never.

Tel	+44 (0)1964 543666
Email	info@ticktongrange.co.uk
Web	www.ticktongrange.co.uk

Tickton Grange,
Main Street, Tickton,
Beverley, HU17 9SH

Judge's Lodging

In the centre of York is a handsome Georgian townhouse with a strikingly luxurious interior. In the cellar: vaulted rooms, cool tunes, stone floors, Farrow & Ball colours, quirky mismatched furniture. Upstairs: a pair of dining rooms, grand, elegant and eye-catching. Vintage grey-blue panelling, tall sash windows, semi-circular sofas, illuminated sculptures. All is cosy but classy, and the service is informal but attentive. The food is impressive too, and packed with flavour so tuck into the likes of slow cooked beef and Thwaites ale pie with clapshot potatoes and buttered kale, or a warming helping of moules frites. The wines are wide-ranging and the beers are Thwaites. Join the punters on the galleried decked terrace and unwind, then treat yourself to a stay in a room with feature wallpapers and fabulous beds. The garden rooms in the courtyard are small and can be noisy, so pay more for the smartest and quietest at the top of the house, one with an original marble fireplace and a York Minster view. Breakfasts are generous.

Rooms	21 doubles: £110-£125.
Meals	Starters from £5. Mains from £12.
Closed	Rarely.

Judge's Lodging,
9 Lendal, York, YO1 8AQ

Tel	+44 (0)1904 638733
Email	relax@judgeslodgingyork.co.uk
Web	www.judgeslodgingyork.co.uk

The Parisi Hotel

This lovely small hotel makes a great base for a night or two in glorious York. It stands within the Roman wall, opposite St Denys Church, which lost its spire to cannon fire in the Civil War. It's all the work of two sisters, Sophie and Maria, who renovated from top to toe, bringing a chic, colourful style to this Victorian rectory. Inside, you'll find original art on every wall in the airy breakfast room, sofas in front of the wood-burner in the beautiful library, then a door that leads out to a gravelled courtyard, where you can sink into wicker armchairs when the sun shines. Bedrooms are just as good: cool colours, smart fabrics, excellent beds, '60s retro furniture. You get lots of art, coffee machines, iPhone players, flat-screen TVs. Some rooms are smaller, all have sparkling bathrooms, one has a free-standing bath in the room. Cross the river, weave through lanes, arrive at York Minster, one of the largest Gothic cathedrals in Europe. Back at the hotel, five excellent restaurants wait within 200 metres. Northern Soul nights take place locally, too. You won't want to leave. *Minimum stay: 2 nights at weekends.*

Rooms	10 doubles: £99-£189.
	1 suite for 2: £179-£229.
Meals	Restaurants 2-minute walk.
Closed	3 weeks in January.

Tel	+44 (0)1904 658815
Email	info@theparisi.com
Web	www.theparisi.com

The Parisi Hotel,
51 St Denys Road, York, YO1 9QD

West Park Hotel

Harrogate made its name in Georgian England as a spa town for the gentry. These days it holds the title of 'happiest place to live in Britain. ' It's also one of the prettiest, with grand houses, leafy streets and the Stray, 200 acres of park and gardens that unfurls itself directly opposite this stylish hotel. Outside, you can sit at tables and watch the world go by. Inside, the bar and restaurant come as one, a lively spot that draws a crowd and comes with leather booths, chic bar stools, lots of colour and style. Cocktails, locals ales, wines from around the world all wait, as does some excellent bistro food, perhaps moules marinière, rack of lamb, apple and caramel tart. Bedrooms are lovely: crisp linen, the best mattresses, smart TVs and cool bathrooms. Bigger rooms at the front overlook the Stray, smaller ones at the back share the same style. Stay on a Sunday night and you can 'eat your bill;' whatever you spend on dinner will be removed from the cost of your room! Don't miss the Turkish baths or the gardens at Harlow Carr.

Rooms	11 doubles, 6 twin/doubles: £125-£245. 6 suites for 2, 2 suites for 4: £205-£365. Singles from £110. Extra bed £10.
Meals	Breakfast from £3.95. Lunch from £6.50. Dinner, 3 courses, £25-£40. Sunday lunch from £14.95.
Closed	Never.

West Park Hotel,
19 West Park Road, Harrogate, HG1 1BJ

Tel	+44 (0)1423 524471
Email	enquiries@thewestparkhotel.com
Web	www.thewestparkhotel.com

The Angel Inn

The old drovers' inn remains staunchly, reassuringly traditional – but offers wines that have come, over the years, to rival the hand-pumped Yorkshire ales. There's even a 'cave' for functions and private-party tastings. Expect nooks, crannies, beams and crackling fires, and a stylish restaurant. Thought has gone into every detail, from the antique furniture in the timbered rooms (one with a marvellous oak-panelled bar) to the fabrics and the colours. Menus change with each season and include dishes ranging from filo 'moneybags' of seafood in lobster sauce – the fish comes fresh from Fleetwood – to their own Yorkshire twist on tapas ('Yapas'!). Vegetarians are well looked after and the sticky toffee pudding is legendary. Exquisite bedrooms, split between the converted barn and adjacent Sycamore House, are all different; perhaps a French armoire, a brass bed, a claw-foot bath, a private garden. All have top-quality fabrics, pretty colours, cosy bathrooms, and, in the newer rooms, a contemporary feel. The glorious up-hill-and-down-dale drive to get here is part of the charm.

Rooms	9 doubles: £150-£175. 5 suites for 2: £175-£200. Singles from £125. Extra beds £25.
Meals	Lunch from £7.50. Bar meals from £15.95. Dinner, 3 courses, £35-£55. Sunday lunch £24.50.
Closed	Christmas Day & 1 week in January.

Tel	+44 (0)1756 730263
Email	info@angelhetton.co.uk
Web	www.angelhetton.co.uk

The Angel Inn,
Hetton, Skipton, BD23 6LT

The Lister Arms at Malham

You'll be hard pushed to find a finer looking pub in a more gorgeous village. The National Trust's Malham is a favourite with potholers (this part of Yorkshire is rich with caverns) but there are many surface pleasures to be had too. Sitting on the edge of the village green, the 17th-century coaching inn was once home to the first Lord of Ribblesdale and very grand it looks too. Don't stand on ceremony: inside are flagged floors, wood-burning stoves and well-kept local ales. Darren also puts an interesting menu together using mostly local produce. You could start with game galantine, and move onto blackened prawn and salmon stroganoff; if you have room, finish with rum soaked apple and sultana crumble. Staying the night? Choose a contemporary new room in the cottage, or head upstairs to one of the comfy bedrooms with calm colours, lovely linen and pristine bathrooms; many have views over the village green to the hills beyond. The barn has beautiful bedrooms, a shared lounge with a wood burner, and a warm welcome for families and dogs.

Rooms	12 doubles, 6 twins: £80-£182. 5 family rooms for 4: £110-£182. Singles £80-£130.
Meals	Breakfast from £5. Lunch from £8. Dinner from £12. Sunday lunch £13.50.
Closed	Rarely.

The Lister Arms at Malham,
Malham, Skipton, BD23 4DB

Tel	+44 (0)1729 830444
Email	relax@listerarms.co.uk
Web	www.listerarms.co.uk

Beck Hall

You'll feel instantly at home here with either Andy or Louise at the helm aided by a happy team of staff. Huge sliding glass doors allow guests to spill out from the restaurant into the pretty streamside garden. Malham is a mecca for walkers with the famous cove just under a mile away and Janet's Foss, Gordale scar and the Tarn not much further. This is some of the most stunning and remote countryside in the UK and it's great for cycling as well as striding.

Wild swimmers will be happy too with rivers, lakes and waterfalls to hurl themselves into. And dogs will love it all as much as their owners. Gird your loins for breakfasts of thick cut back bacon from the local farm shop, bangers from happy pigs and free-range eggs from the Dales. The restaurant, which is also open to the public, specialises in good, seasonal and local food cooked simply. Sleep well in comfortable bedrooms, all very different, all beautifully dressed, and dog-friendly too – beds, mats and bowls can be provided for your hound. *Minimum stay: 2 nights at weekends.*

Rooms	21 doubles, 5 twins: £75-£135.
	5 family rooms for 3: £95-£135.
Meals	Lunch from £6.95. Dinner, 3 courses,
	£56. Afternoon tea from £14.95.
Closed	Never.

Tel	+44 (0)1729 830729
Email	stay@beckhallmalham.com
Web	www.beckhallmalham.com

Beck Hall,
Cove Road, Malham, BD23 4DJ

The Golden Lion

Generations of travellers have enjoyed the welcome at this grand 17th-century coaching inn; following a recent renovation its doors are open to all. Original features have been saved, including smooth oak floors, a fabulous inglenook fireplace in the grand entrance hall and the graceful sweeping staircase; comfortable sofas and chairs are upholstered in checked tartan wool. Locally sourced ingredients dominate a menu which places its emphasis on comfort: try Settle Pudding (tender braised beef with a suet lid) and homemade fish pie with parsley mash, and, if you can find room, the sticky toffee pudding is a must. The elegant but cosy dining room with its pleasingly mismatched furniture, panelled walls and old photos buzzes with friendly chat. If you're a Three Peaks bagger, a devotee of the stunning Settle to Carlisle railway or simply want to get away from it all you can stay in characterful bedrooms with five-star mattresses, white cotton bed linen, immaculate bathrooms, smart TVs and fresh milk for your morning cuppa. The historic town is worth exploring: lose yourself in its cobbled alleyways.

Rooms	14 twin/doubles: £75-£130. Family room from £100.
Meals	Lunch from £6.95. Bar meals from £5.95. Dinner from £8.95.
Closed	Rarely.

The Golden Lion,
Duke Street, Settle, BD24 9DU

Tel	+44 (0)1729 822203
Email	relax@goldenlionsettle.co.uk
Web	www.goldenlionsettle.co.uk

The Traddock

A northern outpost of country-house charm, beautiful inside and out. It's a family affair and those looking for a friendly base from which to explore the Dales will find it here. You enter through the drawing room – crackling fire, pretty art, the daily papers, cavernous sofas. Potter about and find polished wood in the dining room, panelled walls in the breakfast room, then William Morris wallpaper in the sitting room bar, where you can sip a pint of Skipton ale while playing Scrabble. Bedrooms are gorgeous, some coolly contemporary, others warmly traditional. The stars of the show are the suites – sand-blasted timbers, lovely big sofas, stunning free-standing baths – but all are charming, with warm colours, comfy beds and the odd claw-foot bath. Downstairs, a white-washed sitting room opens onto the garden for afternoon tea, while delicious food waits in the restaurant, perhaps seafood chowder, braised lamb shank, apple and calvados mousse. Walks start at the front door, there are cycle tracks, even caves to explore (one is bigger than St Paul's). Unbeatable. *Minimum stay: 2 nights at weekends March-Nov.*

Rooms	8 doubles, 1 twin/double: £95-£165. 2 suites for 2: £180-£235. 2 family rooms for 4: £95-£175.
Meals	Lunch from £9.50. Dinner, 3 courses, around £30. Picnics from £7.50. Afternoon tea from £15.95.
Closed	Never.

Tel	+44 (0)1524 251224
Email	info@thetraddock.co.uk
Web	www.thetraddock.co.uk

The Traddock,
Austwick, Settle, LA2 8BY

The White Bear Hotel

At five o'clock on Friday evenings there's only one place to be in Masham: the tap room of the White Bear, home of Theakston's beer. The great and the good gather to mark the end of the week, the odd pint is sunk, the air is thick with gossip. Interior design is 1920s trapped in aspic: red leather, polished brass, a crackling fire. But there's only half the story. Slip next door and discover this welcoming inn. There's a smart dining room, stripped boards in the bar, a flower-filled terrace for lunch in the sun. Stylish rooms occupy the old Lightfoot brewery and come in contemporary style, with warm colours, comfy beds, chic new bathrooms and attractive prices. Some have views across town, the penthouse is vast and open to the rafters. There's a courtyard for guests, a sitting room, too; staff will bring drinks if you want privacy and peace. Good food waits in the restaurant, perhaps king scallops, duck with red cabbage, treacle sponge pudding. Tours of the brewery are easily arranged, with a pint of your choice at the end. Don't miss the beer festival in June or the sheep fare in September.

Rooms	12 twin/doubles: £130-£125. 1 suite for 2: £200. 2 family rooms for 4: £130-£155. Extra bed £15 per night. Dogs £15 per night.
Meals	Lunch from £5. Bar meals from £11.95. Dinner, 3 courses, about £30.
Closed	Never.

The White Bear Hotel,
Wellgarth, Masham, Ripon, HG4 4EN

Tel	+44 (0)1765 689319
Email	sue@whitebearmasham.co.uk
Web	www.thewhitebearhotel.co.uk

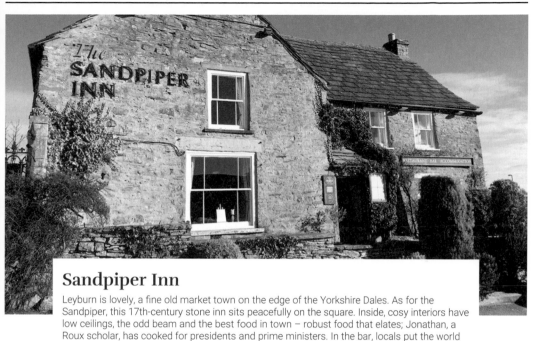

Sandpiper Inn

Leyburn is lovely, a fine old market town on the edge of the Yorkshire Dales. As for the Sandpiper, this 17th-century stone inn sits peacefully on the square. Inside, cosy interiors have low ceilings, the odd beam and the best food in town – robust food that elates; Jonathan, a Roux scholar, has cooked for presidents and prime ministers. In the bar, locals put the world to rights over pints of Black Sheep while contemplating irresistible menus: salted squid or roasted chorizo if you fancy Yorkshire tapas;

battered haddock or omelette Arnold Bennett if you want to explore the bar menu; or the full works in an attractive dining room, perhaps cheese soufflé, Swinton venison, dark chocolate marquise with white chocolate ice cream. Whisky lovers will appreciate the large collection of malts behind the bar. Upstairs, two simple bedrooms have a warm country feel with robes and good showers in the bathrooms. The Dales is one of the most beautiful places in England. Don't miss the roast rib of beef for Sunday lunch or the market in the square on Fridays.

Rooms	2 doubles: £95–£110.
Meals	Lunch from £8.50. Bar meals from £5. Dinner from £10.95. Sunday lunch, 3 courses, £25.20.
Closed	Rarely.

Tel	+44 (0)1969 622206
Email	hsandpiper99@aol.com
Web	www.sandpiperinn.co.uk

Sandpiper Inn,
Railway Street, Leyburn, DL8 5AT

The Burgoyne Hotel

It's utterly peaceful here at this elegant hotel in the North Yorkshire Dales and you're looked after beautifully by a friendly team. You can set up camp in the lounge in front of a roaring open fire where there are books, games and magazines. Bring bikes or hire them from two minutes away (there's a lockable shed for when you get back) and head to the hills, pack a picnic and walk all day without meeting another soul, spot rare birds including lapwings, explore 14th-century Bolton Castle or historic Richmond. Stroll along the river or visit the craft shops in town, return to a big tea of sandwiches and scones with cream or save yourself for pre-dinner drinks and canapés then à la carte in the smartly renovated 1783 Bar & Restaurant.

Rooms	7 doubles, 2 twin/doubles; 1 double, 1 twin both with separate bathrooms: £105-£250. Singles £105. Extra beds for children under 12: £40.
Meals	Dinner, 3 courses, £38. Tasting menu £60.
Closed	3-31 January.

The Burgoyne Hotel, Reeth, Richmond, DL11 6SN	**Tel** +44 (0)1748 884292
	Email enquiries@theburgoyne.co.uk
	Web www.theburgoyne.co.uk

Middleton Lodge

You'll think you've washed up in Tuscany or Provence. These gorgeous stone barns were crumbling a few years ago, now they're home to one of the loveliest hotels in the north. In summer, life spills onto the courtyard for lunch in the sun, but step through the arched glass doors and find a spectacular restaurant open to the rafters, where contemporary design mixes with rustic bricks and mortar. There's a funky bar, an open fire, a sitting room for guests that opens onto a terrace. Rooms are just as good, with chic fabrics, radios, super-comfy beds, and robes in cool bathrooms. Five open onto a terrace, most have claw foot baths. Elsewhere, you'll find a couple of treatment rooms, a two-acre kitchen garden where you can get married, and six beautiful new rooms in the renovated farmhouse. Good food waits, some home-grown, much from Yorkshire, perhaps cured sea trout with horseradish, slow cooked lamb with onion broth, chocolate with caramel and banana ice cream. The Dales wait to the west, the Moors to the east. Don't miss the Bowes museum in Barnard Castle.

Rooms	15 doubles: £160-£240. 2 family rooms: £210-£270. 12 suites for 2: £210-£360. Cot available.
Meals	Lunch from £5.50. Dinner, 3 courses, £30-£35. Not Mon or Tue mid Oct to mid-March. Sunday lunch from £12.50.
Closed	Never.

Tel	+44 (0)1325 377977
Email	info@middletonlodge.co.uk
Web	www.middletonlodge.co.uk/coach-house

Middleton Lodge,
Middleton Tyas, Richmond, DL10 6NJ

The Durham Ox

Find this cosy pub at the picturesque top of the Grand Old Duke of York's hill – it's the heart of the village. There's a lot of space to enjoy – sit outside in the beer garden, sample one of their locally brewed gins in the bar with a board-game or book the private dining room with its own pre-dinner sitting area and log burner. Food is excellent – classic British from fresh, local ingredient; try queenie scallops followed by steak cauliflower and cumin fritters with roasted monkfish. There's plenty for vegans too. Sleep in country-house style rooms in the old farmworkers' cottages, wake up to a Bloody Mary and a buffet breakfast. There are great walks straight from the door; the hour long Crayke estate Walk takes you across the Howardian Hills, through beautiful woodland, over the river Foss and past views of Crayke Castle – bring the dog too.

Rooms	4 cottages for 2, 1 cottage for 4: £120-£180. 1 studio for 2: £150. Singles £100-£150. Extra bed £30 p.p.p.n.
Meals	Lunch & dinner £8.95-£26.95. Bar meals from £6.95. Sunday lunch from £15.
Closed	Never.

The Durham Ox, Westway, Crayke, York, YO61 4TE	**Tel** +44 (0)1347 821506
	Email enquiries@thedurhamox.com
	Web www.thedurhamox.com

The Talbot Malton

A 17th-century coaching inn owned by the Fitzwilliam estate, not far from Castle Howard. It stands on the edge of town with Malton's streets on one side and country views on the other. There's a croquet lawn, a terrace for lunch, and paths that lead down to the river. Inside, an easy elegance abounds. A fire burns in the drawing room, you find fresh flowers, lovely art, the daily papers and cavernous sofas. Bedrooms have chic fabrics, warm colours and botanical prints on the walls. Several have the view, all have robes in gorgeous bathrooms. Now to the serious stuff – delicious local food. Malton, an ancient market town, is the food capital of Yorkshire, with a festival every May that was started by the estate. No surprise then to discover the hotel serves the best Yorkshire produce. They also run a cookery school and have food trails to follow – to pie shops, vineyards, local farms and breweries. Dinner, predictably, is a treat, perhaps twice baked cheddar soufflé, roasted cauliflower and salsa rosso or venison and claret pie. There's a farmers' market every other Saturday. *Minimum stay: 2 nights at weekends.*

Rooms	23 doubles: £110-£190. 2 suites for 4, 1 suite for 2: £270-£320.
Meals	Lunch from £4.95. Bar meals from £10.95. Dinner, 3 courses, about £35. Sunday lunch from £20. Afternoon tea from £19.50.
Closed	Rarely.

Tel	+44 (0)1653 639096
Email	reservations@talbotmalton.co.uk
Web	www.talbotmalton.co.uk

The Talbot Malton,
45-47 Yorkersgate,
Malton, YO17 7AJ

The White Swan Inn

A characterful old building that stands on Market Place, where farmers set up shop on the first Thursday of the month. The exterior is 16th century and flower baskets hang from its mellow stone walls. Inside, you find stripped floors, open fires, a tiny bar, beautiful windows. The restaurant is at the back – the heart and soul of the inn – with delicious food flying from the kitchen, perhaps Whitby fishcakes, rack of spring lamb, glazed lemon tart with blood-orange sorbet. Excellent bedrooms are scattered about. Those in the main house (which may be noisier) are old-fashioned with padded bedheads, Osborne & Little fabrics and flat-screen TV/DVDs; bathrooms have robes and Bath House oils. Rooms in the courtyard tend to be bigger and come in crisp contemporary style with black-and-white screen prints, mohair blankets and York stone bathrooms. You'll also find the Bothy here, a quiet residents' sitting room, with a huge open fire, cathedral ceilings and an honesty bar. The moors are all around: fabulous walking, Castle Howard and Whitby all wait. *Minimum stay: 2 nights at weekends.*

Rooms	Singles £115-£179. Dinner, B&B £105-£125 per person. Extra bed/sofabed £20 p.p.p.n.
Meals	Lunch from £5.25. Dinner, 3 courses £25-£35. Sunday lunch from £12.95.
Closed	Never.

The White Swan Inn,
Market Place, Pickering, YO18 7AA

Tel	+44 (0)1751 472288
Email	welcome@white-swan.co.uk
Web	www.white-swan.co.uk

The Horseshoe Inn

This handsome old pub takes pride of place at the head of lovely Levisham, a magnet for train enthusiasts – the North Yorks Moors railway runs through the bottom of the valley. You're guaranteed the warmest of welcomes in the Horseshoe with its beamed bar and pleasing pub menu which promises the likes of Whitby haddock with chunky chips, and steak and ale pie. Well-kept Black Sheep Best Bitter and Yorkshire Moors from the local Cropton Brewery keeps the real ale lovers happy – park yourself in front of a roaring fire with a pint and the paper after a stroll through nearby Dalby Forest. There's so much to do and see locally you'll want to make a night or two of it; opt for one of the lofty and light 'garden rooms' with big beds and spanking new bathrooms. If you fancy a fabulous view down the village, take a cosy room above the pub. The elegant suite has its own garden, a wood-burner, honesty wine rack and big sofa to snuggle on; take the spiral staircase to your airy bedroom under the eaves. Either way, this is the ideal base for some serious yomping or a trip on the steam train.

Rooms	6 doubles, 5 twin/doubles: £90-£150. 1 suite for 2. £150. 2 singles: £45.
Meals	Lunch from £5.50. Bar meals from £6.95. Dinner from £11.50. Sunday lunch, 3 courses, £23
Closed	Rarely.

Tel	+44 (0)1751 460213
Email	info@horseshoelevisham.co.uk
Web	www.horseshoelevisham.co.uk

The Horseshoe Inn,
Main Street, Levisham,
Pickering, YO18 7NL

Broom House at Egton Bridge

As lovely a place to stay on the moors as you could hope for. You wind your way in – up dale, down hill – with a carpet of purple heather in late summer and a golden fleece of bracken in autumn. As for this attractive house, it sits on the edge of a pretty village, with fine views of Esk Dale from the garden terrace. Inside, airy interiors are stylish and comfortable, the perfect tonic after a day in the hills. Downstairs, there's a sitting room with garden views, then a dining room for Michael's delicious breakfasts – Whitby kippers, Glaisdale bacon, smoothies from garden strawberries. In summer, you decant onto the terrace for birdsong with your bacon and eggs. Stylish rooms have warm colours, comfy beds, white cotton, perhaps a sofa or doors onto the terrace. All have fine bathrooms, one with a free-standing bath. By day you explore the moors, spin over to Whitby or try a leg of the coast-to-coast path, which passes outside. At night you follow the river into the village for dinner at one of its pubs. Michael and Georgina look after you in style. Pure bliss. *Minimum stay: 2 nights at weekends.*

Rooms	4 doubles: £89-£130. 1 suite for 2, 1 suite for 4: £139-£200.
Meals	Two good pubs in village.
Closed	1 November – 1 March.

Broom House at Egton Bridge,
Broom House Lane,
Egton Bridge, Whitby, YO21 1XD

Tel	+44 (0)1947 895279
Email	mail@broom-house.co.uk
Web	www.broom-house.co.uk

Estbek House

A cute little find on the Whitby coast, a friendly restaurant with rooms ten paces from the beach at Sandsend. It's small, intimate and very welcoming. Tim cooks brilliantly, David talks you through his excellent wine list and passes on the local news. Cliffs rise to the north, the beach runs away to the south, ducks on the river occasionally waddle across the road. There's a terrace at the front for drinks in summer and a small bar on the lower ground, where you can watch Tim at work in his kitchen. Upstairs, two dining rooms swim in coastal light and come with stripped floors and white tablecloths. People come from miles around for the seafood – the lobster thermidor is a big draw – but carnivores are well looked after, so try home-smoked salmon with a gin and tonic jelly, stuffed pork tenderloin or Whitby crab, strawberry and champagne trifle. Bedrooms – smallish on the first floor, tiny on the second! – have crisp linen and shuttered windows. Breakfast is delicious, David's mum makes the marmalade. Cliff walks and the moors wait, and you can follow the river up to Mulgrave Castle.

Rooms	5 doubles: £200-£255. Price includes dinner.
Meals	Dinner, 3 courses, included; non residents, about £35.
Closed	2 January – 12 February.

Tel	+44 (0)1947 893424
Email	info@estbekhouse.co.uk
Web	www.estbekhouse.co.uk

Estbek House,
East Row, Sandsend, Whitby, YO21 3SU

North East

Rose & Crown, page 338

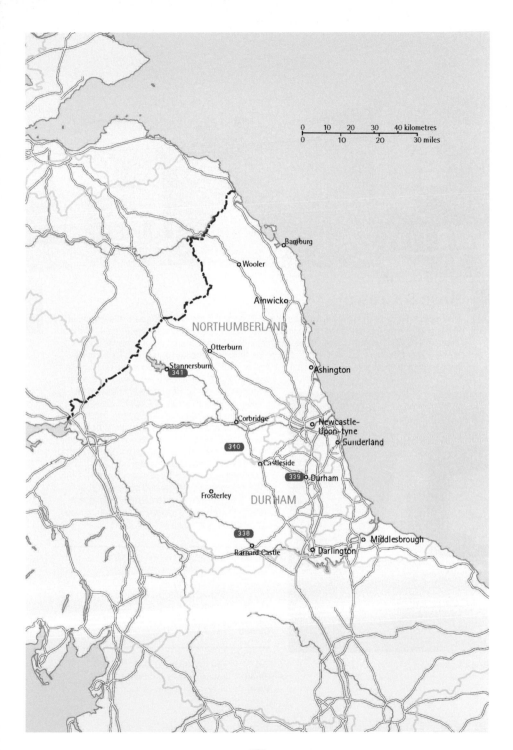

0   10   20   30   40 kilometres
0   10   20   30 miles

Bamburg

Wooler

Alnwick

NORTHUMBERLAND

Otterburn

Stannersburn
341

Ashington

Corbridge

Newcastle-
Upon-tyne

Sunderland

310

Castleside

339 Durham

Frosterley

DURHAM

338

Middlesbrough

Barnard Castle

Darlington

Rose & Crown

Romaldkirk is one of those lovely villages where little has changed in 200 years. It sits peacefully in the north Pennines, lost to the world and without great need of it. As for the Rose & Crown, it dates to 1733 and stands on the village green next to a Saxon church. Roses ramble across stone walls at the front, so grab a pint of local ale, then sit in the sun and watch life pass by. Inside, you can roast away in front of a fire in the wonderfully old-school bar while reading the *Teesdale Mercury*. There's a peaceful sitting room for afternoon tea, then a panelled restaurant for excellent food, perhaps local Raby Estate venison pie followed by white chocolate panna cotta and pistachio ice cream. Thomas and Cheryl bought the place in 2012 and have been spending money on it ever since: it has never looked better. Stylish rooms – some in the main house, others out back, a couple in a cottage next door – have warm colours, comfy beds, Bose sound systems and super bathrooms. Don't miss High Force waterfall, the magnificent Bowes Museum or the sausage sandwich at lunch. Dogs are very welcome.

Rooms	7 doubles, 3 twins: £115-£160. 2 suites for 2: £180-£200. 1 cottage for 4: £115-£200. Singles £95. Dinner, B&B from £79 per person.
Meals	Lunch from £10.50. Dinner, 3 courses, from £27. Sunday lunch £19.50.
Closed	23-27 Dec & 1 week in January.

Rose & Crown,
Romaldkirk, Barnard Castle, DL12 9EB

Tel	+44 (0)1833 650213
Email	hotel@rose-and-crown.co.uk
Web	www.rose-and-crown.co.uk

The Victoria Inn

An old-school drinking bar in the middle of Durham: no music, no fruit machines, just original Victorian interiors trapped in aspic. There's a roaring fire, ancient wallpaper, pints of Big Lamp and lots of local banter. In the old days, shawled ladies would pop in to retrieve an errant husband. These days it's students, bar-room philosophers and beers lovers who drop by. It's not to everyone's taste – if you want boutique interiors and impeccable service, look elsewhere – but those who like to quaff a pint or two with the odd portrait of Queen Victoria hanging on the wall will love it. Bedrooms upstairs aren't huge and those by the road can get noisy, but all have honest prices and are a good base for exploring the city. Most have been partially refurbished in the last two years and come with lots of colour and good bathrooms. Some have brass beds, others Fleur de Lys wallpaper; the family room up in the eaves is large and airy with a contemporary style. Big breakfasts wait downstairs, Durham starts at the front door: cobbled streets, riverside walks, university and cathedral. Good restaurants wait nearby, Hadrian's Wall is close.

Rooms	4 doubles, 1 twin: £70-£90.
	1 family room for 4: £85.
	Singles £70-£87.
Meals	Toasted sandwiches £1.50.
Closed	Rarely

Tel	+44 (0)1913 865269
Email	mwebstervictoria@gmail.com
Web	www.victoriainn-durhamcity.co.uk

The Victoria Inn,
86 Hallgarth Street, Durham, DH1 3AS

Lord Crewe Arms at Blanchland

Originally the abbot's lodge and kitchens (and its garden the cloisters), the Lord Crewe Arms has become a Grade II*-listed inn. The village, in a sheep-clad valley on the moors' edge, was built with stone from the abbey's ruins. Inside: ancient flags, inglenook fireplaces, fortress walls and a classy country décor. Public areas range from lofty to intimate and the atmospheric bar is in the vaulted crypt. With a head chef from Mark Hix's 'stable', the robust

modern British menu includes steaks, chops and spit-roasted meats, fresh crab salad and ruby beets. Puddings hark back to ancient times: sea buckthorn posset, rhubarb fumble. Wines include great burgundies and clarets, ales range from Allendale's Golden Plover to Nel's Best from High House Farm, and there are water bowls for dogs in the garden. If you stay, you're in for a treat. Most bedrooms are divided between The Angel, a simple, beautiful, listed ex-inn across the way, and the former tied cottages. Some rooms have exposed stone walls and real fires, all have soft carpets, fine fabrics, divine beds and deep baths.

Rooms	19 doubles: £119-£192.
	1 suite for 2: £144-£212.
	1 family room for 4: £189-£252.
Meals	Lunch & dinner from £12.75.
	Sunday lunch, 2-3 courses, £18-£24.
Closed	Rarely.

Lord Crewe Arms at Blanchland,
The Square, Blanchland, DH8 9SP

Tel	+44 (0)1434 677100
Email	enquiries@lordcrewearmsblanchland.co.uk
Web	www.lordcrewearmsblanchland.co.uk

The Pheasant Inn

A super little inn lost in beautiful country, the kind you hope to chance upon. The Kershaws run it with great passion and an instinctive understanding of its traditions. The bars are wonderful. Brass beer taps glow, 100-year old photos of the local community hang on stone walls, the clock above the fire keeps perfect time. Fires burn, bowler hats and saddles pop up here and there, varnished ceilings shine. House ales are expertly kept, Timothy Taylor's and Wylam waiting for thirsty souls. Fruit and vegetables come from the garden, while Robin's lovely food hits the spot perfectly, perhaps twice-baked cheese soufflé, slow-roasted Northumberland lamb, brioche and marmalade bread and butter pudding; as for Sunday lunch, *The Observer* voted it 'Best in the North'. Bedrooms in the old hay barn are light and airy, cute and cosy, great value for money. You're in the Northumberland National Park – no traffic jams, not too much hurry. You can sail on the lake, cycle round it or take to the hills and walk. For £10 you can also gaze into the universe at the Kielder Observatory (best in winter). Brilliant. *Pets by arrangement.*

Rooms	4 doubles, 3 twins: £110-£120.
	1 family room for 4: £135-£155.
	Singles £80-£85.
Meals	Bar meals from £9.95.
	Dinner, 3 courses, £20-£30.
	Sunday lunch from £12.50.
Closed	Christmas.

Tel	+44 (0)1434 240382
Email	stay@thepheasantinn.com
Web	www.thepheasantinn.com

The Pheasant Inn,
Stannersburn, Hexham, NE48 1DD

Channel Islands

The Old Court House, page 344

Alderney

CHANNEL
ISLANDS

Herm

Guernsey

Sark

Jersey
St Aubin
St Helier

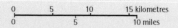
0   5   10   15 kilometres
0   5   10 miles

The Old Court House

This lovely hotel sits on St Aubin's harbour with views across the bay to St Helier and beyond. Outside, there's a sun-trapping terrace where you can watch sailing boats come and go. Inside, you find the star of the show, this beautiful house that mostly dates to 1610, but comes with a 13th-century granite staircase, too. Downstairs, there's an airy bar, then a restaurant split between two rooms. One has the feel of a galleon's dining quarters and featured as Diamond

Lil's bar in the TV series *Bergerac*. The other, the old courthouse itself, has ancient walls of golden stone, then hanging lamps, painted beams and the original fireplace. Both are a delight, as is the food: lots of fresh seafood, delicious duck, sticky toffee pudding; a bistro below is popular with locals. Cute rooms have a soft, chic style: a wall of beautiful paper, white linen for Hypnos mattresses, super little bathrooms with big power showers. Two have slipper baths, one has a hot tub on a private terrace. As for Jersey, expect sandy beaches, gardens and galleries, castles and cliff-top walks. You can surf, sail and kayak, too.

Rooms	7 twin/doubles, 1 four-poster: £100-£300. 2 singles: £50-£75.
Meals	Lunch from £4.95. Restaurant: Dinner, 3 courses, about £35. Bistro: mains from £10.95. Sunday lunch from £14.95.
Closed	Never.

The Old Court House,
Le Boulevard, St Aubin,
St Brélade, JE3 8AB

Tel	+44 (0)1934 863963
Email	info@oldcourthousejersey.com
Web	www.oldcourthousejersey.com

The Georgian House

Alderney is pristine – miles of sandy beaches, ancient coastal forts, cliff-top walks and nature trails, wild flowers and migrating birds. It's a slice of heaven and where else to stay than this quirky island bolthole, part village inn, part restaurant with rooms, part friendly chic hotel. After 30 years holidaying here, Holly's family bought one of their favourite places, whipped it into shape and now it's the beating heart of the island, a magnet for locals and visitors alike. It sits on St Anne's cobbled high street, opposite the art-house cinema; filmgoers sneak over for drinks in the interval. Downstairs, the bar comes with wooden floors, an open fire and lots of gossip. An airy restaurant spills onto a sun-trapping courtyard in summer, a fine spot for the freshest seafood, delicious steaks, island ice creams. Bedrooms – some in the hotel, others across the road in their sister hotel, The Victoria – are just the ticket: not huge, but deeply comfy, with lovely beds, the odd stone wall and cute bathrooms. Hire bikes, grab a picnic, laze about on the beach. Night skies amaze. A perfect island adventure.

Rooms	2 doubles, 2 twin/doubles: £85-£95. Singles £65-£80. Extra bed/sofabed £30 p.p.p.n.
Meals	Light lunch from £6. Dinner, 3 courses, £25-£30.
Closed	Never.

Tel	+44 (0)1481 822471
Email	info@georgianalderney.com
Web	www.georgianalderney.com

The Georgian House,
Victoria Street, Alderney, GY9 3UF

Wales

Penally Abbey, page 356

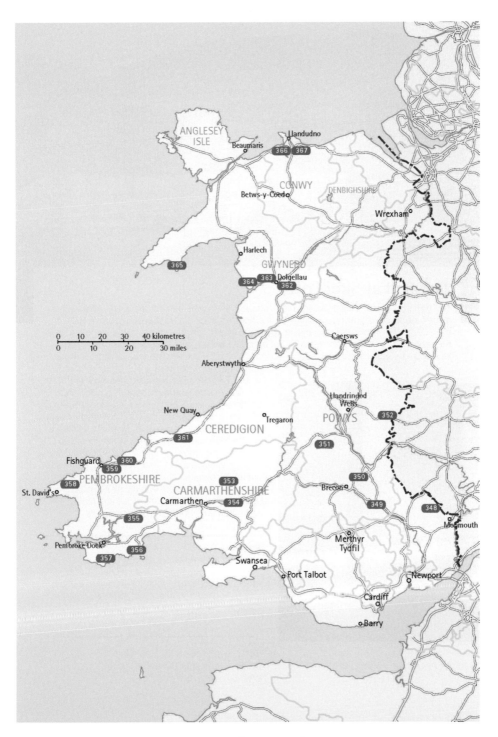

ANGLESEY
ISLE
Beaumaris
Llandudno
366 367
CONWY
DENBIGHSHIRE
Betws-y-Coed
Wrexham

Harlech
GWYNEDD
365
364 363 Dolgellau
362

Caersws

0   10   20   30   40 kilometres
0   10   20   30 miles

Aberystwyth

Llandrindod
Wells
New Quay
POWYS
352
Tregaron
CEREDIGION
361
351
Fishguard 360
359
PEMBROKESHIRE
353
350
358
CARMARTHENSHIRE
Brecon
St. David's
Carmarthen 354
349 348
355
Monmouth
Merthyr
Tydfil
Pembroke Dock
356
357
Swansea
Newport
Port Talbot

Cardiff

Barry

The Bell at Skenfrith

The position here is magical: an ancient bridge, a river snaking through the valley, glorious hills rising beyond, cows grazing in lush fields. It's a perfect spot, not least because providence blessed it with this chic little inn. Inside, you find a locals' bar, sofas in front of a wood-burner in the sitting room, The Dog and Boot bar for dogs and walkers with muddy boots, then an airy restaurant for some very good food. In summer, life spills onto a stone terrace with views, or beside the river Monnow – a fine spot for lunch in the sun. Elegant country-house bedrooms brim with light. Some are beamed, most are big, you'll find padded bedheads, Farrow & Ball colours, perhaps a walnut bed or a claw-foot bath in your room. Those at the front have river views, those at the back look onto the hills, some have sofas, all have robes in excellent bathrooms. Seven circular walks start at the door with maps provided. Delicious food awaits your return, perhaps Welsh rarebit with poached egg, braised beef brisket with dauphinoise potatoes, apple doughnuts with toffee sauce and mulled cider. *Minimum stay: 2 nights at weekends.*

Rooms	5 doubles, 3 twin/doubles, 3 four-posters: £150-£250. Singles £90. Dinner, B&B £190-£270 per person.
Meals	Lunch from £5.95. Sunday lunch from £14.95. Dinner, 3 courses, around £38.
Closed	Rarely.

The Bell at Skenfrith,
Skenfrith, Abergavenny, NP7 8UH

Tel	+44 (0)1600 750235
Email	enquiries@skenfrith.co.uk
Web	www.skenfrith.co.uk

Gliffaes Hotel

A charming country-house hotel that towers above the river Usk as it pours through the valley below. In summer, doors open onto a large terrace, where you can sit in the sun and soak up the view – red kites circle above, sheep graze beyond. You're in 35 peaceful acres of formal lawns and mature woodland. Afternoon tea 'on the house' is served every day in the panelled sitting room – family portraits hang on the wall, logs crackle in the grandest fireplace. This is a well-known fishing hotel and fishermen often gather in the bar for a quick drink and a tall tale. Eventually, they spin into the restaurant and dig into lovely seasonal food (the hotel is part of the Slow Food Movement), perhaps goat's cheese soufflé, fillet of halibut, lemon tart with passion fruit sorbet. Country-house bedrooms wait above. Expect smart fabrics, warm colours, crisp linen, fresh flowers. Several have river views, a couple have small balconies, one has a claw-foot bath that overlooks the front lawn. Outside, beautiful gardens include a small arboretum of specimen trees. Wonderful. *Minimum stay: 2 nights at weekends.*

Rooms	19 twin/doubles: £115-£298. 4 singles: £115-£145. Dinner, B&B £137-£187 per person. Extra bed/sofabed £25 p.p.p.n.
Meals	Light lunches from £5. Sunday lunch £22-£29. Dinner, 3 courses, £42.
Closed	29 December – 25 January.

Tel	+44 (0)1874 730371
Email	calls@gliffaeshotel.com
Web	www.gliffaeshotel.com

Gliffaes Hotel,
Gliffaes Road, Crickhowell, NP8 1RH

The Felin Fach Griffin

Quirky, homespun, colourful: feel like you're staying in the home of a fashionable old friend, with bright art splashed on the walls and pretty bedrooms (some fresh from a spruce up) decked out in antiques. Bring four-legged friends to run around the grassy beer garden, where you can enjoy al fresco lunches. They take food and drink seriously here. Supper is served in the white-walled restaurant, with stock pots simmering on an Aga and a little shop selling homemade piccalilli. Much of what you eat comes from a half-acre kitchen garden, with meat and game from the hills around you, plus a full vegan spread. Breakfast is leisurely: read the morning papers, make your own toast, choose the full Welsh works. A road passes outside, but quietly at night, while lanes lead into the hills. Come to walk, ride, bike, canoe. Hay is close for books galore.

Rooms	3 doubles, 3 twin/doubles: £140-£180. 1 family room for 3: £180-£205. Singles £115-£145. Dinner, B&B £98-£118 p.p.
Meals	Lunch from £12. Dinner, 3 courses, from £29-£35. Sunday lunch from £16.
Closed	Christmas & 4 days in January.

The Felin Fach Griffin,
Felin Fach, Brecon, LD3 0UB

Tel	+44 (0)1874 620111
Email	enquiries@felinfachgriffin.co.uk
Web	www.felinfachgriffin.co.uk

Lake Country House & Spa

An elegant country-house hotel lost in beautiful hills with deep peace all around. Fifty acres of lawns, lakes and ancient woodland wrap around you, there's a spa with treatment rooms, an indoor pool and a tennis court by the lake. You can sit in a hot tub and watch guests fish for their supper, try your luck on the nine-hole golf course, saddle up nearby and take to the hills. Come home to afternoon tea in the old-school drawing room, where an archipelago of rugs warms a brightly polished wood floor and chandeliers hang from the ceiling. The hotel opened over a hundred years ago; leather-bound fishing logs date to 1894 and a feel of the 1920s lingers. Fires come to life in front of your eyes, grand pianos and grandfather clocks sing their songs, snooker balls knock about in the distance. Dinner is a treat, perhaps crab with wasabi ice cream, duck with fennel and honey, blood orange cheesecake with chocolate sorbet. Lovely rooms wait. Most are suites: those in the house are warmly traditional, those in the lodge softly contemporary. The London train takes four hours and stops in the village.

Rooms	6 twin/doubles: £195.
	24 suites for 2: £240-£260.
	Singles from £145. Dinner, B&B from £122.50 p.p.; minimum 2 nights.
Meals	Lunch, 3 courses, £22.50, Dinner, 4 courses, £38.50.
Closed	Never.

Tel	+44 (0)1591 620202
Email	info@lakecountryhouse.co.uk
Web	www.lakecountryhouse.co.uk

Lake Country House & Spa,
Llangammarch Wells, LD4 4BS

The Harp

Chris, Angela and their friendly team run this ancient Welsh longhouse, tucked up a lane near the parish church, as an authentic country pub: unfussy, well-loved and honestly traditional. Find 14th-century slate flooring in the bar, tongue-and-groove in a room that fits a dozen diners, crannies crammed with memorabilia, an ancient curved settle, an antique reader's chair, two fires and a happy crowd. Accompany a pint of Wye Valley or Three Tuns bitter with locally sourced steak and chips, sea bass with salsa verde, or a vegan or vegetarian dish. Or take a simple ploughman's to a seat in the garden and gaze at the spectacular Radnor valley views. The menus change every six weeks. Five comfy rooms have countryside views, colourful Welsh blankets, bright bathrooms (some are just showers) and a farmhouse feel. Big breakfasts set you up for a day of exploring the wonderful Radnor Valley, or dipping into the shops of Hay-on-Wye. Life in this tiny village, like its glorious pub, remains delightfully unchanged.

Rooms	1 double; 1 double with separate bathroom: £105-£115. 1 family room for 4, 2 family rooms for 3: £105-£185. Singles from £70.
Meals	Lunch from £5. Dinner from £10. Sunday lunch, 3 courses, from £22.
Closed	Rarely.

The Harp,
Old Radnor, Presteigne, LD8 2RH

Tel	+44 (0)1544 350655
Email	mail@harpinnradnor.co.uk
Web	www.harpinnradnor.co.uk

Ty Mawr Country Hotel

Pretty rooms, attractive prices and delicious food make this welcoming country house hard to resist. It sits in a very peaceful spot. You drive over hills, drop into the village, then wash up at this 16th-century stone house. Outside, a sun-trapping terrace laps against a trim lawn, which in turn drops into a passing river. Gentle eccentricities abound: croquet hoops take odd diversions, a seat has been chiselled into a tree trunk, there's boules for those who feel inclined. Inside, original stone walls and low beamed ceilings give a warm country feel. There are fires everywhere – one in the attractive sitting room that overlooks the garden, another in the dining room that burns on both sides. Excellent bedrooms, two of which are on the ground floor. You get big beds, warm colours, crisp linen, good bathrooms. Some have sofas, all are dog-friendly, three overlook the garden. Back downstairs, the bar doubles as reception, while Welsh art on the walls is for sale. Steve's cooking is the final treat, perhaps Cardigan Bay scallops, organic Welsh beef, calvados and cinnamon rice pudding. Top stuff. *Children over 10 welcome.*

Rooms	3 doubles, 3 twin/doubles: £115-£130. Singles £80.
Meals	Dinner £25-£30.
Closed	Rarely.

Tel	+44 (0)1267 202332
Email	info@wales-country-hotel.co.uk
Web	www.wales-country-hotel.co.uk

Ty Mawr Country Hotel,
Brechfa, Carmarthen, SA32 7RA

Wright's Food Emporium

This is one of those wonderful places you come across once every ten years, the sort that makes no effort to conform and so brings to life a quirky style that's delightful and authentic. It's a temple to local food – a café, a restaurant, a deli, and a wine shop, though it's not often you can sit in a wine shop, stick on a Bob Dylan LP and dig into glorious food washed down by organic wines. Its legion of fans come from near and far, with staff weaving through the throng to deliver manna from heaven. One room leads to another, all designed to please. You'll find tables crammed with delicious cakes; soups simmering away on the range; a fire and original flagstones in the back room; then a swish lean-to stuffed with curios and pot plants that opens onto a terrace. As for the deli, 'we sell the food we like' says Maryann of her culinary Aladdin's Cave. It's all fresh and local – breads, meat, eggs, vegetables, chutneys, jams, even chocolate. Two rustic-chic cottages are a steal for those wise enough to linger. Both come with kitchens you probably won't use. Don't think, just come, happiness waits.

Rooms	1 cottage for 4, 1 cottage for 6: £110-£280; £700-£1250 per week. Short breaks available.
Meals	Lunch from £6. Dinner, 3 courses, £25-£30.
Closed	Tuesdays.

Wright's Food Emporium,
The Golden Grove Arms,
Llanarthne, SA32 8JU

Tel	+44 (0)1558 668929
Email	maryann@wrightsfood.co.uk
Web	www.wrightsfood.co.uk

32 Townhouse

Narberth is lovely – quirky and colourful, lively and independent. It's wrapped up in Pembrokeshire's rolling hills with the coast and its path waiting ten miles south. As for this stylish restaurant with rooms, it sits on the high street, dates to 1820, and has a smart Georgian exterior with early Victorian bay windows. Inside, the style is hard to miss: Russian red in the bar with a picture of Gorbachev on the wall; then period green in the restaurant, where gilt-framed oils hang by the score. Potter about and find original tiles and ironwork, parquet floors and stained glass windows; the zinc-topped bar was made from a Methodist pulpit. There's a conservatory bistro that opens onto a pretty terrace for strong coffee, homemade quiche and posh burgers. Bedrooms above are soundproofed and come with smart beds, white linen, travertine bathrooms and attractive prices; some interconnect, others in the eaves have the odd beam. Delicious food waits downstairs, perhaps calamari with chorizo and fennel, chicken with braised shallots, toffee apple and blackberry crumble. A great little base.

Rooms	6 doubles, 2 twin/doubles: £85-£190.
Meals	Lunch from £4.95. Light bites from £7.45. Dinner, 3 courses, about £30.
Closed	23-26 December.

Tel	+44 (0)1834 218338
Email	info@32townhouse.com
Web	www.32townhouse.com

32 Townhouse,
32 High Street, Narberth, SA67 7AS

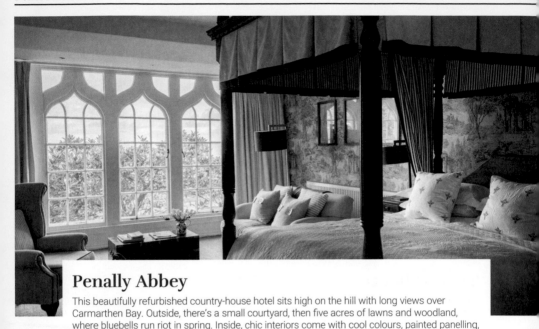

Penally Abbey

This beautifully refurbished country-house hotel sits high on the hill with long views over Carmarthen Bay. Outside, there's a small courtyard, then five acres of lawns and woodland, where bluebells run riot in spring. Inside, chic interiors come with cool colours, painted panelling, parquet flooring and the odd Doric column. There's an elegant bar in deep charcoal with fine art on the walls, then a big drawing room with an open fire and huge sea views. Big windows in the main house flood the rooms with light, while doors in the sunroom open onto a gravelled terrace, where you can read the papers, dig into afternoon tea, or fall asleep in the sun. Bedrooms have a stunning new look: off-white walls, beautiful beds, crisp white linen, elegant fabrics. Big rooms in the main house have vast windows to frame the view, all have sublime white marble bathrooms. You eat in style in the restaurant – period colours, grand chandelier – perhaps steamed clams with lemon and ginger, chicken with chestnuts and a pear tarte tatin, a dark chocolate tort with pistachio ice cream. There's fine coastal walking, too.

Rooms	3 doubles, 6 twin/doubles, 2 four-posters: £145-£265. Extra bed/sofabed £25 p.p.p.n.
Meals	Lunch from £5. Dinner, 3 courses, £30-£35. Sunday lunch from £14.95.
Closed	Rarely.

Penally Abbey,
Penally, Tenby, SA70 7PY

Tel	+44 (0)1834 843033
Email	info@penally-abbey.com
Web	www.penally-abbey.com

Stackpole Inn

This lovely inn sits in a village that's marooned in beautiful country. It's a few miles back from the sea, with Barafundle Bay – one of the finest beaches in Britain – a very short drive away. You can pick up the coastal path, too, and follow it round past Stackpole Quay and St Govan's Chapel to the cliffs at Linney Head, then the surfers at Freshwater West. It's pure heaven, one of those sleepy areas you drop into for a couple of days and hardly use your car.

As for the Stackpole, it's a great little base – stylish and welcoming with tasty rustic food, perhaps deep-fried whitebait, rib of local beef, almond and hazelnut tart. Outside, the pub is drenched in honeysuckle and there's a small garden to the front for a drop of Welsh ale in summer. Inside, you find low wooden ceilings, exposed stone walls, a hard-working wood-burner and four hand pumps at the slate bar. Super bedrooms have comfy beds, stripped floors, seaside colours and excellent bathrooms. All have sofabeds, two have velux windows for star gazing. Dogs and children are very welcome.

Rooms	2 twin/doubles: £90.
	2 family rooms for 4: £90-£120.
	Singles from £60.
Meals	Lunch from £5.
	Dinner, 3 courses, £25-£30.
	Sunday lunch, 3 courses, £18.95.
Closed	Rarely.

Tel	+44 (0)1646 672324
Email	info@stackpoleinn.co.uk
Web	www.stackpoleinn.co.uk

Stackpole Inn,
Stackpole, Pembroke, SA71 5DF

Crug Glas

St Davids is one of the most magical places in Britain. It sits in Pembroke's national park, has an imperious 12th-century cathedral, and is surrounded by magnificent coastline that's dotted with cliffs and vast sandy beaches. As for Janet's wonderful retreat, it's part chic hotel, part farmhouse B&B, stylish yet personal, a great place to stay. The house dates from 1120 and sits in 600 acres of arable and grazing land (they rear cattle and grow cereals). Outside, you find lawns and a small copse sprinkled with bluebells, then field and sky, and that's about it. Inside, there's an honesty bar in the sitting room and a Welsh dresser in the dining room, where Janet serves delicious food: homemade soups, home-reared beef, chocolate mousse with clotted cream. Fancy bedrooms are the big surprise: a vast four-poster, the odd copper bath, old armoires, beautiful fabrics. All have robes in gorgeous bathrooms, bigger rooms come with sofas, one room occupies most of the top floor. Two rooms in an old barn have exposed timbers and underfloor heating. The coast is about five fields to the west.

Rooms	5 doubles, 2 twin/doubles: £150-£190. Singles £110-£140.
Meals	Lunch, 2 courses, from £18. Dinner, 3 courses, £25-£30. Sunday lunch £22.50. Afternoon tea from £12.50.
Closed	22-27 December.

Crug Glas,
Solva, Haverfordwest, SA62 6XX

Tel	+44 (0)1348 831302
Email	info@crug-glas.co.uk
Web	www.crug-glas.co.uk

The Manor Town House

Fishguard is quirky – arty and friendly with a folk festival in May and a jazz festival in August. You'll find great coastal walks, sandy beaches and magical St Davids a few miles south. In short, it's much more than an overnight stop on your way to Ireland and, with a happy vibe waiting at the Manor Town House, hard to resist. Chris and Helen escaped London and have taken to their new world like ducks to water. Inside, you're greeted by a couple of gorgeous sitting rooms – stripped floorboards, cool colours, local art, and crackling fires in winter. One has an honesty bar, you get fresh flowers, lots of books, and comfy sofas from which to plan your day. Homely bedrooms have lots of charm: bold colours, beautiful fabrics, the odd antique, super-comfy beds. Those at the back have sea views, perhaps a sofa or a padded window seat, while compact bathrooms do the trick. Breakfast is a treat, there's a garden for afternoon tea overlooking the harbour, and it's a one-minute stroll up the road to Bar Five for cocktails. Pembrokeshire awaits. Brilliant.
Minimum stay: 2 nights at weekends in summer.

Rooms	2 doubles, 4 twin/doubles: £110-£145. Singles £80-£120. Extra bed/sofabed £15-£20 p.p.p.n.
Meals	Local restaurants within 100m. Packed lunches £10.
Closed	23-27 December.

Tel	+44 (0)1348 873260
Email	enquiries@manortownhouse.com
Web	www.manortownhouse.com

The Manor Town House,
11 Main Street, Fishguard, SA65 9HG

Llys Meddyg

This beautiful small hotel has a little bit of everything: chic bedrooms that pack a punch, a cellar bar for cocktails before dinner, a stylish restaurant for delicious local food. In summer you decant into the garden, where a café/bistro opens up for coffee and cake or pizza from a wood-fired oven. There's a smokehouse out here, too, then a yurt tucked away around the corner that comes with a wood-burner and a hot tub. It's an intimate place, where staff stop to chat, locals pop in for a coffee, and you can take home a jar of quince jelly made by Ed's mum. Food lies at the heart of the affair and you eat in a stylish restaurant with Welsh art on the walls, perhaps home-smoked salmon, slow-cook lamb, caramelised pear with blue-cheese ice cream. Beautiful bedrooms are scattered about. Those in the main house have cool colours, vast beds and fancy bathrooms. Those in the mews have a rustic feel and garden views; all have fluffy bath robes. Pembrokeshire's coastal path waits for windswept cliffs and sandy beaches. Don't miss St Davids or the Preseli Hills. Dogs are very welcome. *Minimum stay: 2 nights at weekends.*

Rooms	8 doubles: £100-£180.
	1 yurt for 2: £100-£120.
	Singles from £85.
Meals	Lunch from £7. Dinner from £14.
Closed	Rarely.

Llys Meddyg,
East Street, Newport, SA42 0SY

Tel	+44 (0)1239 820008
Email	info@llysmeddyg.com
Web	www.llysmeddyg.com

Penbontbren

You're lost in lovely hills, yet only three miles from the sea. Not that you're going to stray far. These gorgeous suites don't just have wonderful prices, they're heaped with comforts, too – this is a great spot to come and do nothing at all. Richard and Huw have thought it all through. You get crockery and cutlery, kettles and fridges, then you're encouraged to bring your own wine or to buy provisions from the farm shop for lunch. As for the suites, expect big beds, super bathrooms, sofas and armchairs in pretty sitting areas, then doors onto semi-private terraces – perfect for lunch in summer. The garden room is a little smaller than the others, but has a big terrace to compensate. Breakfast is served in the main house – the full Welsh works. Beautiful hills, sandy beaches, Cardigan and magical St Davids all wait. Good local restaurants are on hand: lobster from the sea, lamb from the hills. Don't miss The Shed in Porthgain for excellent fish and chips. A great place to unwind with discounts for longer stays. *Minimum stay: 2 nights in high season.*

Rooms	6 suites for 2: £90-£130. 1 cottage for 7: £650-£1150. Singles £95-£110.
Meals	Restaurants within 3 miles.
Closed	Christmas.

Tel	+44 (0)1239 810248
Email	contact@penbontbren.com
Web	www.penbontbren.com

Penbontbren,
Glynarthen, Llandysul, SA44 6PE

Cross Foxes

Nicol and Dewi have worked wonders breathing new life into this stone built former farmhouse. A steel and glass entrance leads through to a modern bar where flagstones, exposed stonework and beams mingle with contemporary sofas, designer bar stools and sleek lighting. In summer, sup Purple Moose's Snowdonia Ale on the terrace and gaze up at lofty Cadair Idris – a giant's seat indeed. Food from the open kitchen comes with impeccable local credentials and the char-grill compliments the meats perfectly. What could be more local than Conwy mussels, leeks and cream followed by confit leg of Welsh lamb, rosemary and honey gravy, potatoes and seasonal vegetables? There are great Sunday roasts too, light bites, and afternoon teas. Upstairs the comfort factor scales new heights as stone, beams and antiques blend with a crisp modernity; there are beds for dreaming in and mountain views through windows. Gorgeous bathrooms, with lotions and thick robes, soothe those who have stretched their muscles in the surrounding hills. A 15-minute drive brings you to delightful Barmouth and the coast.

Rooms	2 doubles, 2 twin/doubles: £90-£135.
	2 suites for 2: £90-£135.
Meals	Lunch from £4.95.
	Dinner & bar meals from £9.95.
	Sunday lunch, 2 courses, £12.95.
Closed	Rarely.

Cross Foxes,
Brithdir, Dolgellau, LL40 2SG

Tel	+44 (0)1341 421001
Email	hello@crossfoxes.co.uk
Web	www.crossfoxes.co.uk

Y Meirionnydd

By day you explore the mighty wonders of Snowdonia, by night you return to this lovely small hotel and recover in style. It's one of those places that delivers just what you want; it's smart without being posh, the welcome is second to none, tasty food hits the spot, the bedrooms are excellent. You're in the middle of a small country town, so sit on the terrace at the front in summer and watch the world pass by. Inside, soft colours and warm lighting create a relaxed feel. There's a cute bar with armchairs and games, an airy breakfast room for the full Welsh works, then a smart restaurant cut into the rock, which was once the county jail; the food is somewhat better these days, perhaps rump of Welsh lamb with rosemary dumplings, Penderyn Welsh whisky and honey ice cream. Bedrooms upstairs fit the bill nicely. Some are bigger than others, but all have the same style: clean lines, cool colours, big beds, beautiful linen. You get the odd stone wall, an armchair if there's room, then super bathrooms. There's secure storage for bikes, too. *Minimum stay: 2 nights at weekends.*

Rooms	3 doubles, 2 twin/doubles: £89-£129. Singles £69-£79. Extra bed/sofabed £20 p.p.p.n.
Meals	Dinner, 3 courses, £25. Not Mondays in low season.
Closed	One week at Christmas.

Tel	+44 (0)1341 422554
Email	info@themeirionnydd.com
Web	www.themeirionnydd.com

Y Meirionnydd,
Smithfield Square, Dolgellau, LL40 1ES

Llwyndû Farmhouse

The view here is fabulous – a clean sweep across Cardigan Bay to the Llyn Peninsula beyond. Below, a ten-mile beach runs north to Harlech Point; behind, the Rhinog mountains rise. As for the farmhouse, it sits high on the hill and dates to 1581. It's a small, homespun world – Peter and Paula do it all themselves – a simple retreat with delicious slow food at the end of the day. Inside, you find thick stone walls, comfy sofas and a wood-burner in the inglenook. Bedrooms are scattered about. Those in the main house have a cosy feel with warm colours, low ceilings, perhaps a four-poster. Those in the outbuildings tend to be a little bigger and have painted stone walls, then ceilings open to the rafters. By day you explore the wonders of Snowdonia – you can climb mountains, take to cycle tracks or merely walk in the hills. By night you return to feast on local delights under ancient beams, perhaps Rhydlewis smoked salmon, Welsh Black steak, apple tarte tatin; if you're still hungry after that, excellent Welsh cheeses wait. Don't miss Portmeirion, or links golf at Harlech and Aberdovey. *Minimum stay: 2 nights.*

Rooms	2 doubles, 2 four-posters: £106-£126. 1 family room for 4: £110-£146. Dinner, B&B from £82 p.p. Singles from £52.
Meals	Dinner £25-£30.
Closed	January.

Llwyndû Farmhouse,
Llanaber, Barmouth, LL42 1RR

Tel	+44 (0)1341 280144
Email	intouch@llwyndu-farmhouse.co.uk
Web	www.llwyndu-farmhouse.co.uk

Porth Tocyn Hotel

This family hotel is set in farmland with wake-up views over Cardigan Bay and the Snowdon mountain range. It's been in Nick's family for nearly 70 years – and the *Good Food Guide* forever. He's passionate about the place and the food, and he and Louise are consummate hosts. Menus change daily: fresh fish aplenty, venison, guinea fowl, fruity puddings, Welsh cheeses. Food is served in the dining room in front of a massive picture window for soaking up the views.

Bedrooms are cosily inviting; some double rooms adjoin twins, easy for families of four or five, and cots are available too. Settle in any of the six interconnecting sitting rooms – all relaxed and friendly with heaps of art on the walls, flowers, books and comfy cushioned places to read; there's a small bar and a children's snug with a games room next door. Spill out onto the front terrace on sunny days; there's an outdoor heated pool and tennis court and the coastal path runs right past the gardens. A great base for exploring the North Wales coast and mountains – seaside towns Abersoch, Pwllheli and Porthmadog are nearby.

Rooms	2 doubles, 12 twin/doubles: £120–£200. 3 singles: £87–£100. Extra bed available.
Meals	Lunch from £11.95. Dinner, 3 courses with coffee & canapés, £49.
Closed	28 October – 16 March.

Tel	+44 (0)1758 713303
Email	bookings@porthtocynhotel.co.uk
Web	www.porthtocynhotel.co.uk

Porth Tocyn Hotel,
Bwlchtocyn, Pwllheli, LL53 7BU

Escape Boutique B&B

A designer B&B with lovely rooms, attractive prices and some seriously fancy bathrooms. The house stands high on the hill, away from the crowds, a short stroll from the buzz of town and its two-mile beach. This is a 19th-century mill owner's villa and its fine old windows, sparkling wood floors and carved fireplace bear testament to its Victorian roots. Other than that it's a clean sweep of funky interiors. Sam and Gaenor scoured Europe for their eclectic collection of colourful retro furniture that fills the rooms – orange swivel chairs, iconic G-plan sofas, beautiful beds wrapped in crisp white linen. You'll find cow-hide rugs, funky wallpapers, big views from rooms at the front. All come with flat-screen TVs, DVD players and iPod docks. Bathrooms are excellent: one room has a shower for two, another has a copper bath in the room. Downstairs, there's an honesty bar in the sitting room, while delicious breakfasts are served in an attractive dining room. Good food waits in town – the Seahorse for fish, Mamma Rosa for Italian. Great Orme waits above for big views of the bay. *Minimum stay: 2 nights at weekends.*

Rooms	8 doubles, 1 twin/double: £105-£160. Singles £90-£145.
Meals	Restaurants within walking distance.
Closed	Christmas.

Escape Boutique B&B,
48 Church Walks,
Llandudno, LL30 2HL

Tel	+44 (0)1492 877776
Email	info@escapebandb.co.uk
Web	www.escapebandb.co.uk

Osborne House

Osborne House – originally the summer residence of a Cheshire brewer – dates to 1850, and was one of the first houses to be built on the promenade. It fell into the hands of Elyse's parents in the mid-1980s, who refurbished from top to toe, turning 23 small rooms into seven enormous suites. They didn't hold back – expect a grand Victorian feel with a dash of Belle Époque. You'll find Corinthian columns, crystal chandeliers, noble portraits on the walls, comfy sofas in front of the fire. Downstairs, there's a sitting room at the front with views of the bay, a bar in the middle for the daily papers, then curtains that open theatrically onto a muralled dining room at the back. Suites are huge – big sitting rooms, brass beds, claw-foot baths and walk-in showers. You'll find rugs on wood floors, ornate marble fireplaces, armchairs and sofas to take the strain; all but one have sea views. Bistro food waits downstairs, perhaps seared scallops, a rib-eye steak, baked toffee and chocolate sponge. There's off-road parking, too, and you can use the pool at the Empire, Osborne House's sister hotel. *Minimum stay: 2 nights at weekends.*

Rooms	7 suites for 2: £135-£195. Dinner, B&B £83-£110 per person.
Meals	Lunch from £5. Afternoon tea from £8.50. Dinner from £10.95.
Closed	Christmas.

Tel	+44 (0)1492 860330
Email	sales@osbornehouse.co.uk
Web	www.osbornehouse.co.uk

Osborne House,
Promenade, 17 North Parade,
Llandudno, LL30 2LP

Scotland

The Airds Hotel & Restaurant, page 393

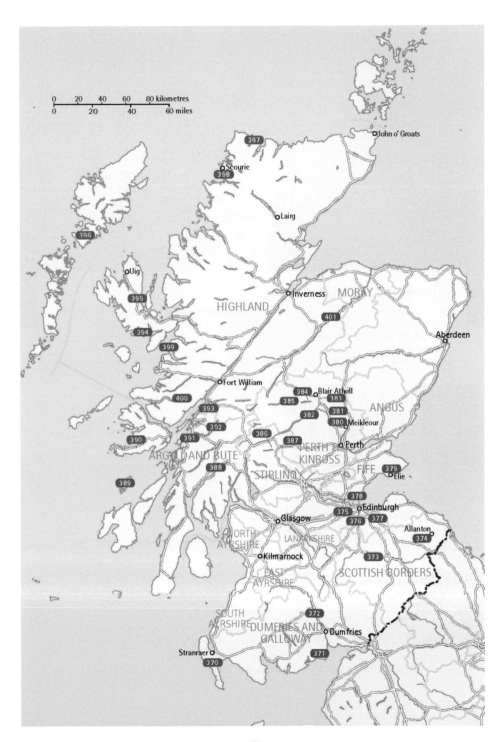

0 20 40 60 80 kilometres
0   20   40   60 miles

397

398 oScourie

396

oLairg

395

oUig

HIGHLAND

oInverness MORAY

401

Aberdeen

394

399

Fort William

400 384 oBlair Atholl 383
393 385 381
392 382 380 oMeikleour ANGUS
390 391 386 387 oPerth
389 388 PERTH Perth
KINROSS
STIRLING FIFE 379
oElie

378 oEdinburgh
375
oGlasgow 376 377
Allanton
NORTH LANARKSHIRE 374
AYRSHIRE
oKilmarnock 373
EAST
AYRSHIRE SCOTTISH BORDERS

SOUTH 372
AYRSHIRE DUMFRIES AND
GALLOWAY oDumfries
Stranraer o 371
370

oJohn o' Groats

369

Knockinaam Lodge

Lawns run down to the Irish sea, roe deer come to eat the roses, sunsets turn the sky red. This beautiful hunting lodge is one of the loveliest country-house hotels in the land. The food is ambrosial, the panelled bar is home to 150 malts, and you'll find a level of service you rarely encounter in such far-flung corners of the realm. There's history, too. Churchill once stayed and you can sleep in his room, then climb into the deepest of baths and read his books. Immaculate interiors abound: gorgeous bedrooms, faultless bathrooms, a morning room where the scent of fresh flowers mingles with wood smoke. You'll find beautiful art, the daily papers, games and books galore. Outside, cliff walks lead over to Portpatrick, peregrine falcons circle on high, bluebells carpet the hills in spring. When it's stormy, waves crash all around. There's golf on the coast at Portpatrick, then Luce Bay for miles of sand. John Buchan knew the house and described it in *The Thirty-Nine Steps* as the house to which Hannay fled. Remote, beguiling, utterly spoiling – grand old Knockinaam is simply unmissable. *Pets by arrangement.*

Rooms	4 doubles, 5 twin/doubles: £215-£450. 1 family room for 4: £360-£430. Singles £190-£330.
Meals	Lunch, 2-3 courses, from £25. Dinner, 5 courses, included; non-residents £70.
Closed	Never.

Knockinaam Lodge,
Portpatrick, Stranraer, DG9 9AD

Tel	+44 (0)1776 810471
Email	reservations@knockinaamlodge.com
Web	www.knockinaamlodge.com

370

Cavens

This small patch of heaven is a delight. You leave the world behind you, take the road south from Dumfries, and soon you're rolling through stunning country with hardly a soul in sight. Sunlight plays in the trees, ridges run down to lush fields, then suddenly you turn a corner and the Solway Firth is sparkling before your eyes. All you need now is somewhere wonderful to stay, somewhere small and beautiful, with kind owners on hand to usher you though to a chic sitting room before pouring you a gin and tonic, dishing up wonderful food and showing you to your delightful quarters. Which is exactly what you find at Cavens, a small country house, where Jane and Angus look after guests in style. Two sitting rooms have open fires, period art and lots of books, then doors onto a garden where only birdsong will disturb you. As for the rooms, three are huge, one has the feel of a library, all have smart fabrics, super beds and garden views. Finally, dinner, an absolute delight, perhaps scallops with lime and Vermouth, venison with a port jus, a thin apple tart. Gardens, beaches and golf wait. Perfect. *Pets by arrangement.*

Rooms	4 doubles, 1 twin: £200-£300. Singles £140-£200. All prices include dinner.Extra bed £40 p.p.p.n.
Meals	Lunch from £6. Dinner, 3 courses à la carte included; non-residents £35. Afternoon tea 'on the house.'
Closed	Rarely.

Tel	+44 (0)1387 880234
Email	enquiries@cavens.com
Web	www.cavens.com

Cavens,
Kirkbean, Dumfries, DG2 8AA

Trigony House Hotel and Garden Spa

A welcoming family-run hotel with good food and nicely priced rooms. There's a small spa in the garden, too, with rather good views from the hot tub. The house dates to 1700 and comes with Japanese oak panelling in the hall, a wood-burner in the sitting room and an open fire in the dining room, where doors open onto the terrace for dinner in summer. Adam cooks lovely rustic fare, perhaps prawns with coconut and coriander, saddle of roe venison, rhubarb and hazelnut crumble; a small, organic kitchen garden provides for the table in summer. Bedrooms – some big, some smaller – have warm colours, crisp linen, good beds and spotless bathrooms. A couple are dog-friendly, those at the back have the view, the suite opens onto a private garden. As for the spa, there's a treatment room, a sauna and a hot tub, so plenty of scope to recuperate after a day walking the Southern Upland Way or discovering the spectacular country between Moniaive and the Galloway Forest, a lost world of huge beauty you'll have to yourself. Don't miss Drumlanrig Castle for its gardens, walking trails and mountain bike tracks.

Rooms	4 doubles, 4 twin/doubles: £120-£140. 1 suite for 2: £165. Singles £90-£120. Dinner, B&B £95-£155 per person. Extra bed/sofabed £15 p.p.p.n.
Meals	Lunch from £7.50. Dinner £25-£35. Afternoon tea £15.
Closed	24-26 December.

Trigony House Hotel and Garden Spa,
Closeburn, Thornhill, DG3 5EZ

Tel	+44 (0)1848 331211
Email	trigonyhotel@googlemail.com
Web	www.trigonyhotel.co.uk

Windlestraw

A small country house with lovely interiors and beautiful views down the Tweed Valley. Hills rise, deer roam, osprey glide through the afternoon sky. John and Sylvia came back from Dubai to do their own thing and have been hard at work presiding over a chic refurbishment. Fires roar, a grand piano waits to be played, there's a sun-trapping terrace for afternoon tea. You find a conservatory sitting room filled with books and curios, a panelled dining room for super food, then binoculars with which to scan the valley –

sunsets turn the hills orange. Country-house bedrooms have a warm contemporary style: smart colours, comfy beds, sofas in the bigger rooms, fine views from those at the front. Spotless bathrooms do the trick: one has a claw-foot bath, bigger rooms have robes. Good food waits downstairs, perhaps scallops from Eyemouth, local lamb, an irresistible tarte tatin. There's lots to do: walking, fishing, mountain biking, even kayaking on the Tweed; if you try your hand on Pebbles golf course, the views may well be better than your game! There's a literary festival at Traquair House in August, too.

Rooms	5 doubles: £180-£240.
	1 suite for 2: £290. Singles from £125.
	Extra beds for children £15. Cots free.
Meals	Dinner, 4 courses, £60.
Closed	10 December – 10 February.

Tel	+44 (0)1896 870636
Email	stay@windlestraw.co.uk
Web	www.windlestraw.co.uk

Windlestraw,
Galashiels Road, Walkerburn, EH43 6AA

The Allanton Inn

Allanton, population 100. Welcome to the sleepy back of beyond, an untouched corner of the rural idyll that most people skip on their rush north. Well, there's no rush here, just patchwork fields, rolling hills and the river Tweed pottering off to the coast. As for this cute little inn, it's a great base from which to explore. The style is charming, the locals friendly, the prices lovely, the food a treat. It sits on the only street in town with a garden that backs onto open country; in summer you can have lunch in the sun while watching the farmer work on his fields. Inside, home-spun interiors have colour and style. There's an open-plan feel, the airy bar flowing into a half-panelled restaurant. You'll find a smouldering fire, fresh flowers, good art, local ales. Rooms have an easy style: padded bedheads, good bathrooms, Farrow & Ball colours. A couple are big, those at the back have the view. Super local food waits downstairs, perhaps an Eyemouth fish platter, rump of local lamb, lavender and raspberry brûlée. There's local honeycomb at breakfast, too. You can fish, walk, play a bit of golf. Perfect.

Rooms	3 doubles, 2 twin/doubles: £85-£105. 1 family room for 4: £110-£155. Singles from £70.
Meals	Lunch from £6.75. Dinner, 3 courses, £25-£35. Sunday lunch from £12.50.
Closed	Christmas.

The Allanton Inn,
Allanton, By Duns, TD11 3JZ

Tel	+44 (0)1890 818260
Email	info@allantoninn.co.uk
Web	www.allantoninn.co.uk

The Bridge Inn at Ratho

This lovely inn sits in a small village directly above the Union Canal. Footpaths head west into the country, after tucking into Sunday lunch you can hire bikes and follow the tow path into Edinburgh. If all that sounds too strenuous, then plonk yourself down on the terrace and watch the odd boat chug past while sipping a pint of good ale. Inside, the view is weatherproofed by big windows in the dining room. An easy style runs throughout. You'll find woodburners, smart colours, a whisky bar, the odd sofa.

In summer, there are barbecues on Friday nights, an ice cream shed in the garden, even a small festival in May with live bands and lots of beer. Rooms aren't huge, but hit the spot. They're stylish and comfy with smart beds and crisp linen. All but one has the view, three have walk-in power showers, one has a claw-foot bath. The airport is ten minutes away, but you're not on the flight path, so peace reigns. Finally, don't miss nearby Jupiter Artland in summer, a wonderland of beautiful things. Children are very welcome, as are dogs in the popular bar area.

Rooms	3 doubles, 1 twin/double: £80-£120. Singles from £65.
Meals	Lunch & dinner £5-£35. Sunday lunch from £12.95.
Closed	Christmas Day.

Tel	+44 (0)131 333 1320
Email	info@bridgeinn.com
Web	www.bridgeinn.com

The Bridge Inn at Ratho,
27 Baird Road, Ratho, EH28 8RA

23 Mayfield

A great base for all things Edinburgh. This attractive villa, in the shadow of Arthur's Seat, was built in 1868 for a coffee merchant. Outside, much prized, off-street parking waits. Inside, Victorian splendour at every turn: original fireplaces, ornate ceilings and a stained-glass window on the landing. The sitting room comes in dark period colours with newspapers on poles, gilt-framed pictures that hang on chains, and you can grab a drink from the honesty bar, then sink into a chesterfield sofa and watch an old movie. In winter you eat breakfast by candlelight, a candelabra on each table, and it's a feast of Scottish produce: porridge with honey, Arbroath smokies, rare breed sausages, marshmallow pancakes. Bedrooms have style and comfort in spades: white linen, excellent beds, fancy bathrooms, maybe wood floors or a brass chandelier. One has panelled walls, all have good art, iPod docks and smart TVs; the family room has a Nintendo Wii. You can jump on a bus and whizz into town, excellent restaurants wait nearby. A very friendly place. *Minimum stay: 2 nights at weekends May-September*

Rooms	3 twin/doubles, 2 four-posters: £110-£185. 1 family room for 4: £130-£200. Singles from £90.
Meals	Restaurants within half a mile.
Closed	24-26 December.

23 Mayfield,
23 Mayfield Gardens,
Edinburgh, EH9 2BX

Tel	+44 (0)131 667 5806
Email	info@23mayfield.co.uk
Web	www.23mayfield.co.uk

94DR

Close to Holyrood and Arthur's Seat, this super-friendly designer B&B is not only popular for its contemporary style, but for Paul and John, who treat guests like friends and make sure you see the best of their city. A traditional Victorian exterior gives no hint of the chic interiors that wait within. You'll find original floor tiles and ornate ceilings, but other than that it's a clean sweep of modern splendour: deep charcoal downstairs; pure white above. There's a sitting room with iPads in case you want to book a restaurant, then an honesty bar, an espresso machine and lots of handy guide books. Upstairs, stylish, well-priced bedrooms wait. Some are big with claw-foot baths, others smaller with walk-in power showers. All come with comfy beds, bathrobes, beautiful linen and fine contemporary art. The family suite (two rooms) has bunk beds and a PlayStation for kids. Delicious breakfasts are served in a conservatory overlooking the back garden, a memorable feast orchestrated by Paul, with lively conversation that travels the world. Majestic Edinburgh is yours to explore. *Minimum stay: 2 nights at weekends.*

Rooms	3 doubles: £100-£145.
	2 suites for 2: £125-£225.
	1 family suite for 4: £145-£190.
Meals	Restaurants within 0.5 miles.
Closed	Christmas, 4-23 January.

Tel	+44 (0)131 662 9265
Email	stay@94dr.com
Web	www.94dr.com

94DR,
94 Dalkeith Road,
Edinburgh, EH16 5AF

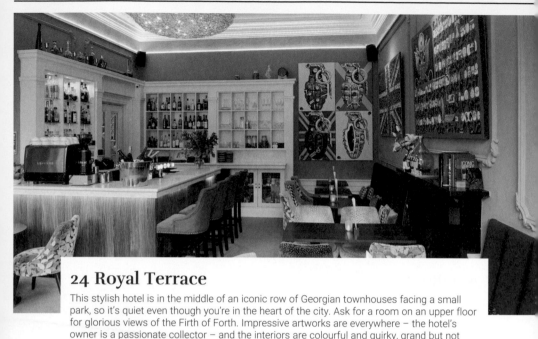

24 Royal Terrace

This stylish hotel is in the middle of an iconic row of Georgian townhouses facing a small park, so it's quiet even though you're in the heart of the city. Ask for a room on an upper floor for glorious views of the Firth of Forth. Impressive artworks are everywhere – the hotel's owner is a passionate collector – and the interiors are colourful and quirky, grand but not pretentious. Generous breakfasts with home baked cakes are served in the front room café and bar; stop by in the evening for a drink or sit out in the pretty terraced garden and, if you book ahead, treat yourselves to a champagne afternoon tea. You can walk, or hop on a bus, to castle, gardens, shops and museums. Paul Kitching's 21212 is a two-minute walk. *Minimum stay: 2 nights at weekends. Pets by arrangement.*

24 Royal Terrace,
Edinburgh, EH7 5AH

Rooms	6 twin/doubles: £118-£328. 3 suites for 2, 2 family rooms for 4: £118-£408. 3 singles: £74-£194. Extra sofabed for children £25pp.
Meals	Breakfast £14. Light bites from £4.50.
Closed	Christmas & one week in January.

Tel	+44 (0)131 297 2424
Email	reservations@24royalterrace.com
Web	www.24royalterrace.co.uk

The Ship Inn

There are few inns where you can sit on the terrace and watch a game of cricket on the beach below. But it's not beach cricket as you know it; this is serious stuff, played at low tide, and Mark Waugh, Viv Richards and Wasim Akram have all tried their hand. As for this cute little boutique inn, it's as good as any in the land, and it doubles as the pavilion... and the venue for post-match celebrations, no doubt. On sunny days, you decant onto the terrace for lunch in the sun and gaze across the Firth of Forth to Edinburgh's hills.

Inside, contemporary rustic design mixes with roaring fires and the odd stone wall. Sofas and armchairs are scattered about, staff weave through the throng delivering delicious food – fish and seafood from local waters, lamb and beef from nearby farms, sinful puddings you can't resist; there are regular barbecues on the terrace, too. Smart rooms have seaside colours, crisp linen, coffee machines, fancy bathrooms with walk-in showers; those at the front have sea views, too. St Andrews waits for golf, the Fife coastal path for excellent walks. A perfect place. *Pets by arrangement.*

Rooms	6 twin/doubles: £120-£185.
	Extra bed/sofabed £20 p.p.p.n.
Meals	Lunch & dinner £5-£35.
	Sunday lunch from £12.95.
Closed	Christmas Day & 2 weeks in January.

Tel	+44 (0)131 333 1320	The Ship Inn,
Email	info@bridgeinn.com	The Toft, Elie, KY9 1DT
Web	www.shipinn.scot	

The Meikleour Arms

With their own ale, over twenty malts and a bevvy of artisan gins, you'll find a toast for every occasion at this lovely country inn where bedroom names (Flahaut, Hortense, Lansdowne) reflect the French and Scottish ancestry of the owners. Much of the food in the restaurant comes from the estate – vegetables and herbs grown in the walled garden, scallops hand-dived on the west coast and venison from the Meikleour Forest. You can sample some quirky finds from the less well known vineyards in Bordeaux. Walk to the Tay for salmon or trout fishing – book a fly-fishing lesson with the head ghillie. Spot ospreys, otters, kingfishers. The Blairgowrie Golf Course is a five-mile drive, with three others within 30 miles. Book a tour of a couple of whisky distilleries too – Blair Athol and Edradour are in Pitlochry (a 40-minute drive). Scone Palace, Glamis and Balmoral are all within reach. You stay in the 19th-century inn or the serviced cottages in the grounds – a short drive or walk from the main building. The cottages have small kitchens, but you can wander over for breakfast. *Minimum stay: 2 nights in the cottages.*

The Meikleour Arms,
Meikleour, PH2 6EB

Rooms	10 doubles, 1 twin/double: £100-£130. 2 cottages for 2, 2 cottages for 4, 1 cottage for 6: £110-£225. Singles £90-£120.
Meals	Light bites about £8. Lunch & dinner à la carte, 2 courses, about £20.
Closed	Never.

Tel	+44 (0)1250 883206
Email	contact@meikleourarms.co.uk
Web	www.meikleourarms.co.uk

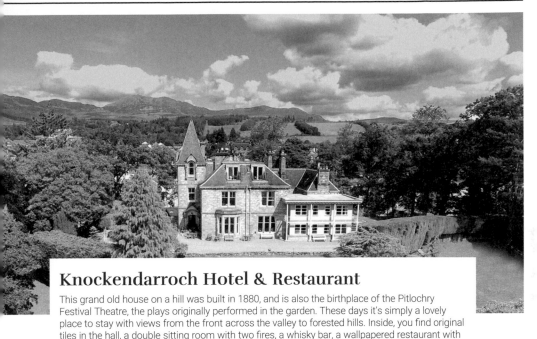

Knockendarroch Hotel & Restaurant

This grand old house on a hill was built in 1880, and is also the birthplace of the Pitlochry Festival Theatre, the plays originally performed in the garden. These days it's simply a lovely place to stay with views from the front across the valley to forested hills. Inside, you find original tiles in the hall, a double sitting room with two fires, a whisky bar, a wallpapered restaurant with views of Ben Vrackie and plenty of original contemporary art. Good paths lead up through forest and moorland for big Highland views, not a bad way to work up an appetite for some very good food, perhaps fillet of hake with chilli and lemongrass, Perthshire lamb with parsnip purée, elderflower panna cotta with pear sorbet. Bedrooms are lovely, it really doesn't matter which you choose, though the big ones at the front do have exceptional views. You'll find comfy beds, smart fabrics and tartan throws, perhaps a cushioned window seat or a sofa if there's room. Two have balconies, most have binoculars to scan the hills. There's a drying room too. *Minimum stay: 2 nights at weekends. Children over 10 welcome.*

Rooms	12 twin/doubles: £140-£195. Dinner, B&B £100-£173 per person.
Meals	Lunch from £5. Dinner, 3 courses, £25; £42 non-residents.
Closed	Rarely.

Tel	+44 (0)1796 473473
Email	bookings@knockendarroch.co.uk
Web	www.knockendarroch.co.uk

Knockendarroch Hotel & Restaurant,
Higher Oakfield, Pitlochry, PH16 5HT

Craigatin House & Courtyard

Craigatin is one of those lovely places where beautiful rooms have attractive prices and hands-on owners go out of their way to make your stay special. It stands peacefully in two acres of manicured gardens on the northern shores of town; good restaurants are a short stroll. Smart stone exteriors give way to warmly contemporary interiors, where beautiful windows flood rooms with light. There are shutters in the breakfast room, which overflows into an enormous conservatory where sofas wait in front of a wood-burner and walls of glass open onto the garden. Big uncluttered bedrooms – some in the main house, others in converted stables – are super value for money. Expect comfy beds, crisp white linen, and pretty shower rooms. Breakfast offers the full cooked works and tempting alternatives, perhaps smoked haddock omelettes or apple pancakes with grilled bacon and maple syrup. As for Pitlochry – gateway to the Highlands – it's a vibrant town with lots to do: castles and mountains, lochs and forests, its famous Festival Theatre. You're on the whisky trail, too. *Minimum stay: 2 nights at weekends.*

Rooms	11 doubles, 2 twins: £109-£118. 1 suite for 2: £136. Singles £99-£126.
Meals	Restaurants within walking distance.
Closed	Christmas.

Craigatin House & Courtyard,
165 Atholl Road, Pitlochry, PH16 5QL

Tel	+44 (0)1796 472478
Email	enquiries@craigatinhouse.co.uk
Web	www.craigatinhouse.co.uk

Killiecrankie House Hotel

No Highland fling would be complete without a night at Killiecrankie. Henrietta runs the place with great charm and has spent the last twelve years pouring in love and money; now it shines. Outside, gardens galore: one for roses, another for vegetables, and a fine herbaceous border. Further afield, you'll find much to please: Loch Tummel, Rannoch Moor and magnificent Glenshee, over which you tumble for the Highland Games at Braemar. Return to the indisputable comforts of a smart country hotel: 52 malts at the bar, views at breakfast of red squirrels climbing garden trees. There's a snug sitting room where a fire burns in winter; in summer doors open onto the garden. Delightful bedrooms come in different shapes and sizes. All are smart with pretty linen, warm colours, chic fabrics and lovely views. Dinner is predictably delicious, perhaps pea and mint soup, Highland venison, sticky toffee pudding. There's porridge with cream and brown sugar for breakfast. Castles, hills and distilleries wait. A great wee place with staff who care. *Minimum stay: 2 nights at weekends. Pets by arrangement.*

Rooms	3 doubles, 5 twin/doubles: £250-£340. 2 singles: £140-£170. Singles £155-£180. Dinner, B&B £135-£175 per person. Extra bed £35-£75 p.p.p.n.
Meals	Lunch from £6.95. Dinner included; non-residents £45.
Closed	3 January – 23 March.

Tel	+44 (0)1796 473220
Email	enquiries@killiecrankiehotel.co.uk
Web	www.killiecrankiehotel.co.uk

Killiecrankie House Hotel,
Killiecrankie, Pitlochry, PH16 5LG

The Inn at Loch Tummel

You weave through the forest, then arrive at this 200-year-old inn to find views of field, hill, loch and sky. It's a magical spot, with a small garden to the front that drinks it all in. As for the inn, Alice and Jade rescued it from neglect, poured in love and money and now it shines. Interiors mix contemporary flair with Highland charm, the very definition of rustic chic. You'll find a cool little bar, painted beams and a wood-burner in the restaurant, then a first-floor sitting room with fat sofas, books and games, goatskin rugs and Jade's guitar. Bedrooms are a treat: chic fabrics, beautiful beds, cool colours, woollen throws. Some are big, none are small, one is dog friendly, most have the view. All have good art, decanters of whisky and spotless bathrooms, some with walk-in showers. By day you explore the hills, whizz down mountain bike trails or climb Schiehallion, the local munro. At night you return for delicious food, perhaps calamari with chilli and lemon, rack of local lamb, an espresso brownie with beetroot meringue. Queen's View, up the road, has one of the best views in Scotland. *Children over 5 welcome.*

Rooms	2 doubles, 4 twin/doubles: £95-£140.
Meals	Dinner with wine £27.
Closed	Rarely.

The Inn at Loch Tummel,
Queens View, Strathtummel, PH16 5RP

Tel	+44 (0)1882 634317
Email	info@theinnatlochtummel.com
Web	www.theinnatlochtummel.com

Dunalastair Hotel Suites

Rannoch Moor is one of those magical places where the hand of man has hardly touched the landscape. You're encircled by hills, with a couple of lochs thrown in for good measure. As for the road, it peters out at the station 20 miles west, where the London train stops and passengers disembark, bicycle in hand. Some, very sensibly, spin down to this chic hotel and check in for a night or two of luxury. You'll find a roaring fire in the hall, a dram or two in the wee bar, colourful art in the big sitting room, then delicious food in the restaurant, perhaps Scottish scallops, loin of roe deer, apple parfait with rosemary and sage. In summer you decant into the courtyard for breakfast, lunch and dinner. Chic suites offer more than most: the best beds, sofas and smart TVs, well-stocked kitchenettes, then dining tables for room service. Swish bathrooms have walk-in showers, some have baths, too. Kind staff are the best, nothing is too much trouble. You can kayak, fish, hire bikes or bag a munro.
Minimum stay: 2 nights July-August.

Rooms	22 suites for 2, 8 suites for 4, 2 suites for 6: £155-f299.
Meals	Lunch from £6. Mains from £7.95. Dinner, 3 courses, £35. Afternoon tea £18.
Closed	Never.

Tel	+44 (0)1882 580444
Email	bookings@dunalastairhotel.com
Web	www.dunalastairhotel.com

Dunalastair Hotel Suites,
1 The Square,
Kinloch Rannoch, PH16 5PW

Monachyle Mhor

Monachyle is unique – a designer hotel on a remote hill farm that started life as a B&B. Today it's one of the hippest places to stay in Scotland and it's still run by the same family with the children at the helm. Dick farms, Melanie designs the magical rooms, Tom cooks some of the best food in Scotland. It sits in 2,000 acres of blissful silence at the end of the track with the Trossachs circling around you and Loch Voil shimming below. Sheep graze, buzzards swoop, the odd fisherman tries his luck. Inside, there's a cool little bar, a fire in the sitting room, then a slim restaurant that drinks in the view. Bedrooms ooze 21st-century chic: big beds, cool colours, fabulous design, hi-tech gadgets. Bathrooms are equally good, perhaps a deluge shower in a granite steam room or claw-foot baths with views down the glen. Loft-house suites are enormous, but the smaller rooms are lovely, too. Dinner is a five-course feast with beef, lamb, pork and venison all off the farm. Rob Roy lived in the glen, you can visit his grave. The hotel holds a festival in May – fabulous food and cool Scottish tunes.

Rooms	9 twin/doubles: £195-£225.
	5 suites for 2: £285.
	1 family room for 4: £195-£265.
Meals	Lunch from £5.50. Dinner, 5 courses, £65. Sunday lunch £32.
Closed	Two weeks in January.

Monachyle Mhor,
Balquhidder,
Lochearnhead, FK19 8PQ

Tel	+44 (0)1877 384622
Email	monachyle@mhor.net
Web	www.monachylemhor.net

Mhor 84

The entirely benevolent expansion of the Mhor empire has mastered the Midas touch, turning this old roadside inn into the coolest motel in the land. Outside, the glen shoots down to Loch Voil, with mountains to climb and bike tracks to follow. Inside, chic white minimalism mixes with warm Scottish tradition, a perfect blend of relaxed 21st-century living. There's style and humour in equal measure – boarded floors, tractor seat bar stools, curios hanging on the walls, the odd sofa for afternoon tea. Fires roar, cake stands bulge, happy staff weave through the throng delivering fabulous food that you eat at old school tables – porridge with honey for breakfast, sourdough and hummus for lunch, Scotch rarebit, Tyree lobster and plum crumble for dinner. There's live folk music every Thursday and a fine selection of malts. Simple bedrooms have white walls, contemporary art, small armchairs and honest prices; spotless bathrooms are 1980s originals, all part of the fun. There's a games room, too, with a juke box and pool table.

Rooms	2 doubles, 4 twin/doubles: £70-£80. 1 family room for 4: £80-£110.
Meals	Breakfast from £4.50. Lunch from £3.90. Dinner, 3 courses, £25-£35.
Closed	Christmas Day.

Tel	+44 (0)1877 384646
Email	motel@mhor.net
Web	www.mhor84.net

Mhor 84,
Balquhidder, Lochearnhead, FK19 8NY

The Creggans Inn

If you're looking for a small hotel in a great position with lovely rooms and excellent food, you'll find it here. There's a little history, too – the inn was once owned by the real James Bond. Sir Fitzroy Maclean was one of a cast of characters on whom Ian Fleming based his hero; the fact the Royal Navy send their big ships into Loch Fyne is purely coincidental. These days, life at the inn is decidedly restful. Views from the front stretch for miles, the loch eventually giving way to the distant peaks of the Kintyre peninsular. Inside, an airy elegance abounds. There's a first-floor sitting room with big views; a locals' bar which doubles as the clubhouse for the shinty team; then picture windows in the smart restaurant, where you dig into super food while watching the sun set, perhaps Ramsay haggis with whisky sauce, pot roast chicken with a thyme jus, bread and butter pudding with honey glazed figs. Comfy bedrooms have lots of style: warm colours, pretty fabrics, delicate wallpapers, robes in sparkling bathrooms; most have loch views. Castles and gardens, golf and boat trips wait.

Rooms	3 doubles, 11 twin/doubles: £100-£150. Singles £115.
Meals	Lunch from £5.95. Bar meals from £12.95. Dinner, 3 courses, from £25.
Closed	Never.

The Creggans Inn,
Loch Fyne, Strachur, Cairndow, PA27 8BX

Tel	+44 (0)1369 860279
Email	info@creggans-inn.co.uk
Web	www.creggans-inn.co.uk

The Colonsay

Another fabulous Hebridean island, a perfect place to escape the world. Wander at will and find wild flowers in the machair, a golf course tended by sheep and huge sandy beaches across which cows roam. Wildlife is ever present, from a small colony of wild goats to a rich migratory bird population; the odd golden eagle soars overhead, too. At low tide the sands of the south give access to Oronsay. The island's 14th-century priory was one of Scotland's finest and amid impressive ruins its ornate stone cross still stands. As for the hotel, it brims with an easy style – airy interiors, stripped floors, fires everywhere, friendly staff. There's a locals' bar for a pint (and a brewery on the island), a pretty sitting room packed with books, a dining room for super food, a decked terrace for drinks in the sun. Bedrooms have local art, warm colours, lovely fabrics and the best beds; some have sea views, all have good bathrooms. Spin around on bikes, search for standing stones, lie in the sun and stare at the sky. There's a festival in May for all things Colonsay. Wonderful.

Rooms	4 doubles, 3 twins: £90-£160.
	1 family room for 4: £110-£150.
	1 single: £75-£85.
Meals	Lunch from £4.50. Packed lunch £7.
	Bar meals from £11.50
	Dinner, 3 courses, about £25.
Closed	Nov, Jan after New Year & Feb.

Tel	+44 (0)1951 200316
Email	hotel@colonsayestate.co.uk
Web	www.colonsayestate.co.uk

The Colonsay,
Scalasaig, Isle of Colonsay, PA61 7YP

Tiroran House

The setting is magnificent – 17 acres of gardens rolling down to Loch Scridian. Otters and dolphins pass through, buzzards and eagles glide above, red deer visit the garden. As for this 1850 shooting lodge, you'll be hard pressed to find a more comfortable island base. There are fires in the drawing rooms, fresh flowers everywhere, games to be played, books to be read. Airy bedrooms hit the spot: crisp linen, beautiful fabrics, the odd chaise longue; some have watery views, all have silence guaranteed. You eat in a smart dining room with much of the delicious food from the island or waters around it, perhaps mussel and oyster broth, saddle of lamb with carrot purée, chocolate torte with vanilla ice cream. Wander to the Whitetail Coffee Shop for afternoon tea. You're bang in the middle of Mull with lots to do: Tobermory, the prettiest town in the Hebrides; Calgary and its magical beach; day trips to Iona and its famous monastery; cruises to Staffa and Fingal's Cave. If you want to be more independent there are two self-catering cottages in the grounds.

Rooms	5 doubles, 5 twin/doubles: £175-£220.
Meals	Dinner, 4 courses, £48.
Closed	Rarely.

Tiroran House,
Tiroran, Isle of Mull, PA69 6ES

Tel	+44 (0)1681 705232
Email	info@tiroran.com
Web	www.tiroran.com

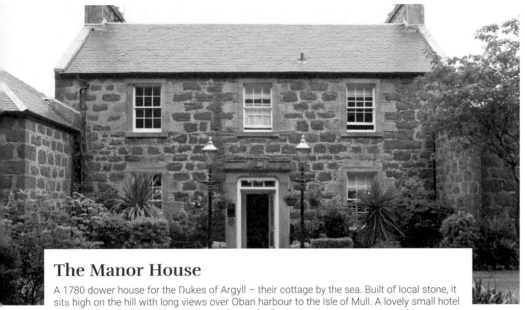

The Manor House

A 1780 dower house for the Dukes of Argyll – their cottage by the sea. Built of local stone, it sits high on the hill with long views over Oban harbour to the Isle of Mull. A lovely small hotel with a stylish old-school feel; lounge in front of a fire in the drawing room, scramble up to McCaig's Tower for sunsets over the Hebrides, spot wildlife through binoculars from your bedroom. Breakfast on traditional porridge, French toast, pastries and Loch Fyne kippers.

Hike and bike from your doorstep; walk down to the harbour for boat trips in search of whales, porpoises, and dolphins. There are lots of islands close by – find long stretches of sandy coastline, rambling forests and mountains to climb. Drink whisky at the Oban Distillery, or head back up the hill to the Manor House for afternoon tea on the terrace. You can dine on a five-course feast at the restaurant; perhaps the west coast sea bass, saddle of lamb or squid ink tagliatelle – the menu changes daily. *Children over 12 welcome.*

Rooms	9 doubles, 2 twins: £120-£260. Dinner, B&B from £87.50 p.p.
Meals	Lunch from £6. Dinner, 5 courses, £44.
Closed	Christmas.

Tel	+44 (0)1631 562087	The Manor House,
Email	info@manorhouseoban.com	Gallanach Road, Oban, PA34 4LS
Web	www.manorhouseoban.com	

The Pierhouse

The original pier house for the village, this small hotel is at the end of a single track on the shores of Loch Linnhe, with glorious views across to Lismore and rising mountains beyond. You'll be warmly greeted by hotel staff and the manager lives next door. Find a sun-trapping terrace from which to watch the odd boat chug past, a smart bar for a dram, a white-washed snug with sofas in front of a wood-burner, lovely bedrooms and a restaurant for some of the

best seafood on the west coast – oysters, scallops and salmon, lobsters kept fresh in creels at the end of the pier. Breakfasts have a Scottish flavour: haggis, black pudding and smoked salmon, croissants with homemade preserves. There's lots to do: the ferry across to Lismore for fine walking, Ben Nevis, magical Ardnamurchan, the simple pleasures of the village itself. Wander to the shoreline at Appin Rocks or up the wooded hill for even more breathtaking 360-degree views, return to the Ferry Bar for a latte and scone.

Rooms	4 doubles, 4 twin/doubles: £100-£275. 2 suites for 2: £145-£325. Extra beds: children 2-12 £30, 12+ £40.
Meals	Lunch from £4.95. Bar meals from £12.50. Dinner à la carte £30-£50.
Closed	Christmas & Boxing Day.

The Pierhouse,
Port Appin, Appin, PA38 4DE

Tel	+44 (0)1631 730302
Email	reservations@pierhousehotel.co.uk
Web	www.pierhousehotel.co.uk

The Airds Hotel & Restaurant

This chic country-house hotel on the Appin peninsular stands above Loch Linnhe with views across the water to the Morvern Mountains. It came to life in 1750, an inn for passengers taking the paddle steamers up to the Caledonian canal. These days, it's one of the loveliest places to stay on the West Coast. Its whitewashed exterior gives no hint of the wonders within. You enter through a small conservatory, then find yourself in a world of smouldering fires, freshly cut flowers, beautiful wallpapers and soft sofas. Bedrooms are divine: beautiful fabrics, warm colours, Frette linen on Vi-Spring beds, sparkling marble bathrooms with robes; in short, the best of everything. Those at the front have the view, bigger rooms have sofas, some at the back have terraces, all spoil you rotten. Best of all is the exceptional food, perhaps West Coast langoustines with pea purée, sea bass with clams and a lemongrass cream, apple terrine with salted caramel and cinnamon doughnuts. There's a garden for croquet and afternoon tea with views to the water. Worth every penny.

Rooms	8 twin/doubles: £260-£325; price includes dinner. 3 suites for 4: £365-£410. 1 cottage for 5: £4865 per week; three-day stays from £210.
Meals	Dinner included. Lunch from £7. Sunday lunch £29.95.
Closed	Mon & Tues Nov-Jan. First 2 weeks Dec.

Tel	+44 (0)1631 730236
Email	airds@airds-hotel.com
Web	www.airds-hotel.com

The Airds Hotel & Restaurant,
Port Appin, Appin, PA38 4DF

Coruisk House

Enjoy a wonderful drive down the glen, past tiny cottages and wandering sheep, around the loch and over the mountain to the wild side of Skye, to this restaurant with rooms at the end of the track, where a glass of prosecco greets you on arrival and Belgian hot chocolate is offered before bed. The breakfast room runs along the front of the converted croft house with a string of windows that frame the view, and the restaurant is in the conservatory. While the wood-burner keeps things cosy, the small daily-changing menu is testimony to the chef's exceptional food. The bedrooms and suites – simple and stylish – are divided between Coruisk House and The Steading next door. Drop down to Elgol harbour, where Bonnie Prince Charlie fled for his life, and gaze upon the mighty Cuillin rising from the sea – you might also glimpse seals and puffins. You can roam the heather-covered hills for miles to spot deer. *Children over 14 welcome. Pets by arrangement.*

Rooms	3 doubles £150-£250. 1 suite for 4: £370-£400.
Meals	Dinner £40-£45.
Closed	20 October – 28 February.

Coruisk House,
26 Elgol, Elgol, IV49 9BL

Tel	+44 (0)1471 866330
Email	info@coruiskhouse.com
Web	coruiskhouse.com

Viewfield House Hotel

It's a family affai here, and all the better for it. Iona is at the helm, but as Hugh is the only person on Skye who understands the plumbing system, he has been retained as a vital asset, and rightly so. As for their ancestral pile, it stands high above Portree Bay with long views across the Sound of Rassay. Twenty acres of gardens and woodland wrap around you; there's croquet on the lawn and a hill to climb for 360º views of peak and sea. Inside, aristocratic fixtures and fittings come as standard: hunting trophies, cases filled with curios, a grand piano and open fire in the drawing room.

Bedrooms have a country-house feel: colourful fabrics, crisp linen, pretty furniture, sea views from those at the front; bathrooms do the job nicely and are in the throes of refurbishment. Majestic Skye waits: mountains, sea lochs and beaches, wildlife, castles and distilleries. Dinner is available by arrangement, but there are good restaurants in Portree, too. Highland porridge for breakfast is a treat. An old-school, island delight.

Rooms	4 doubles, 4 twin/doubles, 1 twin: £129-£200. 2 singles: £77-£90. Dinner, B&B £90-£125 per person.
Meals	Dinner, 3 courses, £25-£30; price dependent on pre-booking. Packed lunch £9.
Closed	Mid-Oct to Easter.

Tel	+44 (0)1478 612217
Email	info@viewfieldhouse.com
Web	www.viewfieldhouse.com

Viewfield House Hotel,
Viewfield Road, Portree, IV51 9EU

Scarista House

All you need to know is this: Harris is one of the most beautiful places in the world. Beaches of white sand that stretch for a mile or two are not uncommon. If you bump into another soul, it will be a delightful coincidence, but you shouldn't count on it. The water is turquoise, coconuts sometimes wash up on the beach. The view from Scarista is simple and magnificent: field, ridge, beach, water, sky. Patricia and Tim are the kindest people. You'll be cosy by peat fires, there are books galore and a first-floor drawing room that floods with light. You'll find walking sticks and wellington boots to help you up the odd hill and a set of golf clubs by the front door in case you wish to play (the view from the first tee is one of the best in the game). Kind staff may speak Gaelic. The food is exceptional, perhaps quail with an armagnac mousse, Harris langoustine with garlic and butter, tarte tatin with cinnamon ice cream. Don't miss Uig Sands or the standing stones at Callanish. A perfect place. *Pets by arrangement.*

Rooms	2 doubles, 1 twin: £213-£233. 2 suites for 2: £230-£243. 1 family room for 4: £235-£248. Singles £153.
Meals	Dinner, 3 courses, £44. Packed lunch from £7.50.
Closed	Christmas, New Year, 1 January – 28 February.

Scarista House,
Scarista, Isle of Harris, HS3 3HX

Tel	+44 (0)1859 550238
Email	timandpatricia@scaristahouse.com
Web	www.scaristahouse.com

Mackay's Rooms

This is the north-west corner of Britain and it's utterly magical: huge skies, sandy beaches, aquamarine seas, cliffs and caves. You drive – or cycle – for mile upon mile with mountains soaring into the heavens and ridges sliding into the sea. If you like big, remote landscapes, you'll love it here; what's more, you'll pretty much have it to yourself. Mackay's – they have the shop, the bunkhouse and the garage, too – is the only place to stay in town, its earthy colours mixing with stone walls, open fires and stripped floors to great effect. Bedrooms (some big, others smaller) are extremely comfy. They come with big wooden beds and crisp white linen, while Fiona, a textiles graduate, has a fine eye for fabrics and upholstery. You also get excellent bathrooms, iPod docks, flat-screen TVs and DVD players. Breakfast sets you up for the day – grilled grapefruit, whisky porridge, venison sausages, local eggs – so head east to the beach, west for great golf or catch the ferry across to Cape Wrath and scan the sea for whales. There's surfing for the brave and the beautiful.

Rooms	6 doubles, 1 twin: £125-£189. 4 cottages for 6: £800-£1600. Singles £129.
Meals	Restaurants in village.
Closed	October to May. Cottages open all year.

Tel	+44 (0)1971 511202
Email	stay@visitdurness.com
Web	www.visitdurness.com

Mackay's Rooms,
Durine, Durness, Lairg, IV27 4PN

Scourie Hotel

This famous old fishing hotel is a treat from top to toe. It's a quirky place run with great panache by the Campbell's, who bought it recently, refurbished in style and now it shines. It's supremely comfy – smart without being swanky, very much a country hotel. You'll find golden wallpapers, antique furniture, beautifully upholstered armchairs, then an open fire in the sitting room. It's a remarkably friendly place. Fishermen tend to come for the same week each year, re-booking when they leave, so everyone knows everyone but also they all go out of their way to welcome interlopers into the fold. There's great tradition, too; a board master allocates fishing beats each morning, a gong announces dinner. Stylish rooms have comfy beds, pretty fabrics, beautiful new bathrooms and no TVs; bliss. Dinner is a treat, perhaps ham hock terrine, fresh local salmon, profiteroles with chocolate sauce. There are two bars, a pretty garden, paths that lead down to the sea. This is a wildly beautiful corner of Scotland: spectacular walking, wildlife tours and golf all wait.

Rooms	6 doubles, 6 twins: £145. 2 family rooms for 3: £160. 6 singles: £95. 1 chalet for 4: £200-£250. Dinner, B&B £135 per person.
Meals	Lunch from 4.95. Bar meals from £10. Dinner, 3 courses, £32.
Closed	7 October – 1 April.

Scourie Hotel,
Scourie, Lairg, IV27 4SX

Tel	+44 (0)1971 502396
Email	stay@scouriehotel.com
Web	www.scouriehotel.com

Doune Knoydart

This is a special place – a thrilling landscape of boundless peace and ever-changing light. You're surrounded by much wildlife: killer whales, Golden eagles, red grouse, otters, seals on rocks and in the water, snuffling badgers, red deer – around 120 species live here. As for Doune, it sits in a unique spot on the Sound of Sleat with views across to Skye, Rum and Eigg. You can see it all from the dining room hub, pine-clad from top to toe and hewn from the mottled stone of a former blackhouse, with a stove to keep you warm and games in case it rains. The food is delicious – freshly baked rolls, crab from the bay, roast lamb from the hill, chocolate tart with homemade ice-cream and the best rhubarb cheesecake, plus oatcakes of course. Once here you'll be part of a tiny community of happily stranded souls and Martin, Jane and Liz look after you with great generosity. Bedrooms along the veranda are simple; cabins with mezzanine bunks for children, showers and armchairs for weather watching. The walking is magnificent, swimming sublime and boat trips can be arranged. *Minimum stay: 3 nights.*

Rooms	2 doubles, 1 twin, all with mezzanine bed for children £90. 1 single with separate shower. £33. Dinner, B&B & packed lunch £82-£100 per person.
Meals	Dinner £35.
Closed	October – March.

Tel	+44 (0)1687 462667
Email	martin@doune-knoydart.co.uk
Web	www.doune-knoydart.co.uk

Doune Knoydart,
Knoydart, Mallaig, PH41 4PL

Kilcamb Lodge Hotel & Restaurant

Another stunning West Coast setting with Loch Sunart at the end of the garden and Glas Bheinn rising beyond. Kilcamb – a barracks during the Jacobite uprising – is a perfect base. There's a smart drawing room with an open fire, an elegant dining room for super food, a cool little brasserie for a spot of lunch, then a handful of deeply indulging rooms. A 12-acre garden rolls down to the water, where you might spot otters and seals. Ducks and geese fly overhead, if you're lucky you'll see eagles. Back inside, you'll find a whisky bar that does a good line in gin, then driftwood lamps, flowers, good books and local art. You can eat in the restaurant or the brasserie, either a five-course tasting menu or something simpler, perhaps hand-dived scallops, Highland lamb, raspberry bavarois with champagne sorbet. Bedrooms have a country-house feel, some with a contemporary twist. You'll find warm colours, smart fabrics and excellent beds. One has a balcony, most have the view, all have spotless bathrooms, some with separate showers. Don't miss Ardnamurchan or Sanna Bay at the end of the road.

Rooms	2 doubles, 6 twin/doubles: £220-£380. 2 suites for 2: £300-£435. 1 family room for 4: £390-£435. Prices include dinner.
Meals	Lunch from £7.50. Dinner included. Tasting menu £75. Sunday lunch £25.
Closed	January & first 2 weeks in December. Limited opening November & February.

Kilcamb Lodge Hotel & Restaurant,
Strontian, Acharacle, PH36 4HY

Tel	+44 (0)1967 402257
Email	enquiries@kilcamblodge.co.uk
Web	www.kilcamblodge.co.uk

Culdearn House

Grantown is a great base for Highland flings. You can fish the Spey, jump on the whisky trail, check out a raft of castles, even ski in Aviemore. Loch Ness is close, as is Royal Deeside, there's golf everywhere and the walking is divine; in short, expect to be busy. As for Culdearn, it stands in a row of five identical houses that were built in 1860 by Lord Seafield, one for each of his daughters. These days it's a lovely small hotel where William and Sonia look after guests with unstinting kindness. There's an open fire and facing sofas in the smart sitting room, panelled windows and a marble fireplace in the dining room, then stylish bedrooms that offer the sort of comfort you hope for after a day in the hills. You get the comfiest beds, the crispest linen, then decanters of sherry, fresh flowers and robes for spotless bathrooms. Back downstairs, William looks after a tempting wine list and 60 malts, while Sonia whisks up delicious four-course dinners, perhaps West Coast scallops, bramble sorbet, fillet of beef, a walnut and maple syrup parfait. Don't miss the ospreys at Boat of Garten. *Children over 10 welcome.*

Rooms	4 doubles, 1 twin/double, 1 twin: £160-£180. Singles £120-£150.
Meals	Dinner, 4 courses, £48.
Closed	Rarely.

Tel	+44 (0)1479 872106
Email	enquiries@culdearn.com
Web	www.culdearn.com

Culdearn House,
Woodlands Terrace, Speyside,
Grantown on Spey, PH26 3JU

Middleton Lodge, page 329

Index by town

Index by town

Index by town

Who are we?

Alastair began publishing books quite by chance – which explains a lot. Twenty-five years ago he was a tour guide in France, exploring the country and getting to know its secrets and its characters. Eventually he turned his scruffy, wine-stained notes into a book about unusual places to stay, so that other travellers could engage with authentic owners and guests in interesting and soul-filled places.

We're now over sixty people working from an office overlooking the eclectic Bristol harbourside, but we're still committed to reflecting our values in our culture. We will continue to rail against the iniquities of bland corporate travel by seeking out special places, visiting them personally, writing about them honestly and making no apology for our choices. We celebrate quirkiness, generosity of spirit and all the good, nurturing things that encourage small, local businesses to flourish.

In 2018 we entered into a unique version of Employee Ownership, in which the company was divided between the employees (52%), a Charitable Trust (24%) and the Sawday family (24%). Over the next few years, the Charitable Trust will grow with the company, developing into a real force for good and suppporting causes we all decide on and believe in.